Translating Israel

Judaic Traditions in Literature, Music, and Art

Ken Frieden and Harold Bloom, *Series Editors*

TRANSLATING ISRAEL

*Contemporary Hebrew Literature
and Its Reception in America*

ALAN L. MINTZ

SYRACUSE UNIVERSITY PRESS

First Edition 2001
01 02 03 04 05 06   6 5 4 3 2 1

The paper used in this publication meets the minimum requirements of
American National Standard for Information Sciences—Permanence of
Paper for Printed Library Materials, ANSI Z39.48–1984.∞™

Library of Congress Cataloging-in-Publication Data
Mintz, Alan L.
Translating Israel : contemporary Hebrew literature and its reception in America / Alan Mintz.
p. cm.—(Judaic traditions in literature, music, and art)
Includes bibliographical references and index.
ISBN 0-8156-2899-4 (alk. paper)—ISBN 0-8156-2900-1 (pbk. : alk. paper)
1. Israeli fiction—Appreciation—Unitd States. 2. Agnon, Shmuel Yosef,
1888–1970—Criticism and interpretation. 3. Zionism in literature. 4. Israeli
fiction—History and criticism. I. Title. II. Series.
PJ5029.M46 2001
892.4'3609—dc21   00-049263

Manufactured in the United States of America

Contents

PART THREE | REWRITING THE ZIONIST NARRATIVE

Preface

THIS VOLUME IS A GATHERING of acts of engagement with Israeli literature by one American Jewish reader. For some twenty years I have been writing about Israeli fiction for American journals and editing collections and studies aimed at presenting this literature to an American readership. Some of my best efforts in this endeavor have been brought together here. I make no apologies for the book not being a scholarly monograph; my aims in it are different as are the conditions under which the various chapters came into being. The chapters represent concrete events in the complex process whereby the culture of one country becomes known to that of another. My experience as a working critic has led me to think more theoretically about the reception of Israeli literature in America, an issue I examine in "Israeli Literature in the Minds of American Readers," which I wrote especially for this volume.

Many of my first encounters with the books written about in these pages took place in passionate discussions among the members of a Hebrew reading group on New York's Upper West Side. Anne Golumb Hoffman and Walter Dubler were my constant interlocutors, and I thank them and the other members of the group for stimulating ideas and fresh perspectives. I also thank Neal Kozodoy and Leon Wieseltier for their editorial acumen and for the hospitality afforded by their distinguished journals. To my friend and mentor Gershon Shaked I owe a debt of gratitude for his inspiring studies of Israeli fiction. To my wife, Susanna Morgenthau, and my daughters, Amira and Avital, go my affection and appreciation for making space within the family for my creative work.

Alan L. Mintz is Kekst Professor of Hebrew Literature at the Jewish Theological Seminary of America. He has served as the coeditor (with David G. Roskies) of *Prooftexts: A Journal of Jewish Literary History* since its founding in 1981. He is the author of *George Eliot and the Novel of Vocation, Ḥurban: Responses to Catastrophe in Hebrew Literature, "Banished from Their Father's Table": Loss of Faith and Hebrew Autobiography,* and *Popular Culture and the Shaping of Holocaust Memory in America.*

Translating Israel

Introduction

Israeli Literature in the Minds of American Readers

THE PAST TWENTY-FIVE YEARS have been a heady time to be an observer of cultural developments in Israel. In the 1960s the literary scene began to explode, especially in fiction. Poetry had long been at the center of the action with fiction playing a secondary role. Agnon's eminence, rooted in a different place and a different time, persisted while the native-born writers who began to produce stories and novels after 1948 never seemed able to carry their efforts much beyond the struggles and controversies of the hour. But then suddenly there were the short stories of Amos Oz, A. B. Yehoshua, Aharon Appelfeld, and Amalia Kahana-Carmon and then their first and second novels. They were joined by Shulamith Hareven, Yehoshua Kenaz, Yaakov Shabtai, and David Grossman. Into the eighties and nineties the debuts of good new writers became more frequent and the productivity of by-now established ones only intensified. What was different about this new literature was the quality and inventiveness of its fictional techniques and its ability to explore universal issues through the milieu of Israeli society. There was also a new audience for this literature; children of immigrants had become sophisticated Hebrew readers. Many of the best books became not only critical successes but best sellers as well.[1]

An earlier version of this chapter was published as "Israeli Literature and the American Reader" in the *American Jewish Year Book*, 1997. Reprinted with the kind permission of the American Jewish Committee.

Was this a party to which outsiders were invited? Very, very few American Jews knew Hebrew well enough to read a serious modern Hebrew book, so even if they were aware of the celebration, they could not hear the music. But soon English translations began to appear: Yehoshua's short-story collection *Three Days and a Child* (Shlosha yamim ve-yeled) in 1970 and his novel *The Lover* (Me'ahev) in 1978, Oz's *My Michael* (Michael She'li) in 1972, Appelfeld's *Badenheim 1939* (Badenheim ir nofesh) in 1980, Shabtai's *Past Continuous* (Zikhron devarim) in 1985, and Grossman's *See Under: Love* (Ayien erech: Ahavah) in 1989, with many others between and after. The translations were generally of high quality and were published by good houses, and they mostly received enthusiastic and discerning notices in major critical venues such as the *New York Times Book Review* and the *New York Review of Books*.

This was a special moment for someone like myself who was devoted to modern Hebrew literature as a teacher and a scholar. That literature had reached its first great flowering in Eastern Europe at the turn of the twentieth century in the works of Mendele, Bialik, Brenner, and Berdichevsky; it had attained another high point with Agnon and Uri Zvi Greenberg in Palestine between the two world wars. In this early phase of the Zionist revolution, it was often literature that led politics. Long before the Yishuv (the new Zionist settlement in Palestine) prospered, sophisticated masterworks in modern Hebrew were being written and read. With the establishment of the State of Israel, the roles were reversed, and it took time for the impressive social, political, and military accomplishments of the new enterprise to be matched by the same resourceful innovation on the literary imagination front. When the two finally came together, as happened in the seventies and eighties, the combination was very powerful. One had the feeling of living through a moment of immense creativity in the life of the Jewish people. Never since the time of the Bible and the ancient liturgical poets had so much that was so good been written in Hebrew. When, after a while, the English translations began to appear, a unique opportunity presented itself. Those who had been following these developments in Hebrew could finally turn to their students, their readers, and their friends, put something in their hands, and say, "Look here! This is what we've been talking about; this is what has been so exciting!"

The response, to put it mildly, was underwhelming; the excitement turned out not to be infectious. Now, it might be said that those who were advocates and special pleaders for Israeli literature to begin with were bound to be disappointed by the absence of an answering enthusiasm. Yet even judged by more objective measures, it is difficult to argue that Israeli literature has enjoyed anything more than a very limited success in America. Despite very favorable notices, Israeli novels in translation have not sold very well.[2] A few have done respectably and gone into paperback, but many of the key texts are out of print entirely, as anyone who tries to put together a syllabus for a college course in the field soon discovers. Even if commercial criteria are put aside, the record remains equivocal at best. When it comes to the generality of committed Jewish laypeople who are affiliated with Jewish institutions and are involved with the life of the community, it is difficult to find much recognition of the names of Israeli writers, not to mention experience reading their works. In the elite of the community—the rabbis, the educators, the lay and professional leaders of organizations and federations—the name recognition may be there, but familiarity may extend only to the political views of the writers, say those of Oz or Grossman, and not to their main literary works. Even university teachers of Jewish Studies tend to regard Hebrew literature not as a source of current cultural creativity that makes claims upon them as intellectuals but as one area of academic specialization among many others. In the end, however, the muted reception of Israeli writing in America is less a reflection of the absolute number of its "users" than a sign of a failure of these writings to become part of the intellectual discourse of the American Jewish community and its cultural repertoire.

Should one be surprised? Is this not just another expression of a pervasive strain of anti-intellectualism in American Jewish life? This is not the case, I argue. One might have reasonably hoped for more, especially because of the relationship of involved American Jews to Israel. The Zionization of American Jewish life has been one of the most remarked upon developments since World War II.[3] Although only a small number of American Jews are Zionists in the classical ideological sense of the term, a substantial majority are pro-Israel in their attitudes, and a significant number are attached to Israel in a variety of ways. Moreover, American Jews buy books. A greater proportion of Jews buy fiction and works of general interest than do the general public and other ethnic groups, and they buy many more books of Jewish interest than they used to, judging from the explosion of titles relating to Jewish life and the Holocaust in recent years. It is, also, not as if the Israeli novels under discussion are unapproachable or unenjoyable. Quite the contrary. That it is by no means a punishment to read them is indicated by their enormous sales in Israel. Sales of forty to fifty thousand, which are not uncommon for a successful novel in Israel, a country of some five million, would still be counted a substantial success in America; given the tiny proportion of readers in Israel to readers in America, the numbers are astounding.

That there is, in fact, something to wonder about in the American situation is supported by a look at the reception of Israeli literature in Europe. Since the early 1990s, the sales of Israeli literary works (these occasionally include volumes of poetry in addition to novels) translated into European languages have been steadily increasing. Again, the exact sales figures are difficult to come by, but the number of new titles translated each year gives some indication. In Italy, for example, during the seventies and eighties only two or three titles appeared on average; beginning in 1989, the number began to climb in increments to twelve in 1994. In Germany, five or six titles appeared yearly until 1988 when the number began to climb dramatically to twenty-seven in 1994. In America, by contrast, translations reached their height in 1989 when twenty-seven were published, but then dropped to fewer than twenty in 1994.[4] It is rather startling to contemplate the fact that in Germany, a country with a tiny Jewish population, the same number of translations of Israeli literature is appearing as in America. After Germany comes France in number of titles translated, and then Italy, Spain, and Holland with a scattering of titles in Polish, Swedish, Portuguese, Arabic, Greek, and Chinese.

More important, perhaps, than the quantitative dimension is the fact—to me the ironic fact—that important new writers in Israel can become familiar to European readers while American readers, especially American Jewish readers, have no inkling of their existence. Orly Castel-Bloom, for example, is regarded as the most brilliant practitioner of an audacious, postmodernist sensibility in Israeli writing. French, Dutch, and German readers can sample four of her titles; none of her books have appeared in English. Itamar Levy's *Otiot Ha-Shemesh, Otiot Ha-Yareah* (Letters of the sun, letters of the moon) is the most important recent contribution in Israeli letters to the representation of the inner experience of the Arab; it will soon appear in Italian, French, German, and Spanish along with two other books of Levy's. Savyon Leibrecht is an accomplished short-story writer who is central to the rise of women's writing in Israel. She is being translated not only into Italian and German but also into Chinese. Until very recently none of Leibrecht's books have appeared in English, and Levy's work still awaits translation. There are many other examples.

The European comparison helps to bring a question to the forefront: Why is it that when Hebrew literature has come of age and finds itself in the midst of its greatest boom that American Jewish readers, so cultured and so committed to Israel, should have so little use for it? This is a question to which I believe there are answers, some obvious, some less so. The answers have to do, in part, with the differences in the reading habits of Americans and Europeans, with the general fate of the audience for serious fiction in America, and with the deep ambivalence American Jews feel at the prospect of encountering the realities of Israeli society. These are explanatory conjectures that are worth probing and developing with care. I defer that task to the end of this chapter to concentrate first on the substance of the record of the reception of Israeli literature in the United States so far. To sharpen and define the issue, I have emphasized the failure of Israeli literature to secure a broad audience in America. But that is only one dimension of the "career" of these books on these shores. These Hebrew novels are acquired and translated and published by prestigious commercial houses without subsidy; they are reviewed thoughtfully in respected journals; they make their way into bookstores and public, synagogue, and university libraries and onto the lists of book clubs and reading circles and the syllabi of college courses and adult education offerings. And, of course, they are purchased and actually read by thousands of people. So, even though the impact of Israeli literature has been circumscribed, the substance of what that impact has been—what these books have meant to whom in which circles—is the first order of business. One is likely to form better conjectures about force and volume if one understands more about the trajectory so far.

Taking that measurement turns out to be a deceptively difficult thing to do. In the interplay of forces and mediations, the reception of a work of art is an enormously complex process, no less so than, say, the ways in which foreign policy is shaped in government or certain ideas become central to a society's discourse. In the limited compass of this introduction I aim to accomplish two goals. My first objective is to sketch an account of the reception process as it applies to Israeli literature in America. How does a piece of writing written in Hebrew and produced in Israel get translated, published, reviewed, distributed, read, and discussed in America? What are the constraints and mediations that favor some works over others? My second objective is to see what can be learned from a closer look at a number of case studies. I have chosen ten books by six writers (Oz, Yehoshua, Shabtai, Hareven, Appelfeld, and Grossman), which generally represent the first publication of the authors' works in English, and I have analyzed the reviews written about them in national journals. What I have looked for is not so much the evaluations given by the reviewers ("Is this a good novel?") although these judgments are obviously not unimportant. Rather, I have focused on the reviewers' encounters with the books as works of Israeli literature. What are the reviewers' implicit assumptions about Israeli society? What awareness is shown in the reviews about the existence of Hebrew literature and its institutions, and what expectations are placed upon that literature? What themes are brought to the forefront, and in what way do they express the concerns of American and American Jewish readers?

The Dynamics of Reception

One of the consequences of living in an advanced consumer society is that one has little sense of either the prehistory of the commodities one consumes before one acquires them or of the forces that tend to determine one's choice of one object over another. When one purchases a car or a computer or a suit of clothes, one is unlikely to be fully conscious of the stages of research, design, engineering, manufacture, marketing, and distribution that took place under highly competitive conditions, eliminating many possibilities and advancing a limited set of others, with the result that one chooses from the several models made available. That final choice, in turn, is shaped by advertising and consumer journalism (reports and reviews of products). The commodity one finally acquires has undergone what Marxian theorists call a process of reification; the object has become a thing stripped of the labor invested by many hands in producing it.

When one reads a newly published book, whether bought or borrowed, one tends to be similarly innocent of the Darwinian provenance of the object held, unless, perhaps, one is involved in the business of writing or publishing. This is particularly true of a translated book, which has an imposing hurdle to clear before it comes into the world altogether. In the case, then, of the English translation of an Israeli novel, one is dealing with a book that is, in a sense, doubly a survivor. The book first has to be published in Israel before it becomes a candidate for the exceedingly smaller ranks of books published in a foreign language. How it joins these ranks and is reviewed and read abroad is the story that is of interest here, but one should not be unmindful of how the publishing scene in Israel has changed over the years.

During the first decades of Israel's existence, the key players were large publishing houses established by the political parties and the kibbutz movements: Sifriyat Poalim, Hakibbutz Hame'uhad, Am Oved, and others. Beginning in the seventies, these institutionally backed publishers were made to share the market with commercial houses such as Keter and Zemora-Beitan, which conducted themselves much more like their American counterparts. This shift, which echoed the larger re-

treat from ideology and the move to an open-market economy, produced complicated consequences. On the one hand, it made it easier
for women and Oriental Jews and other marginalized groups to get
their voices heard in the literary marketplace and to connect with new
audiences for literature. On the other hand, quality writing had to pay
its own way and could no longer depend as much on institutional sub-
sidies. The publishing scene became more driven by the search for best-
sellers, whose appearances were attended by intensive public relations
campaigns.

How then are writers' works chosen for translation once they have
achieved some success in Israel? It is easier for some writers than for
others, of course. Established writers such as Oz and Yehoshua and, by
now, Grossman have long-term contracts with publishing houses that
have become their "homes" in America: Oz with Harcourt Brace Jovanovich, Yehoshua with Doubleday, and Grossman with Farrar Straus
and Giroux. Anything major that they write will almost automatically
appear in English. (The justice of this arrangement is another matter;
many critics think that the last several novels that Oz has written are in-
ferior to the work of several younger writers who remain untranslated.
But his arrangement appears to be a general state of affairs that is not
special to the case of translation.) Another factor is genre. Short stories
have always been difficult to sell in translation although Israeli publishers and readers are more sympathetic to first books of stories than are
their American counterparts. Often, as was the case with Oz's *Where
Jackals Howl and Other Stories* (Artsot hatan), the stories that were
written and published at the outset of the writer's career have to wait
until there is a successful novel (Oz's second novel *My Michael* was his
debut work in English) before a publisher agrees to bring out the earlier
stories. Although the "serious" novel has long reigned as the genre of
choice in translation, mysteries and thrillers are now mounting a challenge. Until recently, Israeli readers have been able to satisfy their appetite for detective novels and *romans policiers* by recourse to the many
translations into Hebrew from English and French, two languages in
which this genre of writing has reached high levels of sophistication and

variety. Now accomplished Hebrew writers such as Yoram Kaniuk, Shulamit Lapid, and Batya Gur have been turning out mysteries rooted in the particularities of Israeli life. In the tradition of Ruth Rendell and P. D. James, they aspire for these works to be something much more than entertainment. The success of Batya Gur's recent detective series, including *The Saturday Morning Murder, The Literary Murder,* and *Murder on a Kibbutz,* is a case in point.

Then there are works that resist translation and writers who resist having them translated. Amalia Kahana-Carmon is one of the key figures in the New Wave that reshaped Israeli fiction in the sixties and seventies and the most import precursor of the current boom in women's writing; she is usually grouped with Oz, Yehoshua, and Appelfeld and is spoken about with the same high regard. Yet whereas interested readers of English are familiar with the work of the latter, Kahana-Carmon is locked away in a secret garden. It is a concealment of her own making, in part. It is said that she has never permitted her work to be rendered into English because she believes it is untranslatable.[5] Although her stance is idiosyncratic, it is not entirely a conceit. Her classic work explores the imaginative and fantasy life of female protagonists; the highly lyrical and figurative language used to represent these inner states is indeed difficult, although, to my mind, not that much more so than the style of Oz's early stories. What has kept her from being translated—beyond her own reported unwillingness—has more to do with the fact that the lives lived by Kahana-Carmon's women seem unconnected to the Zionist master plot (the struggles with the aftermath of ideology and collective purpose) that animates much of the other writing of her generation.

Sometimes the size and subject matter of a book may simply be too imposing. Even if the translation is paid for by the author or is subsidized by a foundation or is aided by some other kind of subvention and comes free of charge, as it were, a publisher is likely to balk when presented with a project that has little prospect of selling. By most accounts, S. Yizhar's *Yemei Ziqlag* (The days of ziklag) (1958) is the best Hebrew novel of the fifties, the first important native Israeli novel, and

the only work of the Palmah-generation writers to transcend the strictures of socialist-positivist aesthetic. Yet despite the importance of the
work, it runs to some 1,143 pages in Hebrew (Hebrew usually translates up to one-third longer in English), and although the story is set
during the War of Independence and follows a fighting unit in the
southern campaign, there is no conventional plot and no stirring battle
scenes. The enormity of the novel consists almost entirely of the internal monologues of the young soldiers and the elaborate nature description of the northern Negev. *The Days of Ziklag* has never been translated
into English although the German rights have been bought by
Suhrkamp in Frankfurt. Another example is Haim Be'er's *'Et Hazamir*
(The time of trimming) (1987), a long novel (560 pages) that examines
the boundaries between Orthodox and ultra-Orthodox Judaism by focusing on a small army unit staffed by religious Jews and charged with
burying soldiers who die in action or in training accidents. Be'er is one
of the best of a small group of writers who probe the religious world of
Israeli society using novelistic tools. His first (and shorter) novel *Notsot*
(Feathers) (1980) is set in the ultra-Orthodox Jerusalem neighborhood of Geula during the fractious controversy about accepting German reparations monies in the fifties. (Hillel Halkin's translation of
Feathers exists in manuscript, but it has never been published.) Although centering a long novel such as *The Time of Trimming* on the
business of an army burial unit may work well with Israeli readers—the
book was, in fact, quite successful—it simply may not translate in a way
to engage American readers. Or, at least, it has not done so up to now.
Some years ago I was contacted by a junior editor at a major New York
house who could read Hebrew and was enthusiastic about the novel. In
the hope of persuading her bosses to bring out the novel, she asked me
to write a reader's report. I was happy to do so; I, too, was enthusiastic
if less hopeful. That was the last I heard of it.

Personal relations, personal contacts, and personal presence should
not be underestimated as factors that help to get a book translated.
There are literary agents who represent Israeli writers, and the Institute
for the Translation of Hebrew Literature in Tel Aviv acts as an agent on

behalf of individual writers to promote and negotiate contracts for publication abroad, more in Europe than in America. Many of the deals are done at the industry's great trade show, the Frankfurt Book Fair. But the exertions of authors in their own behalf remain important. Yoram Kaniuk, a writer of comic grotesque fictions, lived in New York for many years in the fifties and sixties and was involved with the Israeli bohemian scene there. He is one of the best published Israeli writers in America with six or seven books from *The Acrophile* (Ha-yored lemala) in 1961 to the more recent *His Daughter* (Bitoh) (1989) appearing here. I know little about the people he met and the contacts he made during those years, but I would be surprised if his long sojourn in New York did not make it easier for him to get his work published here. He is an important writer, but his hefty representation in English is out of proportion to the standing he is accorded by most critics and readers in Israel. Yehoshua Kenaz and Yeshayahu Koren, by contrast, are two very highly reputed writers who have been writing for as long as Kaniuk but who have just very recently seen some of their work appear in English: Kenaz's *After the Holidays* (Aharei ha-hagim) (1987) and *The Way to the Cats* (Ba-derech la-hatulim) (1994) and Koren's *Funeral at Noon* (Levaya ba-tzohorayim) (1996). How their work came to be translated makes a related point. Both authors have been published in America by Alan Lelchuk's Steerforth Press, a small quality house located in Hanover, New Hampshire. *(After the Holidays* was published by Harcourt Brace Jovanovich). Lelchuk is an American writer who for a long time has taken an interest in Israeli writing; together with Gershon Shaked he edited the important collection *Eight Great Short Hebrew Novels* (1983). Lelchuk's familiarity with the literary scene in Israel— and the flexibility afforded by a small press—have drawn him to some very fine writers who have been overlooked by the industry giants. Ted Solataroff, who for many years was Yehuda Amichai's editor at Harper Collins, is another example of a powerful editor within the publishing world whose commitment to Israeli writing has been an important fact in establishing careers and advancing reputations.

Authors also have to be lucky in their translators, and I think that

Israeli writers by and large have been. S. Y. Agnon and Haim Hazaz, from an earlier generation, were less well served. Although he is regarded by many as the greatest Hebrew prose writer, Agnon wrote in a learned pseudonaive style that laid many traps for translators; two of his great novels, *The Bridal Canopy* (Hakhnasat kalah) (1937) and *A Guest for the Night* (Ore'ah natah lalun) (1968), do not come across as particularly magisterial in English.[6] The native writers discussed here write in styles that are more recognizably novelistic and are laden with fewer allusions to classical texts. Therefore, with some of the exceptions noted above, their work does not throw up obstacles to good translations. The standard has generally been very high. The life of a professional translator, as is well known, is a very difficult one on many scores, and this is particularly the case for a "minor" language such as modern Hebrew in which there is vastly more translation *into* Hebrew from Western languages than there is from Hebrew into Western languages. It is a hugely unequal balance of trade in which export is by far the weaker side. In the corps of translators into English are two preeminent figures. Dalya Bilu is a translator of enormous energy and scope who has worked with most contemporary Israeli writers; born in South Africa, her translations have a slight Anglo rather than American hue. Hillel Halkin, who is American, has also worked with a wide spectrum of current writers although he has devoted considerable time to translating the classics of modern Hebrew and Yiddish literature, including the works of Mendele, Shalom Aleichem, Feierberg, Brenner, and Agnon. Another group of translators are principally associated with single writers: Nicholas De Lange with Amos Oz, Betsy Rosenberg with David Grossman, and, recently, Jeffrey Green with Appelfeld. In each of these cases, a writer (and his publisher, one supposes) has found a translator who has a special affinity for his or her work and who can be relied upon to provide a continuity of voice from work to work. Other accomplished translators include Zeva Shapiro, Seymour Simckes, Richard Flantz, Philip Simpson, and Barbara Harshav. Whatever problems Israeli literature has had in connecting to the American audience, in sum, cannot be attributed in any extensive sense to the quality of translation into English.

Getting Noticed

Once a Hebrew book is translated into English and published in the United States, it embarks upon the uncertain journey of dissemination. One can usefully speak of a book proceeding along two tracks. One is a commercial track, involving marketing, advertising, shipments to booksellers, and sales. The other track involves the growth of the book's critical reputation as formed by published reviews, word-of-mouth comment, and standing within the academy. The two sometimes go together, and sometimes they do not. As noted previously, it has often happened that an Israeli novel has enjoyed a considerable success d'estime here but has simply not sold well. Of course, certain publishing projects can be born into more privileged circumstances than others and be given better chances before they enter the world. An enthusiastic editor can build momentum for a book by exciting the sales people about it, and their interest makes a great deal of difference when it comes to convincing the large chains such as Barnes and Noble, in whose hands book selling has been increasingly concentrated, to carry the book and display it prominently. An advertising budget certainly helps, as does a budget for a book tour. If the author can present him- or herself respectably in English, then personal appearances at bookfairs, talk shows, campus and bookstore readings, and consulate-arranged parties can make a difference.

There is no denying that published reviews play a role in the commercial dissemination of a book. A glowing notice in the *New York Times* is good business. Not to be underestimated also are the low-profile but influential services that preview new books for libraries and book stores such as *Publishers Weekly,* the *Kirkus Report,* and *Library Journal.* Book reviews, like movie and restaurant reviews, certainly function on one level as consumer reports read to decide whether a given book may be worth acquiring. Yet on another level reviews have a life of their own in the making of reputations and the general circulation of ideas that is quite separate from commercial success or failure. For the curious literate person, the ritual of sitting down, bagel in hand, of a Sunday morning to read through the *New York Times Book Review* is not an activity whose goal is to locate a desired commodity in a catalog; it is an opportunity to eavesdrop on culture and to find out what people are talking about in the world of ideas. The old saw that people read book reviews nowadays rather than read the books is true on many levels.

This truth gets truer the more thoughtful the review is. The book supplements and daily reviews of the *New York Times,* the *Washington Post,* the *Los Angeles Times,* and the *Chicago Tribune* probably have the most impact on sales. But in intellectual and literary circles they carry little weight compared to a number of smaller journals that, to begin with, usually publish their reviews too late to have an effect on the crucial initial sales of a book. Reviews in the *New York Review of Books, Commentary,* the *New Republic,* the *Nation,* the *New Leader,* and *Midstream* tend to be longer and more nuanced and more ambitious in seeking to relate the book at hand to larger complexes of ideas and cultural phenomena. Sometimes the book under review serves more as a pretext for airing broader issues. In these intellectually influential journals the main challenge is getting noticed. Only a small number of the serious books published in a given season are chosen to become the subjects of these deeper and more extensive essays. Israeli literature has been moderately successful in competing for this scarce intellectual air time. It has been aided by the fortuitous fact that some editors are not only familiar with the Israeli cultural scene but also read Hebrew. Neal Kozodoy at *Commentary* and Leon Weiseltier at the *New Republic* are two cases in point. It has also helped that figures of immense intellectual authority are actively concerned with Hebrew literature. Chief among them is Robert Alter, whose interest in Hebrew literature is particularly persuasive because of his distinguished contributions to many other areas of the humanities. The late Irving Howe, who also was an enormous presence in so many areas, developed a strong interest in Israeli literature in the seventies and eighties; although Howe could not read in the original language (Yiddish yes, but Hebrew no), his third wife, Ilana, is an Israeli with interests in literature.

Insiders such as Howe and Alter call attention to the role of reviewers and reviews as mediators between cultures. Translation is surely the great step in the process by which a work of literature written in one language and culture reveals itself to another language and culture. But reviews serve as the forward stations that first receive and process the messages sent by a foreign culture. It makes a significant difference, to my mind, if these stations are manned by "insiders," who are conversant with the cultural discourse of the foreign society, or by "outsiders," for whom the foreign culture remains foreign. In reality, of course, there is a continuum between the two, and in no sense is this an evaluative distinction that privileges the perceptions of one over the other. Nevertheless, being an insider is different because it brings with it a special burden of judgment. Knowing not just the work itself that one is asked to review but the societal and cultural formations from which it emerged forecloses a kind of innocence and opens another set of responsibilities.

At least, I know this to be true of myself. Although I do not presume to probe the motives of others, I pause to take advantage of my own status as an insider reviewer to turn myself into a kind of "native informant" and to reflect on the experience of at least one practitioner in the field. Most often, to begin with, I already know a fair amount about the book and the public discussion it engendered. Because of the gap between the Hebrew publication and the appearance of the translation, I usually have had a chance to read the original before I read it in English. (My reading, incidentally, is often not solitary; for many years I have participated in a Hebrew reading group made up of other English speakers, almost all of whom have no academic or professional involvement in the subject. My first responses to a book are affected by the group discussion.) There are some books whose reception in the Israeli press is difficult not to notice. Israel has a lively culture of weekend literary supplements and passionate, feisty readers. When a novel such as Grossman's *See Under: Love* or Yehoshua's *Mr. Mani* (Mar Manni) or Orly Castel-Bloom's *Dolly City* (1992) provokes noisy controversy, it does not take much to catch the reverberations. Best-sellers such as Meir Shalev's *Blue Mountain* (Roman rusi), although less provocative, call attention to themselves through their conspicuous success. The quieter waves made by important books by newer authors such as Itamar Levy or Leah Aini usually become known through word-of-mouth consultations with colleagues and friends or in the pages of *Modern Hebrew Literature,* an English-language journal edited by Gershon Shaked and published by the Tel Aviv-based Institute for the Translation of Hebrew Literature, which publishes reviews of new poetry and fiction and excerpts from them. Because my discretionary time for reading, like that of most people, is circumscribed and because it takes me longer to read in Hebrew than in English, I limit the Hebrew books I can read in a given year to those that are truly significant and put me in touch with the best products of Israeli culture. I may not in retrospect have chosen wisely in a given season, but I remain impatient to get it right next time.

If I find a particular book exciting, if it has been an "important" event in Israeli culture, and if it is being translated into English, then I consider writing about it. Most of the substantive review essays I have written have been initiated by me rather than solicited from me. I have phoned an editor and made a case for a book to be given attention if such attention is not self-evident, and I have asked to have the book assigned to me if no one else is doing it. What this means is that I am already a partisan before I embark upon the task of assessing the book. This does not mean that I will not be critical, but the criticisms I have will be presented within a space of cultural importance that has already been cleared for the book in my mind. Not having the responsibilities of a regular critic has also made it possible for me to avoid writing about books that are disappointing. This selectiveness, I think, does not stem from an arrogant insistence that only certain books are prestigious enough for me to devote time to them. It comes, rather, from a kind of necessary ruthlessness imposed by the constraints of time. In my university job, I am paid to teach and conduct research; reviewing is an elective adjunct, something done "on the side." The time given to reviewing must, therefore, be justified by the inherent interest of a project and by what I can learn by undertaking it.

Once the arrangements for the assignment have been made, I become supremely aware of the dimension of audience. This is determined in some measure by the profile of the publication in which the review is to appear. The differences between writing for the *New York Times Book Review* and *Commentary* and the *New Republic* have to do with a great deal more than great disproportions in the size of reader-ship. The smaller journals have well-known political and cultural differ-ences, as well as distinct editorial cultures, although the "back of the book," the cultural reviews, are often more weakly linked to the jour-nals' political stances. A reviewer perforce becomes a participant in the kind of invisible community determined by the journal; the way in which an argument is framed, however unconsciously and however slightly, is likely to be affected by the signature constellation of conven-tions and expectations associated with the journal. The "Jewishness" of the imagined community is also a key fact, yet a very elusive one. If one is writing for *Hadassah Monthly* or the *Jerusalem Report*, on the one hand, or for *Commonweal*, on the other (as I have done at various times for all three), then the identity of the audience is more in focus. In other instances it is more blurry. Even though *Commentary* is published under the auspices of the American Jewish Committee and regularly in-cludes comments on developments in Jewish culture, the editors are more insistent on avoiding insider references and allusions than are those at the *New Republic*, which, despite the Jewish identity of its owner, has no communal affiliation and has historically been more fo-cused on the political affairs of the republic.

Apart from these differences of milieu, I have found myself over the years remarkably consistent in the audience I imagine myself address-ing. That audience is modest and almost always a small subset of a journal's broader subscription base. These diminished expectations de-rive from a skepticism about the very possibility of a large general audi-ence in America for serious Israeli literature or, for that matter, for serious Jewish scholarship, thought, and criticism. Although I am per-suaded as much as anyone that Jewish culture is a wonderful thing and has much to say to the world, I believe that it will speak most eloquently to those who already hold some brief for its importance. Writing about Israeli literature in national journals brings a number of secondary gains. It keeps the discussion from becoming parochial, and it forces connections to be made to general literature and currents of ideas. It enhances respect for the subject and legitimizes its inclusion in the discourse of American culture. And there is always the hope that, having found the matter of a review intriguing, readers with no previous associations with Israeli literature will pick up the book, read it, and take an interest in the subject.

My primary imagined audience, however, remains circumscribed. In my mind's eye I see friends and colleagues and, by extension, other involved participants in the American Jewish community who regard my subject, Israeli literature, as surely legitimate and, perhaps, even important but largely irrelevant and unread. My goal is to interest them, to get them to pay attention, and to persuade them that Israeli literature has something to say to them and that they should be open to the intellectual claims it makes upon their lives.

But this role of advocate—perhaps even cheerleader—has another side to it. To the degree that I represent Israeli literature to American Jewish readers, I also represent diaspora Jewry to Israeli culture. I read the novel before me with the eyes of the American Jew that I am—although granted, not the typical American Jew. I know a great deal about the cultural milieu out of which the work emerged, and I have "gone native" in my partisanship of this foreign literature. Yet in the end I speak from here rather than from over there. Two examples illustrate how "situated" is my understanding of this material. I greeted the publication of David Grossman's *See Under: Love* as a major event and as the most important exploration of the Holocaust in the generation after Appelfeld.[7] At the same time, for all of the many conspicuous influences on Grossman's writing from Bruno Schultz to Gabriel García Márquez to postmodernist fabulists, I was struck by the utter failure to make use of any of the rich imaginative resources contained in the responses to catastrophe in Jewish tradition. Similarly, in writing about A. B. Yehoshua's *Open Heart* (Ha-shiv'a me-hodu), a novel that describes the turning toward Eastern mysticism by a group of young Israelis who are disaffected from the growing consumerism of Israeli society, I remarked on the sense of déjà vu this provoked in American readers. In rejecting the materialism of American life, I pointed out, Jews who had once looked eastward were more recently turning toward the resources of their own spiritual traditions, whereas the characters in Yehoshua's novel do not give that inheritance a second look.

Observations such as these locate the act of reading Israeli literature in English translation as part of the rough-and-tumble dialectic between Israel and American Jewry. It is part of that dialectic which is, to my mind, irreplaceable. Reading Israeli fiction and poetry provides one of the only ways possible to probe beneath the political emergencies, the newspaper stories, and the organizational pronouncements to get at the existential core of Israeli experience. That most American Jews are deeply ambivalent about wanting to probe so deeply and to see so clearly helps to explain, incidentally, the muted reception of Israeli literature here. For those who do welcome the engagement, then reaction, response, and criticism become integral parts of the process of "active knowing" that the literature enables. In my reviews I try to model this kind of engagement by mixing an empathic presentation of the subject in the context of its own milieu together with a response that is shaped by the very different reality lived here.

What turns out to be the reality of *there* is often not very handsome, and despite myself I often feel apologetically mobilized by this fact. The scenes of Israeli life and the adventures of its psyche as depicted in contemporary Hebrew fiction are not inspiring: Oz's ideological monsters and enfeebled sons, Yehoshua's alienated intellectuals who wound others in trying to confirm themselves, Appelfeld's seedy and emotionally arrested survivors, and, above all, that great epic of folly and dissipation, Shabtai's *Past Continuous*. The much-discussed double standard that is routinely applied to Israel's political behavior operates on the literary front as well. Readers of contemporary American fiction have been socialized into maintaining a certain separation between art and life and abandoning expectations that serious literature should provide exemplary models of family life. If one finds murder or adultery in a novel by Joyce Carol Oates or Philip Roth, one does not take it as a description of American society as a whole. Seasoned readers are equipped with various procedures for "recuperating" the violence and venality found in works of art by understanding them as part of the artist's vision and technique in a tradition that goes back to the theatrical blood Shakespeare freely spilled on the stage of the Globe Theater. These decoding procedures sometimes are suspended when American readers approach Israeli literature, or, at least, I fear they do. I then feel called upon to try to do for the readers the work that they might naturally do on their own when reading on native grounds. I point to the long tradition of social criticism in Hebrew literature going back to the critique of the shtetl. I demonstrate how the comic and the grotesque are used to create ironic distance. I speak of how the perfection of artistic form can yield a sense of transcendence even when the subject matter is repugnant. And I extol the virtues of a society that is self-aware and willing to tell itself hard truths.

Am I being an apologist? Perhaps I am, but I do not believe my stance is inappropriate. Israeli literature is not written for export. It is composed in Hebrew as an internal communication among readers who share a similar exposure to risk and a similar burden of citizenship. Although most Israeli writers are happy to be translated into foreign languages, the audience they are addressing resides at home. Reading literature in translation is, therefore, a kind of eavesdropping. My job as reviewer is to supply the rules of the game for the conversation being overheard. It is not to pretty up what is being said but to explain the context in which the dialogue is taking place.

Ten Books/Six Authors

I have selected ten books by six authors and read what has been written about them in prominent journals to generalize about the reception of Israeli literature in translation in this country. As I do this I am well aware that reviews of this sort represent only a segment of a reception process that unfolds on many levels and never approaches closure. There are, I know, other measures and other places to look. It would be revealing to check the acquisitions of libraries (university, city, Jewish community, and, especially, synagogue) and the borrowing patterns of their users. Many groups, especially synagogue sisterhoods and

Hadassah chapters, have book circles or periodic programs in which book reviews are given. It would be informative to know how often Israeli literature is discussed and the kinds of reactions to it that are voiced. Examining published reviews in local Jewish community newspapers would represent a different level of search, but one that, unfortunately, is beyond the resources of the present study. There are dozens of community papers; many carry notices by local reviewers and others carry syndicated columns. I speculate that only certain works of Israeli literature in translation are selected for attention at this level, and it would be telling to find out which are and which are not, not to mention what is said about them. Is the unromantic presentation of Israel in these works more vexatious here, closer to the streets and neighborhoods of Jewish life, than in national publications? In the end the individual reader is the smallest but most important unit in the reception process. I would pay dearly to observe focus groups of ordinary readers reacting to novels such as Yehoshua's *Mr. Mani* or Grossman's *The Book of Intimate Grammar* (Sefer ha-dikduk ha-pnimi).

In the meantime the reviews at hand have not a little to tell. The fact that they are taken from elite publications is a strength and a limitation. The discussions that take place in the venues and settings I have just listed (community papers, synagogue libraries, etc.) are more likely than not to be internal to the Jewish community. But when a review appears in the *New York Times* or the *New York Review of Books* or the *New Republic,* then, even if it is written by an insider, it enters a discursive space that is at once national and ecumenical. This is even true for a reviewer like myself who admits to directing his words to a subset of that ideally broad audience. It is a conversation all can listen to even if I believe only the few are interested, and I must conduct myself with that in mind.

The following are the works I have chosen to track. I have listed the Hebrew publication date first, and then I have listed the American publisher and the date of publication in translation.

Appelfeld, Aharon. *Badenheim 1939.* 1979. Translated by Dalya Bilu. Boston: David R. Godine, 1980.

Grossman, David. *See Under: Love.* 1986. Translated by Betsy Rosenberg. New York: Farrar Straus and Giroux, 1989.

Hareven, Shulamith. *City of Many Days.* 1972. Translated by Hillel Halkin. New York: Doubleday, 1977.

Oz, Amos. *Elsewhere, Perhaps.* 1966. Translated by Nicholas De Lange. New York: Harcourt Brace Jovanovich, 1973.

Oz, Amos. *My Michael.* 1968. Translated by Nicholas De Lange. New York: Alfred A. Knopf, 1972.

Oz, Amos. *Where Jackals Howl and Other Stories.* 1975. Translated by Nicholas De Lange. New York: Harcourt Brace Jovanovich, 1981.

Shabtai, Yaakov. *Past Continuous.* 1977. Translated by Dalya Bilu. Philadelphia: Jewish Publication Society, 1985.

Yehoshua, A. B. *Early in the Summer of 1970.* 1972. Translated by Miriam Arad. New York: Doubleday, 1977.

Yehoshua, A. B. *The Lover.* 1977. Translated by Philip Simpson. New York: Doubleday, 1978.

Yehoshua, A. B. *Three Days and a Child.* 1962. Translated by Miriam Arad. New York: Doubleday, 1970.

I picked these particular books because they generally represent the first appearances of these important writers in English; they afford readers an opportunity to see the beginnings of their American careers and the initial reactions to their works. The periodicals I have surveyed are those tracked by two standard references: the *Book Review Index* and the *Index to Jewish Periodicals.* These guides cover major national and Jewish journals; they do not, however, index most newspapers except for the *New York Times.* In a more comprehensive treatment one would have liked to canvas as well the book supplements and columns of the *Washington Post,* the *Chicago Tribune,* and the *Los Angeles Times.* My goal has not been to document reception case histories of individual works but to look for patterns of response to these works as parts of the larger phenomenon of Israeli literature. So if there is some subjectivity in my choice of books or lack of exhaustiveness in the coverage of periodicals, the general patterns, nevertheless, remain quite noticeable. These organized themselves under four general headings.[8]

The Status of Israeli Literature as Literature

Whether Israeli literature should be taken as a reflection of the embroiled and besieged nature of Israeli society or as a more removed literary artifact is an issue for reviewers encountering these materials for the first time, especially when the first important translations came out in the seventies. Richard Locke's enthusiastic review in the daily *New York Times* (May 25, 1972) of *My Michael,* Oz's first work to be translated into English, begins with an admission of astonishment.

> [A]dvance rumors hardly prepare one for this first translation of his major work. "My Michael" is anything but a provincial achievement; it has nothing to do with noble kibbutzim, Sten guns and sabras, nor with the Talmudic dryness of Israel's Nobel Prize-winner, the late S. Y. Agnon. It's quite the last kind of book one expects from a young writer living in the midst of a melodramatic political situation, for "My Michael" is an extremely self-conscious and serious psychological novel, slow, thoughtful, self-assured and highly sophisticated, full of the most skillful modulations of tone and texture.

One wonders what Israeli writing, suffused with sabras and Sten guns, the *Times*'s reviewer had been reading up to now to make his surprise so stunning. Alan Lelchuk makes a similar point in reviewing Shabtai's *Past Continuous* in the *New York Times Book Review* (Apr. 21, 1985): "No kibbutz utopias here, no Jerusalem mystique, no Zionist uplift, no sabra heroics—in other words, no magical society." A variation on this theme is the offhand comment in the *Times Literary Supplement* brief review (by "A. D.," Dec. 7, 1979) of Yehoshua's *The Lover:* "[T]he translation . . . suggests some—though less than usual—of that prickly-pear quality so often found in Israeli writing."[9] In a review of the same novel in another British publication, the *Spectator* (Aug. 25, 1979), Paul Abelman utters a sentiment that I suspect is more widely shared than one might realize. After complimenting Yehoshua on not "loading every incident with epic significance," he opines, "[a]ctually . . . a touch more of the heroic mode might not have been inappropriate. At the other end of the spectrum, I felt positive nostalgia for good old ghetto humor and the Jewish joke." How unfortunate, he seems to think, that Israeli literature cannot serve up the comic routines of the Borscht Belt or the East End.

This was certainly not the tenor of Israeli literature before the debut of Oz and the other writers discussed here. For all the shortcomings of the Palmah-generation writers, glamorizing kibbutz life or military exploits was not one of them, not to mention their general unavailability in translation. (Aharon Megged's novel *Living on the Dead* (Ha-hai al ha-met), for example, which appeared in English the year before *My Michael,* made a point of deflating these myths.) It is much more likely that these impressions of "Israeli writing" derive not from actual writings by Israelis but from writing about Israel by Americans. There is no exaggerating the impact of popular novels like Leon Uris's *Exodus*—and their Hollywood versions—in forming the literary image of Israel in the American mind. American Jewish organizations labored very hard, and with impressive success, during the first decades of Israel's existence to project an image of Israel as a country that, although beleaguered and vulnerable, was populated by a resilient collection of idealistic soldier-farmers. This, however, is not the world according to Israeli fiction, for as Faiga Levine remarked in reviewing Oz's kibbutz narratives in *Where Jackals Howl and Other Stories* for *Book World* (May 31, 1981), "[t]heir characters are not the joyous prototype kibbutzniks of the United Jewish Appeal posters." So whatever the source of the previous conceptions of Israeli reality and its literary representation, the encounter with genuine Israeli Hebrew literature in translation, experienced as sophisticated and nuanced literary art, comes with the force of a revelation.

Its artistic refinement acknowledged, the new literature was often welcomed for its truth-telling capacity. In writing about Oz's *Where Jackals Howl* in the *Times Literary Supplement* (Sept. 25, 1981), Judith Chernaik states that [Oz's] "fiction is indispensable reading for anyone who wishes to understand the contradictions of life in Israel, the ideol-

ogy that sustains it, and the passions that drive its people." She concludes her review with the claim that the "reader coming to Oz for the
first time is likely to find his perception of Israel permanently altered
and shaped by these tales." Implied in these words is an actively inquisitive but perplexed reader who acknowledges the complexity of Israeli
society but who can penetrate it only with the help of Israeli literature.
This sense of Israeli literature as a key that unlocks a mystery or as a pro-
jectile that penetrates layers of misperception is especially strong for
"insiders," that is, reviewers in Jewish publications who are sensitive to
the ostensibly negative and even scandalous portrayal of Israeli life in
these works. As the longtime director of education and cultural affairs
for B'nai Brith, Lily Edelman was a quintessential insider. Reviewing
Yehoshua's *Early in the Summer of 1970* (Bi-thilat kaiytz 1970) in the
organization's journal, the *National Jewish Monthly* (Apr. 1977), Edelman remarks that "[o]n the eve of the annual celebration of [Israeli]
statehood, there is little to make the heart dance, even less to make the
spirit soar." To understand "the malaise, the despair, the somber reckoning of the soul that constitutes the stuff of the contemporary Israeli
nightmare," one has only the "key" offered by the stories of A. B.
Yehoshua. Although she finds the translation of his stories flawed, they
remain "indispensable for any reader desirous of touching truth about
contemporary Israeli mood and situation."

More ambitious still are the claims made for the truth-telling function of Israeli literature by James S. Diamond in the pages of *Conservative Judaism,* the journal of the conservative rabbinical organization.
Both a rabbi and a scholar of Hebrew literature—he was director of
Hillel then at Washington University and now at Princeton—Diamond
speaks to his fellow rabbis in an attempt to get them to take Israeli literature as something more important than "just" literature. His text is
Yehoshua's recently translated *The Lover,* and after describing the plot
with all its admitted deviance and family dysfunctionality, he abjures his
readers that it would be a "grave misreading" of the book to regard it
"as a pulp novel best serialized in a women's magazine." After a serious
critical discussion of the novel, Diamond concludes:

What I . . . wish to claim is that [*The Lover*] offers as revealing an insight into post–Yom Kippur War Israel as any political, economic or sociological tract of the last two or three years. The novel was written during the months preceding the May 1977 election and can be read as a fictive presentation of the context in which the Labor-led coalition was repudiated. By exposing the immoralities and the emptiness of much of life in Israel today, Yehoshua is tacitly reaffirming a rational Zionism of humanism and moral development. It is antithetical to the mythic Zionism that celebrates Jewish power, blood, and soil.[10]

Diamond's stance, one to which I myself have a close affinity, is that of an American Jewish reader of current Hebrew literature who is striving to convince his fellows, in this case busy rabbis in search of sermon material, that they are ignoring a valuable resource. His claim is actually two claims. The first is that a novel such as *The Lover* provides a window onto the Israeli situation in the sense that it delivers information about the internal operations of that society besides doing something much more. Like a psychoanalyst or psychotherapist, Israeli literature initiates a process whereby a people gains insight about its obsessions and neuroses and, perhaps, release from them too. This is a process that can be observed by American Jewish readers who care to pay attention. The second claim I would categorize as an effort at moral recoupment. Diamond argues that the desperate, alienated, and sordid behaviors described in the novel can be seen as exposing a fallen Zionism and dialectically affirming a rational and humanistic one.[11] Diamond is invoking an element in the explicit self-conception of Hebrew literature from a time long before the State of Israel was ever thought of: social critique as part of the duties of being what Ezekiel called a *tsofeh leveit yisrael,* a watchman for the house of Israel.

Separate from this prophetic horizon, some reviewers discern in Israeli literature a collective dimension that sets it apart in its very conception from American literature. These are arguments that arise largely in discussions of Shabtai's *Past Continuous* and Appelfeld's *Badenheim 1939* but which are generalized to make a statement about the difference of Israeli literature as a whole. For all the vast differences of scale and technique, both novels have a large cast of characters whose actions are returned to over and over again and are narrated from an impersonal distance that renounces interiority. In reviewing *Badenheim 1939* in *Partisan Review* (vol. 49, winter 1982), William Phillips, the editor of the journal, makes the extraordinary statement that "[i]t is the weight of the *Badenheim* theme that forces one to reexamine the ideas about fiction that we have inherited from both the modernist and avant-garde traditions." Those traditions give priority to the reticulations of individual consciousness and to the self-conscious and myth-making properties of language. Writing at a time when there was much talk influenced by structuralism about the "disappearance of the subject" of literature, Phillips sees in Appelfeld's work the centrality of historical events as they are experienced by a people or a society as a whole. At the heart of the fiction are historical and social forces, not individual psyches.

From a different frame of reference, Irving Howe makes a similar claim in his review of *Past Continuous* in the *New York Review of Books* (Oct. 10, 1985). In writing of the dozens of characters who are "glimpsed rather than developed," Howe writes that despite the sparse physical description of them one soon comes to feel that one "knows" a good many of them, for [Shabtai's] is an art of the representative, an art of the group. A community is releasing its experience, a generation is sliding toward extinction: the community, the generation of "labor Israel," socialist Zionism, which was central in the creation of the young country but has by now—say, the late 1970s—succumbed to old age and debility. If there can be such a thing as a collective novel, then *Past Continuous* is one.

Similarly, in the *New Republic* (May 27, 1985) Sven Birkerts speaks of the way in which Shabtai turns the stream-of-consciousness mode of writing, which is "by definition a subjectively centered idiom" "into a means for expressing the collective life of an extended human network." "Identities, and the problematic particulars of time and place, are diffused within the larger life of the clan." Shabtai's and Appelfeld's works are surely distinctive in this regard, yet throughout the critical responses to Israeli literature in translation, even in the adumbrations of the most recent postmodernist and "post-Zionist" narrative to come from Israel, one hears the echoes of a similar perception: this enterprise, despite individual realizations, is about the nation as a whole.

What Is the Subject of Israeli Literature?

As learned long ago, people do not read a work of literature—or encounter any new phenomenon—without bringing some preexisting interpretive framework to the task. That framework may, indeed, be revised by contact with a strong work of art, but the interpretation that ensues has its point of departure in some foundational set of assumptions. Of the reception of Israeli literature in America, it is fair to say that every reviewer reports on a new work in translation from within some previous concept of what the enterprise is about. Readers "realize" the meaning of the work according to what is most relevant to their individual concerns. These concepts, as they are shared in communities of interpretation, are variously called by literary theorists "master plots" or "metanarratives." So for reviewers to state what they believe is the main theme of a novel is not simply to offer informed subjective opinions nor to render accounts of rigorous objective analyses. Whatever else it does, such a statement also discloses something of the framework of interpretation the reviewers bring to the task and within which they work individually to domesticate the foreignness of the artifact laid out for inspection.

In reading through the many reviews of many books, I have tried to look for patterns in how the subject of Israeli literature is construed. (I am deferring the subject of the Holocaust until later and dealing with it on its own terms.) The gross events in a given work, of course, prompt discussions in certain directions; I have attempted to look for points in which the directions taken are not so obvious or in conflict with other readings of the same material. It goes without saying that for many reviewers the overarching story is life in Israel under the conditions of war. Anatole Broyard said it very systematically in the opening paragraph to his review of Oz's *Where Jackals Howl* in *Books of the Times* (vol. 4, Aug. 1981): "What is it like, the emotional life of people who exist in a constant state of crisis? Does the political cheat, or does it intensify, the personal? Do deeply felt causes constrict or expand character?" (The answer, by the way, is that they constrict; Broyard finds Oz's writing powerful but his characters lifeless and controlled by principles and fixed ideas.) This is a very widely applied grid. It expresses a sympathetic understanding of the constraints under which Israelis live their lives, it identifies those constraints (and the unremitting and tragic conflicts that produce them) as the basic truth or dominant fact of Israeli existence, and it expresses a detached inquisitiveness about the nature of behavior under these conditions.

That the "Arab question" should be prominent in the minds of reviewers would seem to be most natural if it were not for the fact the subject has had a rather slight presence in the literature being reviewed. With the exception of some stories by Tammuz and Yizhar, Israeli literature had largely construed Israeli reality internally; the tense constraints under which Israeli live may be the result of Arab enmity, but Arabs were largely excluded from the Israeli literary imagination. With the arrival of Oz and Yehoshua on the scene, the issue was reopened, yet still in sporadic and partial ways.[12] For example, although Oz's *Where Jackals Howl* contains only one story in which an Arab character is portrayed ("Nomad and Viper"), the reviewer for the *New York Times Book Review* (Apr. 26, 1981), A. G. Mojtabai, observes that the "most haunting issue raised" in the book "[i]s that of exclusion, dispossession—the question of Isaac and Ishmael, why one son is favored and the other not." Praising the book as "strong, beautiful, disturbing," Mojtabai locates its distinction in grappling with "a dimension of the Israeli experience not often discussed, of the specter of the other brother, of a haunting, an unhealed wound."

Time magazine is a venue in which very few works of Israeli literature have been noticed. In reviewing Oz's *My Michael* (Jul. 3, 1972) A. T. Baker points to the Arab twins who appear in Hannah Gonen's dreams as an explanation for the novel's "smashing success" in Israel. "The passion that animated the early founders of Zion has cooled. The new passionate people are the Arab fedayeen, and in some small dark recess of the national psyche, the Israelis are jealous." This, of course, reveals much more about the mentality of *Time* magazine than it does about Oz's novel, but it remains significant that this is what gets said in this rare moment of attention given to Israeli literature. Robert Alter, the great "insider" reviewer of Israeli fiction in America, must have been aware of how widely the novel was being read along these lines when he reviewed the book in the *New York Times Book Review* (May 21, 1972) two months earlier. His review is polemically focused on counteracting a political reading of the novel. "Any consideration . . . of a Palestinian Question is irrelevant to [Hannah's] conjuring with the Arab twins, who represent an alluring, threatening *dédoublement* of the male principle, an image of suppressed desire to submit to brutal sexual forces." Between these two poles Alfred Kazin offers something of a mediating position in his remarks on *The Lover*, a novel in which the Arab theme is indeed conspicuous if not central, in the *New York Review of Books* (Dec. 21, 1978). After admiring the portrayal of Naim, the fifteen-year-old Arab boy who works in a Jewish-owned garage, Kazin offers, "What I value most in *The Lover*, and never get from discourse about Israel, is a gift for equidistance—between characters, even between the feelings on both sides—that reveals the strain of keeping in balance so many necessary contradictions." What I think he means when he says "discourse about Israel" is *political* discourse about Israel, the embroiled and polarized assertions and counterassertions that constitute discussion of the Arab-Israeli conflict. The "gift for equidistance" that Kazin finds in Yehoshua's work characterizes a different kind of discourse, an imaginative or novelistic discourse, in which the impacted conflicts are not resolved but allowed to be observed with varying degrees of sympathetic distance. Kazin's is an argument for Hebrew literature as a different mode of knowing the reality in which Israel is enmeshed, and he touches upon a true, extraliterary potentiality of the enterprise as a whole.

Other efforts to identify an essential "subject" of Israeli literature concentrate—to my mind, more appropriately—on the internal changes within Israeli society, especially the transition from what Amos Elon has called the founders to the sons. Although this is the central preoccupation of Amos Oz's excellent early work, the theme is not picked up by most reviewers until Shabtai's magisterial *Past Continuous* placed it unavoidably between the cross hairs of critical focus. That novel begins and ends with both the death of one of the members of the founding generation (Goldman's father) and the suicide of his son (Goldman). In his extraordinarily perceptive review of *Past Continuous* in the *New York Review of Books* (Oct. 10, 1985), Irving Howe argues that the novel takes off from one of the conventions of Western literature—"a myth of historical and moral decline." Stirred in their youth by a "whiff of the absolute," the generation of Goldman's father was seized by "a tremendous yearning for social and moral transfiguration, a leap through history, a remaking of souls" in the struggle to establish a Jewish state. In the aftermath of that state-making enterprise, they have now slumped "into an irritable mixture of rectitude and cynicism" while, in the absence of privation and challenge, their children wander in and out of despair and dissipation. The plight of these belated off-spring of socialist Zionism is seen in the largest possible perspective by Sven Birkerts in the *New Republic* (May 27, 1985): "The transformations that other nations have undergone over centuries have in Israel been compressed into decades. The elders were faced with clear obstacles and did what had to be done. Goldman and Israel and Caesar have had no such luck. To them has fallen the task of defining the values of the culture, and they do not know where to begin." The velocity of that transformation and the violence of the compression that ensued have produced as by-products both nostalgia and a desire to escape history. These are trends I noticed in surveying a broad sampling of Israeli writing from the 1970s *(Commentary,* Jan. 1978). I found many works, es-pecially Shulamith Hareven's *City of Many Days* ('Ir yamin rabim), that gave expression to a yearning for the Mandate Period as a time when the cleavages between Jews and Arabs and among Jews themselves had not hardened and the possibilities of individual identity, even for women, had not yet been overwhelmed by historical necessity.

Between the individual and society stands the family, and for some observers the disintegration of the family is one of the major stories told in Israeli literature. Again, it is Shabtai's key work that draws attention to this theme, for in addition to being "about" the disintegration of families, *Past Continuous* is structured—and held together—at its very core by an interlocking network of family relations. Highly dysfunctional families populate Yehoshua's fiction throughout the long course of his career from his earliest stories such as "Three Days and a Child" to the more recent novels *Mr. Mani* and *Open Heart*. Encountering the stories collected in *Early in the Summer of 1970* leads Nicholas Shrimpton, the reviewer for the *New Statesman* (Feb. 1, 1980), to remark: "Marriages are made in Heaven. The families which spring from them, by contrast, appear to be the product of some wholly owned subsidiary of Hell. . . . Even Israeli fiction, which might seem to have grander subjects under its hand, shares the tendency to turn from the workplace and battlefield to the dolorous events of the life of the hearth." For others, the focus on the family scarcely represents a fall from "grander" themes. Writing of *The Lover* (*New York Review of Books,* Dec. 21, 1978), Alfred Kazin places the vivid dysfunctionality of family described in the novel within a weighty perspective indeed. The family is "the traditional 'center' of Jewish existence," and in Yehoshua's work it is a center that dramatically does not hold.

Societies undergo transformations and families fall apart for a variety of political and historical reasons. Yet the pain that is experienced by individuals in the wake of these collective events knows little of history and politics. When they are not caught up in the "grand" theme of "the conflict," reviewers have been able to discern in many Israeli writers a fidelity to the fundamental contours of human experience. The persistence of the nonrational, the crushing of sons by fathers, the corrosive effects of isolation and repression—these are some of the themes that have been noted by readers in Amos Oz's early work. Yehoshua's early work invites an even greater concentration on the universal. The stories in *Three Days and a Child* conspicuously eschew markers of time and place and present protagonists whose troubles come across as archetypal exercises in deracination and bad faith. As Yehoshua moves from these early stories to *Early in the Summer of 1970* and *The Lover,* the embroiled particularities of Israeli society come into sharper focus and the contours of political allegory become visible around the edges. This shift, however, does not signal a discounting of the universal-

SYRACUSE UNIVERSITY PRESS

1600 Jamesville Avenue, Syracuse, New York 13244-5160

(315) 443-2597   Fax (315) 443-5545

Orders Only 1-800-365-8929
FID 15-0621510

SOLD TO:

PAUL ZAKRZEWSKI, LITERARY DIR
JCC IN MANHATTAN/LOWER LEVEL 3
334 AMSTERDAM AVE @ 76TH ST
NEW YORK NY   10023

ORDER ENTRY DATE	CUSTOMER P.O. NUMBER	TERMS
6 JAN 03	REVIEW	Gratis

CODE	QUANTITY	TITLE
2900	1	TRANSLATING ISRAEL

CODE 7

ORIGINAL INVOICE

ACCOUNT NUMBER	PLEASE REFERENCE BOTH NUMBERS WHEN MAKING PAYMENT	INVOICE NUMBER
20		343581

SHIP TO:
PAUL ZAKRZEWSKI, LITERARY DIR
JCC IN MANHATTAN/LOWER LEVEL 3
334 AMSTERDAM AVE @ 76TH ST
NEW YORK NY   10023

SALES AREA	HOW SHIPPED	DATE SHIPPED
	Sp 4th Class	

	LIST PRICE	DISCOUNT	AMOUNT
	19.95	%	Free

B-TOTAL -   .00

SHIPPING/HANDLING   Free

AMOUNT PAID	
BALANCE DUE	$ .00

INVOICE NUMBER	PLEASE REFERENCE BOTH NUMBERS WHEN MAKING PAYMENT	ACCOUNT NUMBER
343681		20

SHIP TO

PAUL ZAKRZEWSKI, LITERARY DIR
JCC IN MANHATTAN LOWER LEVEL 3
334 AMSTERDAM AVE @ 76TH ST
NEW YORK NY   10023

SALES AREA	QTY SHIPPED	QTY SHIP/BO	DATE SHIPPED

SD Wdl Class

LIST PRICE	DISCOUNT	AMOUNT
19.95	X	Free

SUB-TOTAL

00
R792

SHIPPING HANDLING	AMOUNT PAID	

BALANCE DUE $ .00

existential but its incorporation into a larger vision in which it is situated within the horizon of history and politics. In writing of *Early in the Summer of 1970 (National Jewish Monthly,* Apr. 1977) Lily Edelman caught this dynamic synthesis between the particular and the universal very acutely. "[I]n a masterly mix of realistic detail and bemused perception, Yehoshua raises the particular to the universal. War of husband vs. wife, Arab vs. Jew and national vs. nation is transformed into man's battle against himself, against his ideas, his goals and purposes, man's eternal, unrelenting struggle against nature, society and God Himself."

The Critique of Israeli Literature
from the Standpoint of the Diaspora

Although Israeli literature has been generously received by the reviewers, a sign that it is taken seriously is the fact that it is also routinely criticized on literary grounds. *Elsewhere, Perhaps* is overly melodramatic toward the end. *The Lover* does, in fact, bog down in overplotting. The Bruno section of *See Under: Love* makes unfair demands on the reader. If anything, Israeli literature has been handled delicately and given a free ride in comparison to the rough-and-tumble of literary reviewing in Israel. Another kind of criticism, however, arises from an awareness of the differences between Israel and America and from an acknowledgment of the fact that a work of literature may be read very differently in different communities.

This difference is presented with much prescience by Richard Locke in his review of *My Michael,* the same review in which he expresses his surprise to discover serious writing amid the political melodrama of Israeli life *(New York Times,* May 25, 1972). Aware that the novel was an enormous success in Israel, Locke attempts to offer a differential explanation for its reception here and there. As for Israel, he points out that "Amos Oz is suggesting that in her heart Israel is going mad dreaming of Arabs, while on the surface emotionally stunted 'new Israelis' are going about their nation's business cut off from self and history. It's hardly surprising that the book caused controversy and was a bestseller in Israel." What might stir the blood of Israeli readers is something very different from the qualities that might capture the hearts of their American counterparts. "For American readers, though, *My Michael* is distinguished by its warmth, its lyricism and remarkable technical control, its fluent pattern of repetitions—threads of words and associations that weave and interweave a vast underwater net."

American Jews are diaspora Jews, and the way in which the Diaspora is represented in Israeli fiction—which is, for better or worse, not very frequent—can generate strong responses on the part of readers who have firsthand experience of the subject. Oz's first novel, *Elsewhere, Perhaps* (Makom aḥer; published in translation after his second, *My Michael*), describes the threats posed to a kibbutz by both the irrationality of the human heart and the hostility of the Arab nations. But by far the greatest threat comes from Diaspora in the character of Siegfried Berger, who seems to embody a kind of radical evil that is unlike the nature of any of the other figures in the novel. In *Commentary* (July 1974) David Stern finds Berger's character to be "embellished by Oz with all the grotesque flourishes that once marked the typical anti-Semitic caricature of the Jew." Stern goes on to declare that "Israeli literature, if it is ever to mature, will undoubtedly have to confront the critical issue of the relationship of Diaspora Jewry to Israel and the relation of Israel to Diaspora Jewry, in all its troubled complexity. . . . The novel fails precisely where the imagination might have offered insight into the nexus of Zion and Diaspora." Although Stern's tone ("if it is ever to mature") strikes a note of impatient condescension, the issue he points to is a real one—in 1974 and now. The imagination of the Diaspora in Israeli literature has never been nuanced or deeply probing. Although infrequently demonized as it was in Oz's first novel, the Diaspora is more often a kind of "elsewhere" that merely serves as a foil or an escape.

The unheroic and unromantic nature of the Israeli reality represented in the literature is experienced by some diaspora readers as disquietingly subversive. Jerome Greenfield's review of Yehoshua's early stories in the *Jewish Frontier* (Dec. 1970), the magazine of the Labor Zionist movement in America, records the difficulty in squaring the existential despair reflected in the stories with a constructive and uplifting vision of Israel. Greenfield's sense of disorientation is worth quoting at length because it expressed what must have been a sincerely felt dilemma for many readers.

> In the space of some half century [Israel] has succeeded in creating a new type of society, a new type of man. Granted that the image one gets of this new society and man is often polished over by public-relations efforts of various Zionist organizations or ideology-blinded observers. Yet there is, by common agreement, an irreducible core of truth to this image, attested to not only by the objective achievements of Israel and Israelis in peace and war but also by the thousands of out-siders who have been visiting the country every year over the past decades and come away invariably entranced by the open vigor of its life style, the uncomplicated patriotism of its people, the direct affinity they feel for their natural environment, their simple, unself-conscious ease in the general social milieu—which often stir American Jews so deeply, beset as they are with the many complexities of their own in-tricate, hyphenated existence in the U.S. And the problem that Yehoshua poses is how we are to relate his unrelenting morbidity, the invariable isolation of his protagonists, their destructive self-negation, their total unadjustment to their forests, their deserts, their climate and cities to this other image we have of Israeli life and, indeed, that Israeli have of themselves.

Aware of the respect Yehoshua's work has been accorded in Israel, Greenfield knows that the contradiction cannot be "rationalized away" by taking the stories as "sickly atypical." Instead, he works toward the difficult realization that one's understanding of Israel needs to be en-larged to accommodate what is learned from Yehoshua's writing about the "persistence of human irrationality and destructiveness and the need of such feelings for outlet at the expense of civilized, constructive rationality." This is a learning that is courageously arrived at but scarcely celebrated. Although the reviewer has learned something about how Israelis "deal with their inner lives," the conclusion of the review leaves some question about whether the native admiration of

American Jews for Israel can remain unaffected by the unwished for insights thrust upon them by Israeli literature.[13]

Then there are issues that figure importantly in the minds of American Jews and find little resonance in Israeli literature. Feminism is surely one of them. Israeli literature of the 1970s is not rife with portrayals of self-actualizing women, yet this is the lens through which Gloria Goldreich, writing in *Hadassah Monthly* (May 1972), sees Hannah Gonen, the troubled heroine of Oz's *My Michael*. For Goldreich, Hannah is a "woman, programmed into women's work—marriage and motherhood—struggling to free herself and become her own person." Another issue is baldly stated by the unnamed reviewer in *Choice* (April 1979), who, after generally praising *The Lover*, opines—with an enormous reserve of naiveté—that the only weakness in the book "is its rather shallow treatment of Judaism and its religious values." As mentioned earlier, I expressed similar disappointment—less naively, I hope—with Grossman's failure to draw upon the enormous and various repertoire of responses to catastrophe in classical Hebrew sources.

Finally, political values can be used as a position from which to interpret Israeli literature, although this happens less frequently than one might imagine. It goes without saying that political convictions about Zionism as a whole, the Arab-Israeli conflict, and Israel's domestic and foreign policies inform a journal's likelihood to pay attention to an Israeli work of literature and a reviewer's proximity to or distance from the material. Yet I did not find many instances in reviews in which these values came into play explicitly. The exceptions came from voices that are more avowedly identified with the Left or the Right. I adduce two examples that each deal with Grossman's *See Under: Love*. The "politics" of that novel are by no means clear, but because Grossman revealed his own distaste for the occupation of the West Bank and Gaza in *The Yellow Wind* (Ha-zeman ha-tzahov), which was written after *See Under: Love* but published in translation in America before it, a kind of invitation existed to connect the politics of one book with those of the other. In a long review in *Tikkun* (Mar./Apr. 1990) Adina Hoffman makes the connection by averring that although Grossman warns against the costs of forgetting the Holocaust, "[e]qually fierce . . . is

Grossman's admonition against an understandably but woefully mis-
guided reliance on the past as eternal justification for the present. No
doubt he would contend that the bankrupt moral state of Israel's present policies is the result in part of the too-frequent sounding of Holocaust alarms designed to drown out the din of Israel's own aggressive
actions against others." On the other side of the political spectrum,
Ruth Wisse invokes *The Yellow Wind* in a review in the *Sunday Boston
Globe* to identify, in a far more nuanced way, a problem that is explicit in
the journalism but implicit in the novel. While praising the novel on
many scores, Wisse finds Grossman's artistic inventiveness cut off from
an awareness of how the human condition is embedded in history. His
shortcoming lies in his readiness to substitute "imagination for mortal
engagement."

> For all its invention, there is no moral tension in this book of the kind
> that derives from the decisions of protagonists who must take reality
> into account in the conduct of their lives. Instead, the author pits his
> imaginative will and his will to innocence against the human condi-
> tion. In fact, readers familiar with *The Yellow Wind* . . . will recognize
> here the same dilution and avoidance of moral complexity that dis-
> torts his reportage of Arabs and Jews on the West Bank.

Do Books about the Holocaust Receive Special Attention?

The answer is yes, they do. On a sheer quantitative level, one is
struck by the notice taken in a large number of journals of *Badenheim
1939* and *See Under: Love* as opposed to Israeli novels whose focus is
contemporary Israel. These are two impressive works of fiction, but the
breadth of their reception cannot be explained by their inherent artistic
achievements alone. It has been pointed out that good Israeli writing
routinely received serious attention in some of the central forums of
American intellectual life, especially the *New York Times,* the *New York
Review of Books,* and the *New Republic.* Yet despite the salience of this
attention, it was rarely broad. This changed when *Badenheim 1939* appeared in 1980. Publications that had previously barely acknowledged

the existence of Hebrew literature wrote—often glowingly—about Appelfeld's novel. *Newsweek,* the *Christian Century,* the *Jewish Spectator,* the *Nation,* the *National Review, Partisan Review, Present Tense, Punch, Sewanee Review, Tradition,* the *Voice Literary Supplement,* the *Wilson Library Bulletin,* and *World Literature Today* represent an incomplete list of publishing venues to be added to the list of both Jewish and general usual suspects. In the case of *See Under: Love,* one can add to the list the following: the *American Book Review,* the *Boston Review, Commonweal,* the *Los Angeles Times Book Review,* the *London Review of Books,* the London *Observer, Review of Contemporary Fiction,* and the *West Coast Review of Books.*

What is most telling about the reception of these books is that for most reviewers the fact that they are written in Hebrew by Israelis from within the enterprise of the Israeli literate is largely irrelevant and often unsaid. To be sure, Nehama Ashkenazi *(Tradition,* summer 1982) pointed out Appelfeld's connections to the Hebrew writers Y. H. Brenner and S. Y. Agnon; Hillel Halkin *(New Republic,* May 15, 1989) placed Grossman's Holocaust novel in the context of his previous non-Holocaust writing and identified the Hebrew stylistic devices and period echoes in the work; and I placed the novel within the framework of the problematic of the Holocaust in Israeli culture (chap. 8 of this volume). When all is said and done, however, most reviewers approached both novels in terms of the solutions they offer to the problem of representing the Holocaust in literature. It is as if these novels are contributions made to world culture by Israeli literature in which the origin of the gifts, although perhaps noted, is not terribly important. It is also a very privileged circle to be allowed to join. Edmund White concludes his review of *See Under: Love* in the *New York Times Book Review* (Apr. 16, 1989) with this encomium: "In a few mythic books, such as Faulkner's *Sound and Fury,* Gunter Grasse's *Tin Drum,* Gabriel García Márquez's *One Hundred Years of Solitude,* large visions of history get told in innovative ways. *See Under: Love* may be a worthy successor to this small but awesome canon."

Baddenheim 1939 is everywhere compared to Kafka, and after calling the book a "small masterpiece," Irving Howe, also in the *New York*

Times Book Review (Nov. 23, 1980), identifies Appelfeld as a "spiritual descendant of European modernism, though he lives in Israel and writes in Hebrew."

It may be pointless to try to prize apart the two components of this phenomenon: the fact that these are books about the Holocaust and the fact that they are significant literary achievements that depart from the conventions of Israeli literature. It may be fair to say, however, that no work of Hebrew fiction whose subject is Israeli society, no matter how outstanding its artistic realization, is likely to garner the volume of attention and admiration won by Appelfeld's and Grossman's Holocaust novels. In this sense, what is true about Hebrew literature and the world works to confirm what is generally true about the Jewish people and the world: it is holocaust rather than homeland that evokes admiration and empathy.

If It's So Good, Why Don't People Read It?

If this extended sojourn among the reviewers has proven anything, it is that in at least one place in American culture, even if that place is not a broad avenue, Israeli literature is being taken seriously and is being written about thoughtfully. What I have sampled here is only a selection of early books by key writers; the volume of critical discussion would be amplified considerably if I went on to include later works by Oz *(Perfect Peace, Black Box, To Know a Woman,* and others) and Yehoshua *(Late Divorce, Five Seasons, Mr. Mani, Open Heart),* Appelfeld's many novellas, Meir Shalev's *Blue Mountain* and *Esau,* Grossman's *The Book of Intimate Grammar,* and others.

Having documented this solid critical reception, I am brought back to the disproportion described earlier between this kind of success and the relative failure of Israeli literature in translation to sell books and to have an impact on the American Jewish community. I conclude this introduction with some interpretive conjectures about why this is so. These explanations must remain conjectural because I know of no hard evidence that describes the attitudes of Jewish and non-Jewish Americans toward Israeli literature in particular rather than toward Israel as a political entity in general. Although it is possible to assemble the body of published critical responses to this literature and to make coherent analytic statements about it, it is another thing entirely to explain the behavior of the final link in the chain of reception—the reader/consumer, who, in this case, more often than not elects not to receive the message. With these caveats, then, I offer the following salutatory observations.

The relative success of Israeli literature in European countries in comparison to America, to begin with, can tell one something about the reading habits of Americans in general. Because Europe is divided into small countries, European readers have long been accustomed to reading in translation, not to mention the fact that many can read in another language altogether. If one is Dutch or Swiss or even German or French and a reader of literature to begin with, one will as a matter of course find oneself reading translations of serious literature. This is the result of a number of factors. Among them is the awareness of an interdependent European identity and the plain fact that the literary systems of smaller countries are expanded and enriched by translations into that language. The result is that European publishers and readers are not just open to but are often eager for translations of good works of fiction. And this eagerness is completely separate from whatever interest in Israel and the Jews is satisfied by these works.

Americans are very skittish about reading literature in translation, and publishers know this better than anyone. The world of published books already written in English is perceived to be so extensive and so polymorphous that, given the limited time Americans have for reading to begin with, there is no pressing need to look farther afield. Reading literature in translation also reminds Americans of college courses in which they were required to read difficult works of European modernism or long continental novels. This attitude applies to American Jews, as well. Even if they buy more or read more books and even if they are interested in Israel and the Jewish world, there is, nowadays, no lack of domestically produced books to answer their needs.

American Jews who wish to engage Israel through reading fiction, moreover, do not have far to look. Beginning with Leon Uris's *Exodus,* there has been a steady stream of popular novels that have continued to cover this territory. More recently, one sees an increase in multigenerational family sagas written from the point of view of female protagonists. What is common to most of these works is a focus on heroic moments in the history of the state of Israel: its founding struggle against the background of catastrophe and world war, the capture of Adolf Eichmann, the Six-Day War, the raid on Entebbe, and so forth. In reading these paperback sagas, American Jews are using literature to connect to Israel in a way that characterizes a much larger pattern; they are using Israel to buttress their own identities. The glow of the heroic-romantic version of Israel abets this process; the moral realism of the Israeli literature I have been discussing here apparently does not.

From its inception Hebrew literature has always seen itself as a truth-telling literature. In this it is really no different from the serious literature of all advanced cultures that propose to offer a critical representation of the way we live now. As a genre, the novel itself from the days of the knight from La Mancha to the present has taken as its goal replacing illusion with reality. Whatever the perfection of artistry and literary form, truth-telling is an appealing quality only to those who want to know the truth. For American Jews, reading Israeli literature in translation must feel like eavesdropping on the internal squabbles of a family whose dirty laundry one does not want to see because it is too troubling to one's own purchase on purity.

Israeli literature is likely to remain important to those who have a different kind of relationship to Israel, to those who have discovered these writers in college courses, and to serious readers of fiction generally. The circumscribed compass of that aggregate reflects a larger truth about the Jewish people at the beginning of the twenty-first century—the drifting apart, in what seems to be an irreversible tectonic process, of American Jewry and Israeli Jewry.

PART ONE

THE ENTERPRISE OF HEBREW LITERATURE

Introduction

THE TWO CHAPTERS in this section are synthetic attempts to give an account of a major aspect or a major period in modern Hebrew literature rather than focusing on a single author or a single work.

"Nostalgia and Apocalypse: Israeli Literature in the 1970s" considers the images of Israeli society reflected in a wave of new Hebrew writing that reached America for the first time in translation. Amos Oz, Shulamith Hareven, and A. B. Yehoshua were first appearing in English and being recognized not only by general readers but also by serious literary-academic journals such as the *TriQuarterly Review*. Nostalgia and apocalypse refer to two modes of evasion that are explored in the Israeli fiction published in the early 1970s. The time is the War of Attrition after the Six-Day War; the grinding hostility after the triumph of 1967 forms the backdrop for various impulses to escape the desultory contradictions of the present moment. Frustration with the unremitting regime of restraint, preparedness, and renunciation leads to fantasies of apocalyptic abandonment. Disillusionment with the entrenched conflict between Israel and her enemies leads to nostalgia for the mandate period in which Arabs and Jews and other denizens of Palestine interacted—at least in the retrospect of the imagination—more freely.

A literary culture that was emerging in the late sixties and early seventies exploded in the years after the Yom Kippur War. Rather than discussing specific works, in the second chapter in this section, "The Boom in Israeli Fiction: An Overview," I offer a general characterization of the state of Israeli literature—at least novels and short stories—

between 1973 and 1993. The period is marked by a proliferation of good writers and strong works and by significant changes in the way books are published in Israel and in the nature of the audience for serious literature. Genres such as mysteries, thrillers, and romance, which had customarily been imported in translation from European languages, now begin to be written in Hebrew and to be set not in English villages but in native locales. By far the biggest change during this time is the surge in the number of women writers. This increase has had a transformative impact on the themes of Israeli literature, not only placing women's experience at the center of much fiction but stimulating male writers to reexamine the construction of gender in their own writing. The rise of women writers is one component of the assault on what has been called the "Zionist masterplot." From its beginnings, most Israeli literature has centered on the lives of Ashkenazi male heroes whose experience is defined by the great issues of national destiny. From the seventies onward, this masterplot has been broken up into many stories, which include and overlap with the stories of Sephardim and Holocaust survivors. It is not surprising that the *way* these stories should be written, the mode of fiction, should also undergo an transformation, borrowing and adapting freely from international styles of postmodernism and magic realism.

1

Nostalgia and Apocalypse

Israeli Literature in the 1970s

THE STATE OF ISRAEL was conceived by force of a messianic vision, but its existence has been maintained by order, sacrifice, and the rational setting of priorities—and this in the face of another, more ominous vision held by its neighbors. Life under such mixed conditions of ordinariness and dread might well seem cribbed and predetermined, and it is understandable that Israelis would search for various ways of becoming released from it. In Israel's literature that search has often taken one of two forms: a looking back to happier times and a reaching forward toward some new vision of an end, either individual or collective, in which the anxieties of history will be dissolved. Indeed, ever since the pioneer period, one of the chief functions of Israel's literature, especially its prose literature, has been to represent and also to criticize this dual urge toward nostalgia and apocalypse in Israeli consciousness.

A number of works published in the mid-1970s give readers a chance to observe at firsthand this tendency in Israeli writing in the years between the Sixty-Seven and Seventy-Three Wars. Of particular interest are two anthologies. The first, *Contemporary Israeli Literature*, which began as a special number of the journal *TriQuarterly*, is quite substantial, containing ten short stories and the work of twenty-three poets and featuring an introduction by Shimon Sandbank and an after-

This chapter was previously published as "New Israeli Writing" in *Commentary*, Jan. 1978, 64–67. Reprinted by permission; all rights reserved.

word by Robert Alter, both extremely useful. The second anthology, *New Writing in Israel*, is a more modest and uneven affair with an abbreviated poetry section and no introduction. And one should also mention a novel by Shulamith Hareven, *City of Many Days*, and a collection of short stories by A. B. Yehoshua, *Early in the Summer of 1970*.[1]

In Israeli fiction of this time, the period returned to most often as an object of nostalgia is that of the British Mandate, a period when the conflict that was to become the Jewish state's lot after 1948 seemed neither inevitable nor irremediable. Jerusalem between the two world wars is the setting of Shulamith Hareven's *City of Many Days*, a novel whose ostensible focus is the history of a specific Sephardi family but whose real subject is Jerusalem itself, bodied forth in the book through a polyglot cast of eccentrics who make their way through the city's bewildering array of sights and smells. Miss Hareven's Jerusalem catalog (gorgeously rendered in English by Hillel Halkin) is meant to suggest the idyll of possibility that somehow was allowed to flourish in the years before the rise of intensive nationalism in Palestine. Relations between Arabs and Jews during the early mandate are depicted as standoffish but amicable. The British presence is exemplified by an army officer so fascinated by his "colonial" subjects that he throws in his lot with them. And then there is the most vital element of all, the Jews themselves, the half-pious, half-worldly Sephardim whose luxuriant openness becomes all the more precious a quality as it is seen to be eclipsed by the gathering of historical forces.

Unfortunately, the charm of Miss Hareven's picture of Jerusalem—there is no question about the beauty of her evocation—is purchased through her exclusion from it of anything that is *not* charming. Miss Hareven's characters are innocent of history, and their innocence attenuates their charm until it threatens to become mere idealization. The Sephardi community has, it is true, been underrepresented in modern Hebrew fiction, but Miss Hareven tends to err in the opposite direction. There is scarcely a trace here of the large numbers of Eastern European Jews, the pioneers and the socialists, who during these same years were changing the face of the Jewish settlement in Palestine and preparing the greater transformation to come. Lacking a dialectical view, which could comprehend what was being created besides what was being destroyed, *City of Many Days* remains an exquisite piece of literary nostalgia rather than a full evocation of a historical moment that might instruct as much as it delights.

The mandate setting is put to a much different purpose in David Shahar's story "Louidor Louidor," which is included in *Contemporary Israeli Literature*. For Shahar (two of whose books have already appeared in English, a collection of short stories, *News from Jerusalem*, and a novel, *The Palace of Shattered Vessels* [Heichal ha-kelim ha-shvurim]), Palestine of those years is also a landscape of eccentrics, as it is for Miss Hareven, but his eccentrics are driven by the contradictions of history rather than by private idiosyncrasies. Louidor, for example, is a distracted Tolstoyan intellectual who comes to Palestine to realize his rationalist-pacifist principles in a Jewish homeland. Shocked to find the country filled with Arabs, he converts to Islam to have the moral right to appeal to his new "brethren" to leave Palestine for the "blessed lands of Arabia." (As a figure he is a precursor of figures in the fiction of Ruth Almog and A. B. Yehoshua.) Louidor's eventual fate—he is beaten up and dismembered by an Arab gang—is for Shahar a way of suggesting that imported visions will always be rejected by a land so pocketed by historical ironies and crossed national destinies.

Although the tone of Shahar's story is elegiac and nostalgic, what motivates his hero is rather an apocalyptic (and almost psychotic) passion for redemption, a yearning for an impossible future in which all obstacles to moral purity will have finally disappeared. Something of the same passion motivates Joseph della Reina, the hero of a fine story by Dan Tsalka included in *New Writing in Israel*. The story is based on a kabbalistic legend about a fifteenth-century mystic who attempted to bring about the messianic age by capturing Satan but who failed under terrifying circumstances and ended his days as Satan's ally and as the lover of Lilith, the archfemale demon of Jewish folklore. In Tsalka's retelling the legend takes an eerily modern turn by the addition of an existential context with della Reina's passion understood psychologically as that familiar kind of moral zeal in which the unacknowledged element of self-aggrandizement ensures future corruption and failure.

If messianism, even misplaced messianism, is the "positive" paradigm of Jewish apocalypse, the Holocaust, both as an event and as a symbol, is its negative pole. Among Hebrew writers of fiction, Aharon Appelfeld is the one who has most unequivocally taken the Holocaust as a field of imaginative activity. Appelfeld, whose work deserves to be better known in English, is a master of obliqueness; rather than describing atrocity directly, he focuses instead on the historical moments just before and just after the Holocaust and speaks through them of what is in itself unspeakable. (See the chapter on Appelfeld in this volume.)

Appelfeld's story, *Badenheim 1939,* included in both *Contemporary Israeli Literature* and *New Writing in Israel,* is an ingenious and ornate parable about the fall of German-speaking Jewry. The locale is an Austrian resort town whose inhabitants reveal themselves to each other in the course of the story as they are forced to register with the local authorities as Jews. Instead of being panicked and cowed, the Jews assume a kind of calm gaiety. As the registration proceeds and the routine of the resort breaks down, there is an immense sense of relief at being able to confess the deep and troublesome burden of Jewishness "as if they were talking about a chronic disease which was no longer a reason to hide." With the resort finally closed and the transports waiting, the Jews, who believe they are being returned to the simpler life of their ancestral home in Poland, express appreciation to the authorities and look forward to their "repatriation." It is characteristic of Appelfeld's laconic and perverse brilliance that the story ends here with no further comment or elaboration.

Like the State of Israel itself, that ambitious social experiment, the kibbutz, came into being in large part through a messianic drive, and it, too, paradoxically, has been maintained through the antimessianic values of order, rationality, and institutionalization. As setting and theme, the kibbutz has undoubtedly been overworked in Hebrew literature, but in the 1970s it still retained potential for fictional treatment. The isolation and self-sufficiency of the kibbutz offer exactly the kind of manageable and self-contained world that is so desirable to fiction, and the situation of the kibbutz suggests a microcosm of the larger situation of Israel as nation and society. Amos Oz has, in fact, used the kibbutz in just this way (as in his 1966 novel *Elsewhere, Perhaps* and in an earlier collection of stories, *Where Jackels Howl*); he is represented in *Contemporary Israeli Literature* by a kibbutz story from the 1960s. *New Writing in Israel* also contains a story with a kibbutz setting, this one by Yitzhak Ben Ner. Both stories are examinations of the price paid by kibbutz members for, precisely, the rationality of kibbutz existence.

Ben Ner's "A Village Death" is a wonderfully told monologue whose narrator, a forty-three-year-old member of a collective village, has assumed the responsibilities of undertaker and mourner of the dead to expiate an affair he had twenty years earlier with the wife of another member. His death-in-life represents one way of dealing with the persistence of two antagonistic forms of feeling: lust for what is alien and dangerous, and love for one's native ground.

Oz's "A Hollow Stone" concerns the honored memory of a kibbutz founder whose brand of romantic socialism led him to his death in the Spanish Civil War. His wife has been left behind to play the role of a sainted widow of the revolution—a role the kibbutz despises. "Martyrdoms, Mediterranean tragedies, emotional arabesques," remarks the anonymous narrator who represents the community's conventional wisdom, "were irreconcilable with the principles by which we guided our lives." [2]

To escape a life hedged in by principles and responsibilities, a life symbolized in miniature by the kibbutz but characteristic as well of Israel's entire national situation, Israelis flee to zones of imagined freedom such as the United States, a country where there is seemingly no limit to the romance of individual achievement and where a man has room to pursue private dreams of experience, money, sex. The fragility of such dreams is suggested by the novelist Yoram Kaniuk in "They've Moved the House," one of a pair of stories with an American setting included in *Contemporary Israeli Literature*. With enormous linguistic energy Kaniuk evokes the mixture of wide-eyed naiveté and grandiose ambition that marks his two Israeli *schlemiels* as they untiringly conceive new money-making schemes.

In "The Orgy," an amusing and cerebral story by the poet, Yehuda Amichai, America likewise serves as a symbol of liberation from the disciplines of history and holiness that are the conditions of life in Israel but is a symbol heavily charged with irony. Amichai's first-person narrator is an Israeli student, worn down by his doctoral studies, who comes to New York in search of a new source of transcendence. He finds it in sex, something America has abundantly to offer and a commodity that in Amichai's rendering assumes a kind of Sabbatian appropriateness as the supreme value in a transvalued world, a world in which the orgy has become the means of reconstructing the rituals of a collective experience. Amichai's story ends with a jocular account of a road show formed by the narrator and his friends to expound and practice their new Torah.

Nostalgia for an idealized past, the frenzied search for a transcendent future—it is one of the marks of A. B. Yehoshua's achievement as a writer that he refuses to give way to either of these temptations. In his new collection, *Early in the Summer of 1970,* as in a previous collection, *Three Days and a Child,* Yehoshua sticks resolutely to the harrowing confines of the present, even though, within those confines, he often writes with the touch not of a realist but of a fabulist. The stories in the new collection take place between 1967 and 1973, a time of wearying stalemate between Israel and its Arab neighbors punctuated by random, sporadic death. In Yehoshua's imaginative reconstruction of this period, the larger collective purposes of the national existence have lost their clarity; his characters struggle on, but the struggle discloses no meaning to them. If there is any heroism in Yehoshua'a world, it consists in the courage to face facts as they are and still proceed with the business of life.

The nameless hero of "Missile Base 612" cannot muster such courage. Rather, he persists in demanding some revelation that will explain the disorientation of his existence. Like the aimless fighting between Israel and Egypt along the Suez Canal, his life has become a permanent battle fought from fixed positions: although he and his wife share the same house and the same child, they squabble or ignore each other, and at the university where he works, his career has bogged down. Thus, when he is asked to spend a day lecturing in the Sinai to army troops, he is grateful for the chance to break out of his isolation.

Yet he who has come to lecture is actually the one in need of enlightenment. The army is full of people who have adapted to the conditions of
uncertainty and attrition, and his fumbling and grandiloquent over-
tures to the men are met by stupefaction or bemused skepticism.

Finally, he steals a close look at the missiles on the base and is electrified by the spectacle they present of impersonal, erotic power. But he
characteristically fails to grasp the nature of this power. Searching for an
epiphany that will explain and release him from the deadlock of his own
life, he cannot understand that the purpose of the missiles is not to be
fired, that they are there to prevent an apocalypse by remaining in
check.

Loss of meaning and the baffled search for a way to overcame that
loss is similarly at the center of the title story, "Early in the Summer of
1970," Yehoshua's brilliant recasting of the motif of the Sacrifice of
Isaac. The father here is an aging high-school teacher who has stubbornly refused to retire, to accept that his life is over. He looks to his
son, a university lecturer who has recently returned from abroad with a
young American wife, for the enunciation of some new message, the
banner of a new generation. But the son is remote and ungiving. Then
one day, while teaching in school, he is suddenly informed that this son,
who is on reserve duty in the Jordan Valley, has been killed.

When he goes to identify the body, however, it develops that there
has been an administrative error: the dead man is not the son after all. A
frantic journey follows to the outpost where the son's unit is on maneuvers, and a face-to-face encounter ensues in which the son shows himself to be completely unresponsive to the ordeal his father has
undergone; all he can do is mutter bitterly about his military experience, "such a loss of time . . . so pointless."

The story is told with an obsessive, almost painful, allegiance to the
viewpoint of the father, who returns constantly in his mind to the moment when he was given the news of his sons "death." With each repetition, it becomes clearer that instead of reliving a moment of pain, the
father is actually reliving a moment in which his son's life, and his own,
seem finally to have taken on meaning. He sees himself, guilty and
bereft but somehow heroic, offering up his son on the altar of national

existence, and he sees his son as a willing martyr in the same cause. As in the biblical tale, however, the son is allowed to live. But whereas in Abraham's case it was trust in God that was being tested and revealed, in Yehoshua's story what is being tested is only the father's desperate and misplaced faith in a deliverance wrought by others. And whereas in the biblical story, ordeal is followed by covenant, by the striking of a new redemptive relationship between God and His chosen ones, "Early in the Summer of 1970" ends back in a reality without illusions: the ordeal will simply continue.

Yehoshua's stories sound grim and severe when stripped to their moral burden, but as works of art they are marvelously accomplished, rich and precise in language, and startlingly inventive in their use of nonrealistic modes of narration. As a moralist Yehoshua is relentless, and he shows his characters no quarter. Conspicuously absent from his work is just that element of sympathy toward the yearning for deliverance that runs like a scarlet thread through so much serious Jewish writing in the twentieth century—and not only in the twentieth century.

Still, what Yehoshua does share with almost all Hebrew writers of the modern period, and with many contemporary Israeli writers in particular, is a highly charged sense of obligation toward his material, an obligation not only to depict faithfully but also to evaluate and comment upon the twists and turns of the national consciousness as they reveal themselves in character and incident. That so many Israeli writers have been able to transform this sense of obligation into successful works of the imagination is a remarkable achievement and in its own way a tribute to the vigor of the Jewish national spirit.

2

The Boom in Israeli Fiction

An Overview

HEBREW LITERATURE, which began with the Bible, has had a very, very, long history. Modern Hebrew literature, which began with the Enlightenment, has been around for two centuries. Against this time line, the Hebrew novels and short stories written in Israel since the mid-1970s might seem callow and unproven recent arrivals. Yet, in fact, the opposite is true. Readers and critics share the heady realization that they are living through an explosion of literary creativity and that many of the works written during this period not only do not pale in comparison to their strongest precursors but are likely to be studied with close attention in the future.

The point, of course, is not to fix the value of reputations or to speculate in the bourse of literary immortality but to indicate the excitement and sense of moment that have attended the arrival of new works of fiction in Israel since the mid-1970s. Fresh writers have appeared on the scene, and older writers have developed in new ways. The field has also become more crowded. It used to be that a literate Hebrew reader would have to satisfy his or her appetite for fiction largely by reading novels translated from European languages. Each year a few

This chapter was previously published as the Introduction to *The Boom in Contemporary Israeli Fiction,* edited by Alan L. Mintz, copyright © 1997 by the Trustees of Brandeis University. Reprinted by permission of the University Press of New England, Hanover, N.H.

novels written in Hebrew would demand attention and give pleasure, but they did not make for a steady diet of satisfying reading. By the 1980s the trickle had become a steady flow. Not only were there many more conventionally "serious" works of fiction but there were also many more attempts to write "genre" novels in Hebrew: detective novels, thrillers, romances, historical novels. These are just the kinds of works that had previously been imported in translation and now have served to fill out the literary system.

More and better works of fiction also created a new audience for fiction. This had something to do with a general shift from poetry to prose. During most of the twentieth century, throughout the waves of immigration from Europe and the struggle for nationhood, the Hebrew-reading public has carried on a love affair with poetry. Poems were declaimed by national figures at public ceremonies and carried in the rucksacks of anonymous soldier-farmers. For Jews who were only one generation removed from study of the Torah and observance of the commandments, the writing and reading of poetry, as a private communion or a communal sacrament, served as a kind of substitute piety. The national preoccupation with poetry has been on the wane for some time now, however, and one is tempted to point to Yehuda Amichai as the poet whose widely accessible and widely read work signaled the end of an era. Wonderful poetry continues to be written in Israel, but, in a way that parallels the fate of poetry in most Western democracies, the poetry scene is scattered and unsure of itself. New commanding poetic voices have not emerged, and poets find themselves marginalized in the arena of public culture and pressed into a defensive position concerning the prerogatives of their craft.

Why this turn to prose? This is one of those questions that naturally come to mind but about which few satisfying answers can be given. No research protocols or analytic frameworks I am aware of can shed much objective light on this subtle yet fundamental phenomenon in culture. One is left with speculations, and the speculation I would offer, although it is scarcely original, centers on the capacity of prose fiction to give adequate representation to the way in which the individual self is entangled with other selves in the world of social relations. In the decades after independence the Israeli reality became more diverse and less ideologically driven. Whole sectors of the population became established economically at the same time as social, ethnic, and religious cleavages deepened. The move away from labor socialism at the polls and state ownership in the economy were not simply outgrowths of shifting political currents but causes and effects of a deeper change. The construction of the self in Israeli society became less dominated and organized by a national collective myth, and the "story" of the individual became many stories enacted in many arenas with many possible outcomes and many possible interconnections. To be sure, poetry can—and Israeli poetry does—offer abundant insights into these changes, especially through a strong tradition of political verse. But it is my conjecture that prose fiction has proved better suited to comprehend the interwoven strands of this complex society in transformation and give an account of "how we live now."

The new audience for Israeli fiction is in part a creation of a publishing industry that operates very differently now than it did in the past. Since the 1920s and 1930s when the basic institutions of the Yishuv were set up, books of poetry, essays, and fiction were generally put out by publishing houses connected to political movements with varying degrees of insistence on the "political correctness" of the published works and their authors. Private houses, such as Schocken, were a rarity; these were either vanity presses or cooperative ventures by small circles of avant-garde writers. Beginning in the 1970s, large commercial publishing houses entered the scene and introduced more of a free-market model based on profitability and consumer demand. Even the older, movement-based publishers were quickened by this entrepreneurial spirit; as ideological constraints weakened, the desire to connect with wider audiences led to a greater flexibility of publishing arrangements and to many joint ventures with commercial houses.

The publishing marketplace in Israel has come to resemble in many respects the way books are sold and promoted in America. There is a culture of best sellers in which a few books get read by a great many people and benefit from concentrated media attention. This means that some writers are receiving substantial royalties (in Israeli terms), and, although I know of no writer who lives solely from writing serious fiction, money has become a new factor. There is a greater investment in the promotion of books and the manipulation of their reception in the press. A handful of powerful editor-professors attempt to shape the tastes of the serious reading public, and many boundaries are crossed between the academy, the publishing houses, and the media. The "Americanization" of publishing in Israel, in short, has all the merits and demerits of the model it has copied. Undeniably, it has had the general effect of quickening the climate within which fiction is written and read and of engendering excitement about new talents. The best books do not always sell the most copies, but sometimes they do, and the larger number of works that manage to get published creates a wider field of critical play and possibility.

In this connection, it is worth noting that the audience of Israeli fiction is not located only within Israel. (To be sure, hundreds of thousands of Israelis have left Israel and settled in other countries, primarily the United States; like Israelis in their homeland, most do not consume serious literature, but some do.) More to the point, there is a significant audience for Hebrew fiction translated into other languages, mostly (but not exclusively) English and European languages. Interestingly, despite the size of the American audience and the large scale of its Jewish community proportional to other countries, Israeli novels sometimes do better in French or German or Italian than in English. In any case, commercial successes are rare, critical succès d'estime much less so. If the diffusion of Israeli literature in translation is not broad, these works often do have an impact upon intellectual and critical circles. This notice contributes to an awareness of the presence of Israeli literature on the international literary scene. Amos Oz, A. B. Yehoshua, Aharon Appelfeld, and Yehuda Amichai are among the Israeli writers who are acknowledged as significant figures of world literature.

What ends up being translated is not always what is most popular or highly regarded in Israel. Getting translated is the result of a combination of factors: commercial publishing considerations, cultural politics, and the degree of the author's determination to make it happen. Amalia Kahana-Carmon, the important New Wave writer whose work took a pronounced postmodernist turn in the 1980s, has generally declined to allow her work to appear in English or other languages, presumably because of her belief in its untranslatability. In the end, the most important factor lies less inside Israel and more in the way in which Israel and its culture are perceived and are thought to be relevant in the minds of foreign intellectuals and the national culture of which they are part. How Israeli literature in translation is read in different lands—what is chosen for translation, the sales and diffusion, the critical notices, the features that are brought to the fore—in short, everything one associates with the phenomenon of reception is a fascinating subject that awaits exploration.

Does the existence of an international audience change the way in which Israeli writers go about their writing? Certainly writers with major reputations who have had previous works translated must be somewhat mindful that they are not likely to be read by Israelis alone, although this awareness is difficult to separate and measure. Aharon Appelfeld, the prolific author of Holocaust literature in Hebrew who has seen much of his work appear in translation, does, in fact, seem to see himself as an international Jewish writer. This is evidenced, in part, by the fact that he has sometimes published the original Hebrew text of a work in Israel *after* the translation has appeared abroad. In general, however, most Hebrew fiction is intended to be an internal communicative exchange between Israeli writers and Israeli readers and a give-and-take between citizens of a nation who all largely share the same fate and live under a similar set of cultural and historical circumstances.

From its beginnings in the eighteenth century, modern Hebrew literature has always seen itself as discharging an oppositional mission in relation to the established community, a role that carries on the prophets' commitment to be what Ezekiel called a "watchman to the house of Israel" (Ezekiel 3:17). But because Israel is a country constantly under scrutiny by the world, its internal affairs, from the raucous behavior of its politicians in the Kenesset to the protests of the disadvantaged in development towns, cease being solely internal. Such is the case with literature as well. Novels that are written in Hebrew and are meant to affect a single cultural system are read in translation—eavesdropped upon, as it were—by outsiders to that system. Artists may aim their work at a target audience and even encrypt their messages in a code known only to that audience; yet once the art work is released into the world, the artist can have little control over its dissemination and interpretation. Knowing this to be the case, no serious Israeli artist, I think, would or should feel constrained to write differently. But a certain ironic loss of innocence in this knowledge of the complexity of cultural reverberations remains.

One of the main claims for the broader significance of Hebrew literature lies in its success in creating a rich secular culture in the face of antagonistic pressures and in doing so in a way that is instructive relative to both European literatures and other Middle Eastern societies. In contrast to Western societies in which the process of secularization unfolded over several centuries, the Jews emerged from the medieval religious culture of their ancestors much more recently and much more suddenly. This transformation, moreover, took place under extreme conditions of persecution, revolution, and displacement. That under these circumstances a significant number of extraordinary works of modern literature should be written in a revived classical tongue (a story unto itself) is impressive enough. Most important, however, is the fact that literature and the institutions of literary culture became a principal mode of encountering and mediating modernity. Between the claims of religious tradition and the headlong imitation of Western values, the national movement managed to nurture a literature that could appropriate elements of the past in secularized form and then use them in the service of creating a viable civic society. This is especially true in the case of the novel as an institution, which began a continuous line of development in Hebrew in the 1850s and reached the degree of variety and complexity described in this volume. It is not the uniqueness of this achievement that is the point as much as the paradigmatic status of Israeli literature as an instance of enriched rather than impoverished secularization.

It is only natural that a large part of the audience for contemporary Israeli literature in translation is, and will likely remain, American Jews. One wishes the audience were larger. Given the large number of American Jews and their generous book-buying habits and given the generally high quality of Israeli literature, it is surprising that more Israeli fiction is not translated and that which is translated sells only respectably at best. The paradox is just another facet of a selective and ambivalent relationship to Israel on the part of American Jews. Although support for Israel is a widespread sentiment in the American Jewish community, a considerably smaller number of Jews express support by active involvement in Israel affairs and in inquisitive curiosity about the workings of Israeli society. The difficult and problematic knowledge of Israel provided by reading Israeli literature—the nature of serious contemporary literature in all societies, as I have said—is the kind of demystifying knowledge that many American Jews would prefer not to have. The construction of American Jewishness is often dependent upon an idealization of Israel that focuses on the heroic struggle for statehood and the resistance to annihilation. There are whole genres of American popular fiction—Leon Uris's *Exodus* the most famous among them—that rework these themes and seem to keep many Americans supplied with what they feel they need to know about Israel. It is to be hoped that, with the maturing of the relationship to Israel by American Jewry, attentiveness to Israeli literature will play a greater role in the enterprise of mutual understanding between the two communities and will become, at the very least, a norm for literate Jewish leaders.

What is the usefulness of speaking of a boom in Israeli literature specifically during the years 1973–93? It is interesting that in Hebrew literary historiography it has long been the custom to demarcate creative periods by significant historical events rather than by inherent aesthetic developments such as the first appearance of a genre, a technique, or a theme. This is a practice that says much about the close connection between the historical vicissitudes of a nation and the evolution of its literary history. In marking off the twenty years between 1973 and 1993, I have departed from this custom only in making one rather than both dates the years of significant armed conflicts. The year 1973, of course, evokes the Yom Kippur War; the year 1993, however, marks the famous handshake between Yassir Arafat and Yitzhak Rabin, the official end to the intifada, and the beginning of the peace process. All such at-

tempts at periodization, to be sure, are at some level acts of interpretive
intervention that bear a purely heuristic relationship to the ongoing
and crisscrossing flow of human activity. Nonetheless, there is something to be gained from positing a correlation during these years between developments in the social and political arena and developments
in serious literature.

Although the 1973 war ended in a victory for Israel, there was little
of the euphoria that had marked the aftermath of the Six-Day War in
1967. Instead, a sense of aloneness in the world ensued and a feeling of
vulnerability at home that was deepened rather than mitigated by the
occupation of the West Bank and Gaza. The Territories became the
breeding ground for radicalized nationalism fueled by a resurgent
Islam; the Intifada, the loosely organized terror against Israeli soldiers
that emerged later on, deeply scarred the morale of the Israeli public.
The political identity of that public also underwent an abrupt shift. The
Labor Party, which had dominated political life since before the state
was created, was voted out of office. The rout was a sign, among other
things, that Jews who had emigrated from Arab lands had not only
reached a demographic majority in Israel but had now made their numbers count in the political process. The ascendancy of the Likud meant
the dismantling of some of the central institutions of labor socialism
and the privatization of state-run industries. In the new free-market
economy the disadvantaged did worse while the middle classes enjoyed
a steady rise in their standard of living and in the availability of consumer goods. Speculation in the stock market with its attendant risks
became an endeavor for individual investors and institutions as well.

Israeli society in general became more cosmopolitan and Western-
ized; many Israelis traveled abroad, especially young people who had
recently completed their military service. Hundreds of thousands of Israelis left for good, emigrating mostly to America in search of better opportunities. During the same years, large numbers of Russian Jews (and
non-Jews) and smaller numbers of Ethiopians settled in Israel, creating
at once a renewed sense of Zionist mission and a massive economic and
social burden. On the religious scene the moderate Orthodox national-
ists, who had been part of the Zionist enterprise since its inception, lost

ground, both politically and demographically, to ultra-Orthodox groups that promoted separatist interests. The control of domestic relations by religious law helped to spur the emergence of a nascent women's movement and promote feminist reflection in pockets of the society. A momentous shift took place as well in the relations between Israeli Jewry and diaspora Jewry, which since the days of Ben-Gurion had been characterized by the unambiguous hegemony of the Israelis. The Jewish communities of the Diaspora, especially in America, rejected the notion that their communal lives lacked value and vitality and existed only to provide material and human resources to Israel's development, and steps were taken to place the relationship between the two communities on a more equal footing.

This is a hurried overview of complex historical forces, but it is enough to suggest the ways in which the self-conception of Israeli society has broken down and been reshaped since the mid-1970s. Central to that self-conception, which was consolidated during the Ben-Gurion years after the establishment of the state in 1948, were the values of labor Zionism and its pioneering lineage: work on the land, solidarity with comrades, state supported social welfare, a nationalist interpretation of Jewish history expressed in the school curriculum, a devaluing of diaspora values in general and Yiddish culture in particular, and the encouragement of a secular, native Israeli culture. Unofficial but implicit in this ethos was a parallel set of hierarchies that privileged male over female leadership in many areas of politics and culture and extended a similar sense of entitlement to citizens of Ashkenazic background over those from Arab lands or of Sephardi heritage. Religion was also meant to remain a marginal presence that required some concessions but made no substantial claim on the identity of the state. Holocaust survivors were encouraged to suppress their experiences and their stories and assimilate into the nativist spirit. And free enterprise and individual ambition were regarded as necessary evils in a democracy that esteemed solidarity to the commonweal.

Before one, then, is a set of oppositions—male/female, Ashenazic/Sephardic, religious/secular, Eretz Yisrael/Diaspora, collectivism/individualism, native Israelis/Holocaust survivors—whose rigidities were disturbed if not set aside during the period between 1973 and 1993. The crucial role played by Israeli literature, especially fiction, in these years was to interrogate these oppositions and lay them open to scrutiny. Literature performs this task either by giving voice to the suppressed term in the binary opposition or by ironizing the privileged term and, in general, by complicating the relationship between the two. One of the images used by critics to describe this moment in Israeli literature is the breakdown of a single story into many stories. In this image a Zionist master story or plot existed that preoccupied Hebrew literature from the settlement period until the 1970s. This was, with many variants, an account of the national enterprise and the struggle of individuals to create their lives within it. At the center of this story was a male protagonist of European descent, unconnected to religion but connected to the national struggle, whose outlook had been shaped, either sympathetically or antagonistically, by the values of the youth movement or military service or the institutions of the new state. In the great change that followed, the one story became many stories; the dominance-and the representational sufficiency—of the master plot was broken and forced to yield to the stories of those who had until then been kept on the margins. Like all models, this account of Hebrew literary history is an idealized story in itself that disregards numerous antecedents and ancillary developments; nevertheless, it possesses a kind of gross truth that puts large cultural shifts into perspective.

The achievements and innovations of Israeli literature during this period can be described from three different, and at times overlapping, angles: minority discourse, that is, writing by or about ethnic groups that had not previously been the subject of literary representation; women's writing and the reexamination of gender codes; and magical realism, the fantastic and postmodernist narrative techniques in the writing of fiction.

The whole notion of minorities in Israeli society is at odds with the official Zionist ideal of "ingathering." Rather than being seen as ethnic groups or minorities, the Jews who came to Israel from many countries around the globe were meant to be absorbed into a new society in Zion that represents a departure from life in the many and varied Diasporas.

In actuality, however, the culture of the Yishuv and later the state was largely based upon the norms of a single society—the socialist Zionism that had emerged in Eastern Europe—and it was often into that culture that Jews from other lands were, willingly or unwillingly, gathered in. Over time the Israeli Jews whose families had settled in Israel for ideological reasons became themselves a minority, yet the institutions of the state and its literary culture continued to bear the impress of the East European socialist stamp.

Jews from North Africa and the Middle East—together loosely called Sephardim—had long been presences in the Old and New Yishuv, but it was not until the upheavals occasioned by the War of Independence in 1948 that great numbers arrived in Israel. The immigrants from Eastern lands were extremely diverse in their backgrounds. Some came from the secularized urban professional classes of Cairo, Damascus, and Bagdad; others were shopkeepers with a traditional religious outlook; and still others came from small towns and villages that had scarcely been touched by industrial life. Only a small number were Zionists in the modern ideological sense of the term, and for the great majority their sudden arrival in Israel was experienced as an enormous and unanticipated upheaval. Although the Zionist leadership took a romantic and ethnographic interest in the varied and distinct folkways of this exotic population, Eastern Jews were urged to integrate themselves into the dominant civic culture of the new state. After the hardships and indignities of the transit camps hastily set up to absorb this mass immigration, some did succeed in assimilating into Israeli society, whereas others, who had been settled in outlying "development towns" that never developed, slipped into a chronic underclass.

Creating a voice and projecting it within the literary world of the newly adopted country required taking on the challenge of Hebrew. Most of the writers from Ashkenazic backgrounds had either been born into Hebrew-speaking families or had been educated in Hebrew-oriented schools before coming to Palestine. Intellectuals from Eastern lands, by contrast, were at home in Arabic, and sometimes French or Berber or Turkish. Being suddenly transplanted into a Hebrew-speaking culture presented aspiring writers with the enormous challenge of learning to create in an adopted language. Some clung to Arabic and were marginalized; others went through a difficult gestation period and began to write in Hebrew. The first works produced by Sephardic writers dealt with the humiliations of transit camps and were written in the tradition of social outrage. By the period under discussion, Sephardic writing had evolved into a nuanced examination of the complexities of acculturation into Israeli society. The most recent fictional efforts have reached beyond the temporal and spatial boundaries of Israel to reevoke in highly imaginative terms the Jewish life of Baghdad and Damascus before the establishment of Israel and the "ingathering" of Eastern Jewry. The works of Sammy Michael, Shimon Balas, Eli Amir, and Amnon Shamosh moved the Eastern voice toward the center of Israeli literature.

Although not an ethnic minority, survivors of the Holocaust and other Jews who came to Israel as displaced persons also constitute an identifiable group whose voice gained literary expression only belatedly. The specter of political passivity—the contemporary perception of European Jews going to their death "like sheep to the slaughter"—clashed sharply with the heroic myth at the core of Zionism. During the first twenty years after the Holocaust, the survivor was often represented in Israeli literature as morally tainted in contrast to the brave and hard-working sabra. Until the Eichmann trial in 1961 provided a showcase for Holocaust testimonies, survivors were not encouraged to tell their stories—to themselves or to others. Aharon Appelfeld, who began to publish short stories in the 1960s, has been the most imaginatively powerful writer to focus on the Holocaust. Apart from Appelfeld's fiction, the single most important work to address the Holocaust is David Grossman's *See Under: Love,* an ambitious postmodernist novel that employs a variety of story-telling techniques to explore the persistence of the tragic past. Although the novel's central character is a son of survivors, Grossman himself is not, and as such he joins an increasing number of younger Israeli writers who have approached the subject of the Holocaust despite having no direct experience of it.

The minority that by nature stands most apart from the national consensus is made up of Israeli Arabs. Their language of literary expression is, of course, Arabic and not Hebrew although there is the distinguished example of Anton Shamas, who has written a beautiful novel *Arabesques* in Hebrew. Given the intensity of political differences, it is unlikely that there will be a major contribution to Hebrew literature by Arab writers, although the possibility always remains open. As a subject for Jewish writers in Hebrew, the representation of Arabs has played a significant although not central role in Hebrew literature. The image of the Arab most often served as a screen upon which were projected the hopes and the fears and the moral dilemmas of the Jewish settlers in Palestine. In Yitzhak Shami's 1927 novella *Revenge of the Fathers* (Nikmat avot), for example, the Arab is portrayed as the instinctual native son of the land; this was an ideal that the Zionist student pioneers from Eastern Europe could aspire to but not immediately embody. In S. Yizhar's story "The Prisoner," which was written during the 1948 War of Independence, the forlorn, anonymous Arab prisoner serves as a touchstone for the Jewish narrator's struggles with his conscience. In Amos Oz's 1968 novel *My Michael,* Arab twins from the female narrator's childhood occupy her adult fantasy life and mirror her erotic and aggressive obsessions.

The publication of A. B. Yehoshua's first novel *The Lover* in 1977 marked a turning point in the representation of the Arab. Naim is a teenage boy from an Israeli Arab village in the Galilee who works in the garage owned by an Israeli Jew named Adam and who in the course of the story becomes entangled with Adam's family. The novel is composed entirely of monologues, and Naim has his monologues along with the other characters. But when he first speaks one-third of the way through the novel, it has the force of a stunning debut. It is the first time in Hebrew literature that an Arab character is given his or her own voice and is allowed to articulate an inner life that is not largely a projection of a Jewish fantasy or dilemma. Although Yehoshua's *The Lover* was indeed a breakthrough, it would be an exaggeration to say that it opened a floodgate of efforts in this direction. There are exceptions such as Itamar Levy's *Letters of the Sun, Letters of the Moon* (1991), a novel that is told entirely through the consciousness of an Arab boy in a village in the Occupied Territories. In the end, however, the Arab remains very much an other, a flickering presence in Israeli literature.

The role played by women in modern Hebrew literature has been an equivocal one. Although there have been a number of important women poets in the first half of the twentieth century (Rachel, Elisheva, Yocheved Bat-Miriam, Esther Raab, Lea Goldberg), in fiction there has essentially been the lone example of Devora Baron, whose short stories are only now receiving wide critical attention. Like other revolutionary ideologies, Zionism's proclamations concerning the equality of women were true more in theory than in practice. In the core myth of Zionism, it is the figure of the male soldier-farmer that occupied center stage. Women are assigned supporting roles; they are participants in this new historical endeavor but rarely as leaders. In the gendered language of Zionism, the partners in this new grand passion are, on the one side, the Land, as both mother and virgin bride, and on the other, the heroic Hebrew (male) pioneer, who has returned to possess the Land or to be received back into its bosom. Although flesh-and-blood women were essential to the settlement of the country, there were often marginalized by the prerogatives of the Great Mother, the land itself.

It is a sign of the enormous changes in culture and society that by the 1980s women writers had become among the most visible and creative voices in Israeli fiction. These include Savyon Liebrecht, Ruth Almog, Michal Govrin, Dorit Peleg, Yehudit Katzir, Orly Castel-Bloom, and Ronit Matalon. What prepared the way for this belated explosion? The key precursor in women's writing is Amalia Kahana-Carmon (born in 1930), whose first collection of stories *Under One Roof* (Bi-chfifah ahat) was published in 1966. Kahana-Carmon belongs together with Oz, Yehoshua, and Appelfeld to the New Wave in Hebrew fiction that used modernist techniques to interrogate the ideologically laden social realism of their predecessors. Yet whereas Oz and Yehoshua directly engage the Zionist narrative by writing about the kibbutz and war and peace, Kahana-Carmon, like Appelfeld in his own way, writes more subversively by sidestepping the Zionist narrative altogether. Just as Appelfeld writes about Holocaust survivors to whom the heroic posture of the Jewish state is irrelevant, so Kahana-Carmon writes about the inner lives of women as a zone removed from the passions of the national story. Influenced by the style of the Hebrew Chekovian writer Uri Nissan Gnessin from early years of the century, Kahana-Carmon focuses on the inner space of subjectivity where language, fantasy, and desire come together. Yehudit Handel and Shulamith Hareven are women writers of Kahana-Carmon's generation—although they began to publish later than she—whose fiction directly engages the Zionist narrative. Their work features heroines whose spirit and pluck might have carried them in feminist directions if their lives had not been overtaken by the claims of historical emergency.

Less noticed but of equal significance is the interrogation of gender that has been conducted in fiction written by men. The Zionist revolution was as much about a new construction of masculinity as about anything else. Beginning in the late-nineteenth century, Hebrew writers undertook an unsparing critique of the East European Jewish male, the archetypal denizen of the shtetl, as ineffectual, overintellectualized, effeminate, passively sensual, and wife-ridden. The theorists of Zionism presented the new movement as a kind of therapy for these sickly diaspora bodies and minds. The new "muscle Jew," in this scheme, would remake the Jewish male both inside and out. How successful this therapeutic regimen was in practice is difficult to assess, but it is clear that as a masculine ideal it is very much the model for the young men who populate works by such writers as S. Yizhar and Moshe Shamir, who came of age during the War of Independence in 1948.

When Amos Oz and A. B. Yehoshua began publishing in the 1960s, their work was addressed to the issue of ideology itself and the role it played in suppressing or ignoring the exigencies of human needs. From the 1970s onward, it is possible, I think, to detect a shift of focus from a preoccupation with ideology to an exploration of masculinity. This can be seen most clearly in Yehoshua's novels *Five Seasons* (1987) and *Mr. Mani* (1990), which concern male characters who have either taken on feminine characteristics or who seek access to the female mysteries of reproduction. The most conspicuous exploration of these issues takes place in the work of a writer who burst upon the literary scene in the 1970s and died shortly after the publication of his major work. That work is the epic novel *Past Continuous* (1977) by Yaakov Shabtai, which broke new ground in a number of areas. In tracing the daily movements of three men through a series of futile experiences culminating in the suicide of one of them, the novel evokes the vacuum of despair that came after the ideological passions of the generation of the founders of the state. Integral to this entropic slide toward death is a clutching for the remnants of machismo and the muscular myth of Zionist settlers. Shabtai's and Yehoshua's works have initiated among younger writers of both sexes an intense awareness and exploration of the constructed and deconstructed nature of gender in Israeli society.

The third broad category of innovation in Israeli writing between 1973 and 1993 lies in the rethinking of fiction itself. As a modern secular literature, Israeli writing has always been influenced by currents in Europe and America. The so-called Palmah-generation writers from the 1950s were deeply influenced by the canons of socialist realism. The New Wave writers of the 1960s and 1970s were influenced by the high modernism of Faulkner and Kafka. Many of the Israeli writers discussed in the present volume were influenced in part by the techniques of magic realism and postmodernism. Yet, whereas in the first two instances there is a considerable lag between the time of the European influences and their eventual adoption in Israel, in the more recent case the gap is much shorter. Rather than being a belated enactment of European developments, the radically innovative novel *See Under: Love* by David Grossman, for example, is already a participant in an emerging international postmodernist style. The significant question posed by the new Israeli literature, as is the case with any literature that is written at a remove from the traditional centers of culture, is how these "borrowings" are naturalized within the internal traditions and concerns of Israeli culture.

Five areas of fictional experimentation are worth noticing. The first is the use of the fantastic or magic realism, which can be defined as the suspension of one or more of the laws of nature within an otherwise realistically conceived fictional world. Grossman's *See Under: Love* is the chief but not lone example, and it is not coincidental that these nonrealistic procedures have been mobilized to deal with the event that tampers with received categories of meaning—the Holocaust. In his novel *The Blue Mountain* (1988), which deals with the pioneers who settled the Galilee, Meir Shalev makes limited but effective use of magic realism to convey—and simultaneously deflate—the enormous energy and willfulness of the mythic settlers.

A second feature is deliberate derivativeness expressed in the borrowing and recycling of previous literature and other cultural materials. In Grossman's *See Under: Love,* for example, Bruno Schulz's writings are quoted extensively, the juvenile literature of Jules Verne and Karl May is returned to repeatedly, and different historical styles are imitated wholesale. This last practice, the ventriloquizing of discourse from different historical periods, is the very principle around which Yehoshua's *Mr. Mani* is constructed. In earlier periods of Hebrew literature, the relationship to the past centered on the use of allusion, a phrase or a metaphor embedded in the work's contemporary fictional discourse that activated associations from earlier, and usually classical, Jewish literature. In the postmodernist practice, however, the unit of reference is often much larger; rather than a point of concentrated meaning in which past and present texts momentarily engage one another, a postmodernist text may itself be made up of large swatches of earlier works or of playful imitations of them. Moreover, the materials borrowed are likely to come not from the classical tradition but from popular genres of writing and from the materials of everyday life and popular culture.

A third tendency is a movement away from ideology toward storytelling. In some of the key texts of this period—Grossman's *See Under: Love* and the novels of Meir Shalev, for example—such momentous developments as the settlement of the Land of Israel and the Holocaust are used as the stuff of storytelling and mythmaking rather than being taken as events of moral-historical meaning. The shift from history to story is a supremely self-conscious move that becomes thematized within the novels themselves. The subject of Grossman's Holocaust novel is the gravest of the twentieth century, yet its engagement with the event itself is minor relative to the immense preoccupation with the difficulties of writing about it and the extravagant fictions spun from its thread. For many writers, Yaakov Shabtai especially, the failure of ideology and the weakness of the spirit allows for a margin of hope or resolution only on the plane of art rather than within the mire of human affairs. But this is not the sacred art of high modernism with its priestly aspirations. The notion of art and the commitment to it among these Israeli postmodernists are at once as serious and less solemn. The playful and manipulable aspects of the artifice of their art are expressions of a commitment to experiment with the possibilities of narrative and a willingness to lay bare the mechanics and devices of their efforts. The boundary between low hijinks and serious experiment is one that is not infrequently crisscrossed by many writers.

A fourth aspect is the great interest evinced in recent Israeli writing in taking the novel apart and putting it back together differently and variously. These experiments take place at three different levels. The first is the actual discursive fabric of the novel as it presents itself to the reader reading the words on the page. At one extreme is the extraordinary—and, for most critics, extraordinarily successful—effort of Yaakov Shabtai in *Past Continuous* to make the novel into a single paragraph composed of a minimum of sentences. Shabtai's narrative loops back and forth in time and connects the fates of several extended families creating a sense of continuous duration at the level of reading that is missing from the experiences of the characters. At the opposite extreme are the works of Yoel Hoffman *(Bernhardt* [Bernhard] and *Christos of the Fish* [Kristus shel ha-dagim]), which neutralize the epic aspiration of the novel by chopping it into tiny pieces. A diminutive paragraph may appear alone on a page, representing a bubble of consciousness, and on some pages may be nothing at all. Some of the most successful experimentation manipulates the materials that compose the novel. One may not realize how conventionalized are the expectations of readers of novels until one comes across an example of the genre, as is the case with Grossman's *See Under: Love,* in which each of the novel's four sections is written in an entirely different literary style and is based on a different genre model. In A. B. Yehoshua's *Mr. Mani* each of the five chapters features the speech of one person in an extended dramatic dialogue with another; the questions and answers of the other person are unvoiced but inferred; furthermore, the whole of each "half dialogue" is introduced and followed by several pages of biographical and historical background supplied with a tone of factual discursive detachment.

Finally, Israeli writers have also been fascinated by what can be done with, and to, point of view. Amalia Kahana-Carmon is a writer who is identified with an earlier literary generation but whose recent writings have a distinctively postmodern temper. The narrator in her *Above in Montifer* (Lemala be-Montifer) (1984) is a woman who has subjugated herself to a man and tells her story from the vantage point of extreme abasement and obsession. The narrator in Itamar Levy's *Letters of the Sun, Letters of the Moon* (1991) is a probably retarded Arab growing up in a village on the West Bank under Israeli occupation; his radically limited view of the world around him serves as a technique for undoing stereotypes and making strange the ostensibly familiar and threatening. Dorit Peleg's *Una* (1988) and Yoav Shimoni's *Flight of the Dove* (Ma'of ha-yonah) both split the narrative point of view in two and develop each line of sight in different ways.

As in any era of intense experimentation, time will determine which works will endure. There is a potential in postmodernist practice for narcissism and trivialization, and it often depends on the will and the gifts of the individual writer whether a work transcends the effects of technique and creates the aura of a work of art. In the meantime, Israeli fiction continues to thrive, providing readers all the while with challenging writing and an incomparably insightful glimpse into the experience of Israeli society.

PART TWO

THE FACES OF AGNON

Introduction

THAT CHAPTERS ABOUT S. Y. AGNON (1888–1970), who is
widely regarded as the greatest Jewish writer of modern times, should
occupy a section of their own in a book about Israeli literature reflects
the anomalous nature of Agnon's status. He is certainly an Israeli
writer. He came to Palestine as a young man before World War I and
then settled for good in the mid-1920s after a long sojourn in Germany,
and he wrote major works about life there. Yet, at the same time, the
bulk of his very capacious corpus is set in Eastern Europe and Germany.
Most of all there is Agnon's vital connection to the classical sources of
Judaism and to the religious culture of Ashkenaz, which sets him apart
from the secularity of almost all other Israeli writers. Agnon, in the end,
is both. He is a magisterial writer whose imagination is constantly oscil-
lating between his home, the Galician town of Buczacz, and his
adopted homeland, Eretz Yisrael. Although Agnon has exerted some
influence on Israeli writing, there have been few continuators of his
style. He stands as a monumental presence within Israeli literature but
alongside its major trends.

The first and longest chapter in this section, "Agnon as Modernist:
The Contours of a Career," coauthored with Anne Golumb Hoffman,
was originally written as part of a self-conscious effort to widen and en-
hance the reception of Agnon's work in America. Agnon's name was
honored, but his works were not read; many titles were going out of
print, and some of the major novels had been badly translated. Anne
Golumb Hoffman and I set out to make a fresh presentation of Agnon

to American readers with the hope that he would be "rediscovered." We took Agnon's strongest genre, the short story, and put together a collection of his strongest stories, adding texts translated for the first time along with previously translated ones. The stories were arranged in sections according to phases of Agnon's autobiographical persona; each section was headed by a critical introduction, and each story was accompanied by notes glossing literary and historical allusions. The purpose of all these editorial interventions was to remove barriers and to create a level playing field upon which American readers could encounter Agnon. Readers can look at *A Book That Was Lost and Other Stories by S. Y. Agnon* (Schocken Books) and judge the success of our endeavor for themselves. The chapter in this section is the general introduction to the anthology, and it is an attempt to present the shape of Agnon's career and to delineate the nature of his modernism.

Shira, Agnon's most contemporary novel, is set in Jerusalem in the 1930s, a city that is awash with scholarly German Jewish refugees. Agnon did not allow it to be published in his lifetime because of the easily recognized portraits of well-known figures from university circles. The novel describes the attraction of Manfred Herbst, a historian who came to Palestine from Germany and who is married with children, for an unmarried nurse named Shira, who came from Poland. The name Shira means poetry or song, and the attraction of this erudite but emotionally constricted scholar to the realm of art opens up fascinating if elusive allegorical reverberations. My essay on the novel, published in *Commentary* when the translation first appeared, examines the German-Jewish ethos embodied by Herbst and his colleagues and its progressive dismantlement during the course of the novel.

Because of the very fact of Agnon's preeminence as a Jewish writer, the absence of much explicit reference to the Holocaust in his work has often occasioned surprise. In the third chapter in this section, I make a case for taking a substantial amount of Agnon's postwar writing as an implicit response to the Holocaust. Agnon devoted much of his time in the fifties and sixties to reconstructing in stories written in different fictional modes the lost world of his hometown, Buczacz. By making Buczacz stand for the spiritual world of Polish Jewry and by revoking it in its vitality and variety, Agnon declines the path of most explicit Holocaust literature, which focuses on destruction and the death-in-life of survivors, and chooses a different path. My chapter offers a reading of a powerful long story in which Agnon relates the mystical moment in which he felt called upon to undertake this commemorative vocation and meditates upon the connection between the destroyed font of his being in Eastern Europe and the fulfillment of his being in Zion.

3

Agnon as Modernist

The Contours of a Career
(With Anne Golumb Hoffman)

When it was his turn to be presented, Mr. Agnon jumped to his feet and enthusiastically shook the King's hand as he received the prize. Then, instead of
the usual single bow to the King, he kept on bowing until he got back to his
chair. He was obviously a very happy and flustered man. When he learned in
October in Jerusalem that he had won the Nobel Prize, Mr. Agnon said that
going to Stockholm would give him pleasure "because there is a special bene-
diction one says before a king and I have never met a king before." Tonight at
the banquet, as the King looked on, Mr. Agnon, speaking in Hebrew, recited
the blessing, "Blessed art Thou, O Lord our God, King of the universe, who
has given of His glory to flesh and blood." The Israeli author said that "some
see in my books the influences of authors whose names, in my ignorance, I
have not even heard, while others see influences of poets whose names I have
heard but whose writing I have never read." The true sources of his inspiration, he went on, were, first and foremost, the sacred scriptures and, after that,
the teachings of the medieval Jewish sages, and the spectacle of nature, and the
animals of the earth.

—*New York Times,* December 11, 1966

This chapter was previously published as the Introduction to S. Y. Agnon, *A Book
That Was Lost and Other Stories,* ed. Alan L. Mintz and Anne Golumb Hoffman, © 1995
by Schocken Books. Reprinted by permission of Schocken Books, a division of Random
House, Inc.

1

THE SIGHT OF THE LITTLE ROUND MAN in the black tails, white tie, and large velvet skullcap receiving an international prize from the king of Sweden was remarkable on a number of counts. Although a sophisticated participant in modern culture, Agnon presented himself as a pious and naive representative of the lost world of East European Jewry who was ignorant of European literature and had been instructed only by the Bible and the spectacle of God's creation. No scene could have provided a more powerful instance of the writer's ability to fashion and refashion his artistic persona. Agnon's construction of an autobiographical myth of the artist, with its deliberate blurring of the boundaries between life and art, is the key to understanding his work.

Over the years Agnon shaped the narrative of his own beginnings to produce an image of an artist as a figure at once solitary and part of a community, both a rebel and a redeemer. He may not have left a formal autobiography, but through his letters and public statements one does have evidence of his engagement in a remarkable process, carried out over most of a lifetime, that amounts to the fashioning of a public name and history of the writer.

The example of James Joyce's artistic self-consciousness and his sense of a mythic renewal through language gives insight into the process through which Agnon created himself as a modern Jewish writer, linking significant markers in his own life to Jewish history and community. Among European modernists, Joyce offers a portrait of the artist who became his own father, an act of self-creation that also links him to his people. Like Joyce, Agnon saw himself as one whose life and art could shape new identities out of old traditions.

Born in Eastern Europe in 1888, Shmuel Yosef Agnon died in Jerusalem in 1970. He offers a life and an art that are emblematic of the century to which he was witness. If one thinks of him as a Jewish writer, it should be in the sense of a confrontation with history that encompasses destruction and rebirth from the stirrings of national consciousness to the extermination of European Jewry and the establishment of the state of Israel.

In Agnon's account of himself, personal biography intertwines with national narrative through recurring themes of destruction, rebirth, and renewal. Most striking in this life story is his designation of the Ninth of Av as his date of birth. The Ninth of Av is a date deeply embedded in the history and eschatology of the Jewish people as the date of the destruction of the first and second Temples in Jerusalem. Its significance is reiterated in the collective memory of the Jewish people as a date of catastrophes throughout history. At the same time, one finds the traditional belief that the Ninth of Av is the date on which the Messiah will be born. Agnon's choice thus carries the meanings of both destruction and redemption. The Ninth of Av holds an essential tension that comes to define the figure of the writer and to constitute a major theme in his work.

Along with the Ninth of Av, Agnon cited the Jewish holiday of Lag B'Omer as the date of his initial immigration to the Land of Israel. In the Jewish calendar, Lag B'Omer marks the date of Bar Kochba's rebellion against Roman occupation of the ancient Land of Israel. A minor festival associated with a struggle for liberation, it is accompanied by a turn to the outdoors that marks the spring season in which it occurs. Evoking the spirit of that day, Agnon was fond of recalling one of his earliest Hebrew publications, "A Little Hero," a poem that pictures a small boy as the savior of his people on the occasion of Lag B'Omer.

In a similar association of life events with the history of a people, Agnon dated his second return to the Land of Israel in 1924 with a reference to the Torah portion of that week, *Lekh lekha* ("Go forth," Gen. 12:1–17:27). That portion of the Genesis narrative opens with God's commandment to Abraham to leave his birthplace and his family for the land that God will show him. Agnon thus intertwines his personal journey with the ancestral narrative. In letters and autobiographical statements, Agnon returned to such evocative coincidences, weaving them into a narrative frame for the life of a writer who lives out the story of his people.

The historical accuracy of these dates is less the issue than the functions they serve as markers in a life story. Agnon may have constructed a biographical myth, but he also held onto the original documents going back to 1908 that allow comparisons of the writer's story to the historical record. Why do both? This is Agnon the modernist, who offers access to the making of a life and to the life that is made as well. He engaged in the narrative construction of a myth while leaving traces of the materials out of which it was fashioned. One sees him as the myth-maker, and he acknowledges his own artifice with a wink and a nod that invite the reader into his workshop.

Out of that workshop came embellishments to the portrait of the writer as a youth who revered his father. In a ceremonial letter to the municipality of Tel Aviv, Agnon observes that "I was born in the city of Buczacz in eastern Galicia to my father Rabbi Shalom Mordecai ha-Levi Czaczkes, of blessed memory, on the Ninth of Av." In the Jewish calendar, the year is signified by the letter of the Hebrew alphabet, each of which has a numerical equivalent. The notation of a date thus offers Agnon the opportunity for recombinations of letters that become the source of new meanings. With inveterate playfulness, he rearranges the Hebrew letters that designate the year in which he was born, *t-r-h-m*, to form the phrase "Zion will be merciful" (Zion *t-r-h-m*). Never losing the opportunity to heighten the personal with bits of exegetical play, Agnon fashions the public face of the writer out of bits and pieces, artfully constructing significance out of odds and ends of tradition.[1]

There is a considerable element of irony in Agnon's designation of dates and coincidences. He may draw upon biblical phrases of rabbinic exegesis to enlarge the horizon of meaning by linking the individual to the nation, but his relationship to his sources is never simple. Wordplays and historical associations work to inflate themes and simultaneously expose his pretension. On occasion, Agnon takes these associations to a playful excess that suggests an element of self-mockery as when he notes that he wrote his first poem on Lag B'Omer, made his first *aliyah* (immigration) on Lag B'Omer, married his wife on Lag B'Omer, received the Swedish translation of one of his novellas on that day, was notified of the award of honorary doctorate on Lag B'Omer, and so on. At such moments as this, Agnon jokingly exposes his game, even as he continues to play it.

Agnon's ongoing self-portrait connects the writer not only to the history of the people but crafts a special relationship to Hebrew as the holy tongue, the language of Creation. Agnon's choice of Hebrew, after experiments with Yiddish and Hebrew, links him with others of his generation who turned to Hebrew as a potent resource in the enterprise of national renewal. But while Agnon's writing draws upon the riches of language and makes one feel keenly the centrality of Hebrew to a worldview centered on Scripture, the relationship of the writer to the universe involves an intricate combination of reverence and subversion, piety, and irony.

The very name "Agnon" is fabrication, a central instance of the interpretive play that identifies the writer's art. It is a name that the writer, who was born Shmuel Yosef Czaczkes, invented by adapting the title of "Agunot," the first story he published in Palestine in 1908. To fashion both the title and his own name, Agnon used the Hebrew noun *agunah*, a term in Jewish law that designates a woman who is not free to marry because her husband has disappeared or left without divorcing her. The *agunah* is an indeterminate figure, at once connected to the community and separate from it. Interestingly, the story "Agunot" itself contains no *agunah* in the technical sense of the term. One must realize, then, the boldness of Agnon's imagination in taking a legal term and spiritualizing it, shaping it into a metaphor for the modern condition. Fertile with meaning, the name suggests an image of the artist as a soul without anchor. Thus, at an early point in his career, the writer arrived at a title and a name that express the longing for completeness amid the awareness of isolation and distance.

Picturing himself as one who maintains a connection to what he has lost, Agnon paints a portrait of the writer as a figure on the margins of tradition. In this passage from "The Sense of Smell," written in the 1930s, he maps out a mythic universe in which Torah—Jewish Scripture—occupies the center while he defines himself by his distance from that language of plenitude and presence:

> For love of our language and affection for the holy, I darken my countenance with constant study of Torah and starve myself over the words

of our sages. These I store up in my belly so that they together will be present to my lips. If the Temple were still standing, I would be up there on the platform among my singing brothers, reciting each day the song that the Levites sang in the Temple. But since the Temple remains destroyed and we have no priests as service or Levites at song, instead I study Torah, the Prophets and the Writings, Mishnah, laws and legends, supplementary treatises and fine points of Torah and the works of scribes. When I look at their words and see that of all the delights we possessed in ancient times there remains only this memory, my heart fills up with grief. That grief makes my heart tremble, and it is out of that trembling that I write stories, like one exiled from his father's palace who makes himself a little hut and sits there telling of the glory of his father's house.[2]

Positioning himself as one who writes in the aftermath of destruction, Agnon subordinates himself to the priestly poets who are his predecessors and effaces his own individuality. Paradoxically, the effect of this denigration is to secure for the writer an affiliation to tradition: the reader has there a mythic portrayal of the writer as one who longs for return and restoration. What disappears from this picture is, of course, his more worldly or modernist face.

In the study of his house in Talpiyot, just outside of Jerusalem, Agnon preferred to write while standing at a lectern, a relic of an Eastern European Talmudic academy. He was fond of gesturing to the scores of volumes of Jewish learning to be found on the shelves lining the walls, noting in passing the presence of a modest shelf of twentieth-century literary works. This arrangement of books suggests an architecture of the imagination in which secular influences play a distinctly minor role. Indeed, one might compare this denial of his own modernism to Agnon's public comments after accepting the Nobel Prize: he acknowledges sacred texts as the sources of his inspiration and disavows the influence of writers whose names he claims never to have heard. In both instances one sees the persona of the writer at play. Agnon, whose works display a range of literary experimentation that links him to the major modernists of the twentieth century, chose to minimize that affiliation and to present instead the image of the writer who subordinates himself to traditional texts. In so doing, he sought to fit his public image to a simpler notion of membership in a community unified by its history.

That mask was also real. Agnon devoted a large portion of his energies to ensuring the survival of cultural documents of European communities that were ultimately destroyed. Indeed, even before the threat of the destruction of European Jewry became apparent, Agnon had come to play a major role as a collector of Jewish books and manuscripts and had compiled several anthologies of Jewish lore. He was an important figure in Mekitze Nirdamim (those who awaken the sleeping), a group devoted to the retrieval, preservation, and dissemination of old Jewish manuscripts.

The cultural influences and traditions into which the writer was born all eventually found their way into an art that is encyclopedic in its references to Jewish life and texts.[3] Shmuel Yosef Czaczkes, son of Shalom Mordecai ha-Levi Czaczkes and his wife, Esther Farb, was born in 1888 in Buczacz, a town of some twelve thousand inhabitants located in eastern Galicia, then part of the Austro-Hungarian empire. Family lineage and traditions on both sides exposed him to a variety of currents in nineteenth-century Jewish life. From his mother's side, Agnon inherited ties to the Mitnagdim, the rationalist opponents of the Hasidism, whereas his father's lineage included Hasidic connections. Thus, within his family he experienced the major currents of life in Eastern Europe, from the joyous pietism of Hasidic traditions to the rigorous intellectual commitments of the rationalists. With his father, who traded in furs, the boy Shmuel Yosef frequented a *kloyz*, a Hasidic house of prayer, that belonged to the followers of the Chortkover rebbe, the leader of a sizable community of Hasidim. It was also through his father that he first studied rabbinic texts.

By his own description Agnon received a traditional education, studying in the traditional one-room Jewish school, the *heder*, then privately with a teacher and with his father, learning the Bible, Talmud, and literature of the Haskalah (the Jewish Enlightenment). The family library was stocked not only with the Talmud and its commentaries but also with the works of Maimonides and the Galician Maskilim, the eighteenth—and nineteenth-century proponents of Jewish Enlightenment. It was in this library and other local collections that as an adolescent Agnon freely educated himself. The comfortable circumstances of his family allowed him the leisure to do so. But the absence of more formal schooling was, in fact, a general trait of Galician-Jewish culture.

In a somewhat nontraditional departure, Agnon studied German with a tutor and gained access to European literature in German translation. Thus one sees that a certain sophistication attaches to the young writer's early education. Nevertheless, his reminiscences tend to dwell on the traditions of Jewish learning in the town of Buczacz, traditions that he associates, most particularly, with his father. Marking an idealization of the father that recurs through his work, the son, in later years, painted a portrait of his father as a figure of radiant piety: "My father, my teacher, Rabbi Shalom Mordecai son of Zvi Aryeh ha-Levi, was a man of wondrous learning. Expert he was in the Mishnah and in early and late commentators. And as learned as he was in the Mishnah and its commentaries, so too was he expert in secular learning. . . . I was not worthy of acquiring even the slightest bit of his knowledge [Torah] or of his qualities. But he taught me love of Torah and those who study it."[4] In a portrait that is already embellished with the touch of myth, the son underscores his own deficiencies through comparison with a father whose learning participates in the plenitude of the Torah.

This juxtaposition of son to father, lack to wholeness, present to past, enters into the writer's depiction of his birthplace, the town that he left as a young man. Destroyed in the Holocaust, the town of Buczacz retains in his imagination the accumulated richness of centuries of Jewish life in Eastern Europe. *Sefer Buczacz* (The book of Buczacz) is the memorial book of the town to which Agnon contributed. It belongs to a genre that was created in response to the Holocaust by the surviving members of communities that were obliterated. Along with histories, photographs, anecdotal memorabilia, *Sefer Buczacz* sketches a portrait of the writer as a young boy of twelve, cataloguing the books on the shelves of the town's house of study, its Beit

Midrash. The Beit Midrash functioned as a center for the study of classical Jewish texts and, thus, can be understood as a central structure in the maintenance of Jewish life.

Sefer Buczacz incorporates its native son into the town's tradition of study and commentary: "Wondrous was that old Beit Midrash—it was not just any Beit Midrash, but the capital of the Mitnagdim, a center for those antagonists of Kabbalah and Hasidism. . . . In this Beit Midrash Sh. Y. Agnon spent his time and nourished his spirit. Until the destruction his notes and comments could be found in the margins of pages of the books that he studied."[5] In this scene the youthful figure of the writer-to-be takes an active role in continuing the traditions of study and commentary that distinguished the town, an enterprise of learning that found its physical and spiritual center in the Beit Midrash.

Compiled after the destruction, *Sefer Buczacz* is unambivalent in its attention to the history, the setting, and the lives of the inhabitants of Buczacz. By contrast, Agnon's maturation as a writer undoubtedly involved a resolution of his relationship to traditional Jewish texts and the communal structures that house them. That resolution produced an ironic stance where the writing constantly plays out themes of rebellion and reconciliation. The disjunctions in Agnon's art are all the more sharply felt in light of the traditions that the writer draws upon so eloquently. Nowhere can this be better seen than in the quasi-autobiographical *A Guest for the Night*. This novel takes note of the writer's youthful rebellion as its first-person narrator describes his early preference for writing poetry rather than studying traditional texts in the Beit Midrash. That bit of personal history is then integrated into the narrator's account of his return for a yearlong stay during which he devotes himself to efforts to revive the dying town and to undo his own early rebellion through a newfound dedication to the study of old texts.

Agnon builds this major novel around the Beit Midrash, which serves as the organizing structure for the efforts of its narrator to bring about a restoration that is both personal and communal. The key to the Beit Midrash provides a symbol for the lost potency of the town and its inhabitants. Nevertheless, the narrator's efforts to reverse that loss and to bring about a renewal of the town are treated with a wry combination of seriousness and irony. Agnon uses the novel to acknowledge the traditions of learning and piety that the Beit Midrash represents but also to mark the futility of attempting to preserve them in Eastern Europe. Written in the 1930s, *A Guest for the Night* is set in the period immediately after World War I. In a sense, it can be said to straddle history by recording the devastation of the period immediately after World War I while in retrospect conveying a sense of the greater destruction that was yet to come.

2

    At the turn of the twentieth century, Buczacz found itself responding to the rumblings of Jewish nationalism. Zionist congresses from 1897 on capture the imagination of young Czaczkes. He would have been part of communal responses to the 1903 massacre in Kishinev, the death of Theodor Herzl in 1904, and the 1906 riots in Bialystok. A development of some importance occurred in the spring of 1906 when Elazar Rokeah came to Buczacz to publish *Der Yidisher Veker,* a Jewish weekly, and took on the young Czaczkes as his assistant. Rokeah's hiring must have given a significant boost to the youth's literary ambitions. Evidence exists of these early years in Galicia of numerous pieces in Hebrew and Yiddish published by the young writer. The Israeli critic Gershon Shaked has analyzed Agnon's maturation through the development of a more complex and ironic relationship to his early romantic tendencies.[6] In later years, Agnon distanced himself from his early romantic effusions, even occasionally inserting an early poem into a novel where it serves to demonstrate a character's youthful enthusiasm and naïveté.

    The first manifest break in the writer's life took place in 1907 when Agnon left Buczacz for Palestine at the age of nineteen. Along the way, he passed through Lemberg and Vienna where he encountered important figures in Jewish public affairs such as the Hebrew writer Asher Barash and the Hebraist and educator Eliezer Meir Lifschütz. But although his visits with these men and others seem to have yielded opportunities for employment and study, Agnon appears to have kept his gaze fixed on the goal of reaching Palestine.

Indeed, he appears to have sustained his resolve in the face of the astonishment of Galician Zionists, who were unaccustomed to actual decisions to emigrate to Palestine. For an insight into the period, one might consider Agnon's account of the *aliyah* of Yitzhak Kummer in the novel *Temol Shilshom* (Only yesterday): this youthful idealist sets sail for Palestine filled with expectations of fraternal solidarity. But despite his fervent echoing of the refrain *kol yisrael ḥaverim* (all Israel are friends), he is set back by encounters with self-important Zionist functionaries in Europe and Palestine.

During his first sojourn in Palestine, from 1907 to 1913, Agnon encountered the pioneers of the Second Aliyah, who had come to work the land. Although he never joined them in their physical labors, he came to know the land intimately over the years. In this first period, Jaffa was his preferred milieu, and he found work as a tutor, as secretary to the editor of a literary journal in which he published his first story, and as secretary to a variety of groups involved in Jewish settlement. The novella *Betrothed* (Shevuat emunim) gives something of the cultural mix of Jaffa in these years. In Jaffa he extended his readings in European literature and, in a striking break with his background, abandoned Orthodox dress and practice. He also spent time in Jerusalem where he drank in the lore of the city's neighborhoods.

These years bear evidence of the impact of relationships with influential older men. In particular, the writer Yosef Hayim Brenner played an important role in the publication of Agnon's early stories in Palestine. Agnon looked up to Brenner as a man of uncompromising integrity. In later years he described their first meeting in Lemberg where he stopped on his way to Palestine and sought an introduction to the older writer whose work he so admired.[7] Noting the brilliance of Brenner that shone from the pages of contemporary journals, Agnon describes Brenner's utterly unassuming figure and mocks his own youthful expectations of the impressive figure of an author. As thoroughly secular a writer as Brenner came to figure for Agnon as the type of uncompromising authenticity.

It was during this first Jaffa period that Czaczkes first adopted the pen name Agnon. During these years several long stories found serial publication in the Hebrew-language newspaper *Hapo'el Hatzair*. Despite these indicators of early success, however, the young writer apparently failed to find firm footing in the Land of Israel, and his abrupt departure for Berlin in 1913 remains something of a mystery. This is the second break in Agnon's development. Unlike the departure from Buczacz for the Land of Israel, this departure appears to be surrounded by confusion, rather than any clear sense of direction.[8]

From 1913 to 1924 Agnon lived in Germany, and these years constitute the writer's major European period. Living in Berlin, with interludes in Munich, Leipzig, and a small town near Brückenau, Agnon absorbed a variety of cultural influences—secular and Jewish—that stayed with him, however he may later have chosen to represent his relationship to them. Gershom G. Scholem, the great scholar of Jewish mysticism, recalled his impression of the young Agnon in Berlin "in the reading room of the library of the Jewish Community Council where he tirelessly leafed through the Hebrew card catalogue. Later I asked him what he had so intensively searched for there. 'Books that I have not read yet,' he replied with a guileless and yet ironic gleam in his eyes."[9]

In the fall of 1913 Agnon attended the Eleventh Zionist Congress in Vienna. Shortly after, he was called home because of the death of his father, but he arrived one day too late for the funeral. Whatever the circumstances, this delay suggests an ambivalence never to be fully overcome, an ambivalence that is as much a part of his character as the unqualified reverence for his father that he expressed elsewhere. Looked at retrospectively, in light of the proliferation in his fiction of themes of lateness and delay in fulfilling important obligations, Agnon's failure to arrive on time for his father's funeral takes on dramatic resonance. Literary reverberations of this theme can be felt in the stories that comprise the last section of this anthology; there one finds stories that vary from the dreamlike to the realistic but convey, nevertheless, a sense of lapses or losses that can never be made good.

During the years of World War I, large masses of refugees from

Eastern Europe arrived in Western Europe. These "Ostjuden" (Eastern Jews) met with ambivalence and hostility from some German Jews and were romanticized as "authentic" Jews by others, among them Martin Buber. Here one must try to imagine Agnon's double perspective: he was and was not one of the Ostjuden, given the acculturation to the West he had undergone. In a study of Agnon's German affiliations, the Israeli critic Dan Miron points out that Agnon's early years in Galicia brought him closer to Jewish-German influence than to contemporary developments in Russian Hebrew culture so that he can be regarded as something of a liaison between the two segments of a divided Ashkenazik Jewry.[10]

Scholem describes the Agnon of this period as an extraordinarily sensitive young man for whom the German Jews were an endless source of fascination. From the vantage point of the present, it seems clear that the differences between Eastern and Western Jews allowed for a cross-cultural fertilization that enriched immeasurably the scholarship of Scholem and the fiction of Agnon. Scholem shows Agnon as a young writer who appeared to inhabit an imaginative universe of his own making: "Every conversation with him quickly turned into one or more narratives, stories about great rabbis and simple Jews whose intonation he captured enchantingly. The same magic could be found even in his colorful but completely incorrect German."[11] Over the many years of their relationship, from Berlin to Jerusalem, Scholem and Agnon would engage in bouts of scholarly banter, each outdoing the other in producing bits of exotic lore from actual or invented sources. Thus Scholem tells the reader that Agnon persisted in claiming that "Agnon" could not be considered his real name because it was only an invention, with no roots in the holy books. In a bit of scholarly play, Agnon claimed that the name "Czaczkes" could be found among the mystical names of angels in the Book of Raziel, an ancient Hebrew book of angelology.

In Scholem's eyes, Agnon appears as something of an aesthete, an Ostjude who enjoyed friendships with German intellectuals. The young writer found himself developing his art amid a linguistic mélange of Yiddish, Hebrew, German, and Russian and an array of ideologies from socialism to Zionism, Jewish mysticism, and Continental philosophy.

Here one sees, also, the Agnon who would frequent the Frankfurt dealers in secondhand Hebrew books, and, indeed, it was a shared interest in old Jewish books that brought Agnon together with the older German-Jewish businessmen and bibliophile Salman Schocken. Agnon and Schocken first met toward the end of 1915 when both were attending philosophy lectures in Berlin. Schocken drew on Agnon's bibliographic knowledge while Agnon benefited from Schocken's familiarity with German and European literature. This remarkable relationship has been documented through the recent Hebrew publication of the correspondence between the two men.[12]

The relationship took shape at a time when Agnon's status as an Austrian citizen subjected him to the possibility of induction into the German army. At one point, in 1916, Agnon sought to fail his physical examination by consuming quantities of pills and coffee and smoking incessantly. Not only did he succeed in flunking the physical, he made himself quite sick and ended up spending four months in a Jewish hospital near the town of Brückenau. During this time Salman Schocken kept Agnon supplied with reading materials. Providing readers with evidence of the scope of his literary interests, Agnon writes to Schocken that he has read Zola's essay on Flaubert in one breath, not because it was so beautiful, but because it was on Flaubert and anything on Flaubert "goes straight to my heart." He goes on to ask Schocken to send him the medieval *Chanson de Rolan,* along with Jakob Burckhardt's writings on the Renaissance.

The relationship between Agnon and Schocken grew in importance for both as the older man commissioned the younger writer to search for Judaica and rare manuscripts. Indeed, part of the uniqueness of Agnon's position in modern Hebrew literature must be understood through his relationship with Salman Schocken and the Schocken publishing house. Schocken became aware early on of the writer's talents and supported his development with a yearly stipend and a commitment to publish his work although Schocken had not yet opened his publishing company. The publication agreement that Agnon signed with Schocken allowed the writer to devote himself completely to his art. The mutually enriching interaction on the young writer and the older patron and collector of Judaica offers an opportunity to study the mingling of East European, German-Jewish, and Zionist elements in the early decades of the century.

In 1920 Agnon married Esther Marx, the daughter of a German-Jewish family prominent in Jewish scholarship and Zionist activities. Together with his wife Agnon established a home in Homburg. Esther gave birth to a son and a daughter during these years. (Agnon's daughter, Emuna Yaron, is responsible for the publication of a major portion of her father's work in the years since his death.) While living in Homburg, Agnon participated in Franz Rosenzweig's Lehrhaus, a center for adult Jewish studies. Rosenzweig, who had briefly contemplated conversion to Christianity, turned instead to an exploration of Jewish learning and committed himself to seek a deeper understanding of Judaism. During these years Agnon also collaborated with Martin Buber on a collection of Hasidic stories that was never published. (A volume of stories of the founder of Hasidism, the Baal Shem Tov, that draws on the collaborative work was published posthumously in 1987.)[13] Agnon also spent a great deal of time with Hebrew writers such as the poet Hayim Nahman Bialik and the Zionist theorist Ahad Ha'am and the publisher Y. H. Ravnitzky as well. Bialik and Ravnitzky had collaborated on the mammoth project *Sefer Ha'aggadah* (The book of legends), an anthology of rabbinic lore.[14] Agnon thus encountered the full spectrum of Jewish life in Germany from assimilationist trends to the search for a more authentic Judaism through study of classical texts. In retrospect, it is possible to discern the contribution of all these currents to his art.

At the same time, stark themes of loss and destruction find their roots in Agnon's experience during these years. In 1925 he suffered a devastating loss when his home in Homburg was destroyed in a fire that consumed all of his books, along with the manuscript of an unpublished autobiographical novel. This fire registered as one of the decisive losses in his life, and its impact can be felt throughout his work in themes of destruction and loss.

Agnon moved back to Eretz Yisrael in 1924, and his family followed him soon after. His letters to his wife during this time express his concern with establishing a home for his family, a concern that appears to coincide with the decision to extend the name Agnon to his personal and public life. Through his letter to his friend and publisher, Salman Schocken, over an eight-month period, one can follow the gradual shifts in his signature from Sh. Y. Czaczkes to simply Sh. Y. and finally to Sh. Y. Agnon. In the letters that date from this time, Agnon expressed his pleasure at resuming his walks through the Old City of Jerusalem and at the recognition he received. Perhaps most important, he looked forward to Schocken's publication of a complete edition of his works. It was in 1931 that the first four volumes of *The Collected Works of S. Y. Agnon* appeared in Hebrew, inaugurating Schocken Verlag, the publishing house in Berlin. Cumulatively, the developments of these years may be considered to be something of an inauguration, heralded by the name shift that extends the domain of Agnon to the personal besides professional life as if to assimilate the writer to his story.

Following his return to Eretz Yisrael, Agnon returned to Orthodox ways. I can surmise a consolidation in the identity of the writer; he has arrived at a sense of himself. There are signs of this settling in to be discerned in his mythologized account of his relationship to the Land of Israel. During a series of conversations that were later published, Agnon told the young writer David Canaani that God had punished him with the loss of the home he established in Germany because he had abandoned the Land of Israel.[15]

Agnon was to lose his home once again, and the historical resonance of this twice-repeated loss with the destruction of the Temple was significant to him. During the year 1929 there were widespread Arab uprisings against Jewish settlement, and Agnon suffered yet again the loss of his home and library, this time in Talpiyot. The story titled "Hasiman" (The sign) conveys the multiple significances of loss and rebuilding. After this second destruction, he built a new house for his family in Talpiyot, and this was where he lived to the end of his life. Today, the house is open to the public: visitors can stand in the writer's study and examine the titles on his shelves.

With the passing of years Agnon became the writer of Jerusalem. A sign on the street in Talpiyot, Rehov Klausner, warned visitors to be quiet because of their proximity to a WRITER AT WORK. The city occupies the central place in the map of Agnon's imagination, as in Jewish tradition, however much his writing may play with ambiguities and paradoxes in the relation of the individual to sacred space. For Agnon, the establishment of a home in Talpiyot acquired significance in terms of the relationship of the neighborhood to the city of Jerusalem. From the roof of Agnon's Talpiyot home, one used to be able to see the Old City. The location expresses something of the identity of the artist whose vision is sustained by Jerusalem and yet who situates himself just outside its gates.

3

The awarding of the Nobel Prize to Agnon was rightly taken by many, especially in Israel, as a belated recognition of the achievements of Hebrew literature and the legitimacy of Israeli culture. As a modern literature, Hebrew had been producing impressive writing for two hundred years, and, since the turn of the twentieth century, a series of great modern writers had emerged (Hayim Nahman Bialik, Yosef Hayim Brenner, Uri Zvi Greenberg, and Natan Alterman, among others) who in no way suffered in comparison to the best artists in European languages. Yet it took the annihilation of the very subject matter of Agnon's epic art—the social and spiritual life of East European Jewry—to prompt international recognition of Hebrew.

Two decades before the Holocaust destroyed the European centers of Jewish culture, the scene of Hebrew writing had already largely shifted to the new Jewish settlement in Palestine, and thereafter it became fused with the fortunes of the State of Israel. Agnon, who settled permanently in Palestine in the 1920s, should be counted in every sense as an Israeli writer, yet not a typical one. His use of traditional Jewish sources, his appropriation of traditional Jewish storytelling techniques, his preoccupation with East European themes—all these choices set him apart from most of Israeli writing at the time, which was realistic in mode and devoted to the depiction of the secular actualities of the new society.

Such is the uniqueness of Agnon. There is no figure in modern Jewish culture in any language whose work is as suffused with the texts and symbols of classical Jewish learning and as steeped in the customs of a thousand years of Jewish life in Eastern Europe. Yet, at the same time, the genius of Agnon's achievement was unleashed only by the rise of modern Hebrew literature. To be sure, European romanticism and modernism contribute to his work. But to understand where Agnon came from and to grasp the cultural matrix that made his writing unique, one must first turn to the specific conditions of time and place. The time was a particular moment in the emergence of the new Hebrew literature after the first challenges of modernity to Judaism had exhausted themselves. The place was the Jewish community of Galicia, the southeastern provinces of Poland that were ruled before World War I by Austria-Hungary.

The origins of modern Hebrew literature entailed a two-phased assault against traditional Jewish culture. In the first phase, which was called Haskalah and took place between approximately 1780 and 1880, the ideals of the Enlightenment in Western Europe were domesticated within the sphere of Hebrew literature and culture, first in Germany and then in Eastern Europe. The social program of the Haskalah called for Jews to cease being merchants and shopkeepers and to enter more "productive" occupations. The educational program sought to introduce the study of arithmetic, world history, and Western languages into the exclusively religious curriculum of Jewish schools. The religious program sought to rid Judaism of superstitious beliefs and practices and to emphasize the foundations of reason in the Jewish creed. The literary program sought to confer prestige on the classical lineage of Hebrew over Yiddish and opened Hebrew writing to the novel, the lyric poem, the essay, and other Western genres. Yet despite these multiple challenges to traditional Judaism, the worldview of the Haskalah remained essentially hopeful: divine reason remained the underpinning of a world that would progress from folly to enlightenment.

This optimism could not be sustained by the events that overtook Jewish life in Eastern Europe in the late-nineteenth century. The pauperization of the Jewish masses, the widespread pogroms of 1881, the virulent anti-Semitic policies of the czarist regime—these and other related causes prompted Jews to take measures ranging from emigration to the West to the more ideological forms of political awareness embodied in socialism, communism, and Zionism. Zionism broke with the Haskalah over the possibility of the Jews' acceptance into European society in exchange for the modernization of their culture. The Jews could realize their national identity, Zionism argued, only in a land of their own and in a language of their own. Zionism broke with religious tradition by rejecting transcendental messianism in favor of a thisworldly politics of self-redemption.

Beneath the political and communal turmoil of those years, an ever graver ordeal was being enacted in the spiritual lives of a generation of young people. For many, the coherent world of the Torah, within which the experience of the individual had been securely inscribed for the thousand years of Jewish settlement in the cities and hamlets of Eastern Europe, broke down in the last decades of the nineteenth century. The daily intimacy with holy texts, the deep texture of study and interpretation, the rhythm of sacred and profane time, the dense patterning of ritual gestures and symbols, the assured authority of teachers and sages—all of these strands in the weave of tradition loosened in the course of a single generation. For some young people, the rejection of religious tradition was the dialectical by-product of a principled espousal of a new faith in one of the revolutionary ideologies of the age. For others, the failure of Judaism had less to do with the adoption of new secular faiths than with a process of internal decline. In the face of modernity the very plausibility of the religious tradition had suddenly collapsed, its authority neutralized and its relevance rendered mute. The world of the Torah had ceased to speak to them.

The crisis of these young people is one of the major themes of Hebrew literature at the turn of the twentieth century. The enormity of their loss was experienced on several levels. For the characters in the fictional world of Mordecai Ze'ev Feierberg, for example, the collapse of tradition is experienced as nothing less than a catastrophe; in the sudden absence of the tradition that had both oppressed and nurtured them, they feel orphaned and hollowed out. For the characters in the fiction of Y. H. Brenner and U. N. Gnessin, the loss of faith is taken for granted as an inevitable rite of passage; the source of their suffering is the ensuing void with its coils of self-consciousness and its temptations to bad faith. For the fictional figure of M. Y. Berdichevsky, the void is invaded by the humiliations of erotic obsession. Taken together, these characters and their creators are members of a generation that was born too late for religious tradition to remain intact and too early for the new order of Jewish national life to delineate itself.

To be sure, the force of experience engendered extraordinary aesthetic gains. The depiction of life in the immediate aftermath of faith in all its existential extremity led these writers to abandon the decorative language and convention-bound techniques of their Haskalah predecessors and to fashion a Hebrew prose far more capable of representing the complexities of modern consciousness and experience. Yet for all these achievements, the loss of the past remained enormous. Thousands of years of Jewish cultural creativity had been rendered irrelevant, compromised, contaminated, and utterly unavailable to the reconstruction of the fractured modern Jewish mind.

Against this background the significance of the precise moment at which Agnon entered the scene of modern Hebrew literature comes into view. Born in 1888, Agnon began publishing in Hebrew and Yiddish while still a teenager. Although not much younger than the other Hebrew writers just mentioned (he was twenty-three years younger than Berdichevsky and only seven years younger than Brenner), this was a sufficient interval in these revolutionary times to make a difference. The small-mindedness and intolerance of the insular Jewish society of the shtetl, the brutalizing medievalism of the *heder* (the one-room elementary school), the repressive and superstitious religion of the fathers, the self-deluded rationalism of the Enlighteners—all the abuses of the old order had already been systematically laid out; the burden of critique had been discharged. For the majority of Hebrew writers, this settled the score with the past and enabled Hebrew writers to proceed to engage the troubling and hopeful realities of the twentieth century. For Agnon's genius, it had the effect of clearing a path to the past and making possible an ambitious examination of the present through the reappropriation of classical Jewish culture.

The area of Galicia in which Buczacz lay was part of the kingdom of Poland until Poland's partition in 1771; from that time until World War I, Galicia was an eastern province of the Austro-Hungarian empire. That the great majority of Polish Jewry to the north came under the rule of the Russian czars while Galicia was governed by the Hapsburgs is a fact of paramount importance. Although life under the Hapsburgs was not easy for the Jews, it compared favorably to the grinding poverty and official anti-Semitism of the czarist government. The Jews of Galicia were spared the kind of pogroms that were visited upon Russian Jewry in 1881 and 1903–5. The Austro-Hungarian administration was also less autocratic than the Russian imperial regime; on the provincial level, socialist and republican movements were allowed to play a role in local politics. When it came to language and culture, Galicia was particularly polyglot. The Jews spoke Yiddish and read Hebrew, the landowners Polish, the peasants Ukrainian, the government German. German was the language of culture, and many Jewish women, even from religious families—Agnon's mother included—read modern German literature.

In Jewish culture Galicia had been the scene of great controversies. Earlier in the nineteenth century it had been a center of Westernization and a home to such Haskalah writers as Nachman Krochmol, Yosef Perl, Yitzhak Erter, and S. Y. Rapoport; some of the fiercest battles between the Hasidim and their opponents took place here. But by the end of the nineteenth century, when Agnon was growing up, these conflicts had been domesticated into a diverse and tolerant religious culture. Galicia lacked the great yeshivot (the Talmudic academies) of Lithuania to the north in which young minds were either inducted into the rigors of rabbinic erudition or provoked by rabbinic authority into rebellion against the world of tradition. Galicia also proved fertile ground for the Zionist ideal. Even before Theodor Herzl created a mass movement, Buczacz boasted several proto-Zionist organizations, and the Zionist cause enjoyed much support among the middle-class religious families of the city. Agnon's departure, at the age of nineteen, to settle in Palestine can be understood at one and the same time as fulfilling a widely held ideal and leaving behind his provincial origins through a sanctioned escape route.

Agnon did escape. He turned first to the heady milieu of young pioneers and cosmopolitan émigrés in Jaffa and then to Germany where he gained intimate knowledge of the stream of modern European culture. Agnon never experienced the extremes of negation that characterized the spiritual world of his Russian counterparts. He was a modern man whose modernity could not be expunged, but the world of classical Jewish culture, in all its dimensions and manifestations, remained for him animated and animating in a way it did not for other modern Jewish writers in Hebrew or in any other language. Agnon's relationship to that heritage had little to do with nostalgia, and he was expert at dissecting the ways in which a person might use religion for self-serving purposes. For Agnon the past exists for the sake of the present, and its stories and symbols exist for the sake of what they offer to the construction of a fuller Jewish self-understanding in the modern world.

4

The Critique of the German-Jewish Ethos in Agnon's *Shira*

AGNON MOST NATURALLY DISPLAYED his narrative genius—and gained his early fame—in short fiction that made ironic use of two traditional Hebrew forms: the midrashic vignette and the Hasidic tale. When it came to writing novels, Agnon similarly constructed them by stringing together cycles of related stories. This resulted in sprawling, epic works that, despite their thematic intricacy and symbolic power, were always in danger of breaking down and breaking apart.

Agnon's transactions with the novel as a form encountered other difficulties as well. As the quintessential literary expression of the secular middle classes, novels required close attention to a particular set of themes: domestic relations, individual ambition, and, classically, adultery. This presented an immense challenge to a writer who had deliberately cultivated the persona of a pious storyteller; yet as a modern writer Agnon could scarcely avoid this challenge without dooming his work to provincialism. In a novel of fairly limited scope, such as *A Simple Story* (Sipur pashut) (1935), Agnon's grasp of the medium is masterful. The bigger novels, *The Bridal Canopy* (1937), *A Guest for the Night* (1939), and *Only Yesterday* (1945), are always fascinating yet sometimes challenging reading.

Shira is Agnon's problem novel.[1] He began writing it in the late

This chapter was previously published as "Agnon Without End" in *Commentary*, Feb. 1990, 59–60. Reprinted by permission; all rights reserved.

1940s and published many chapters in periodicals; then it was consigned to his drawer. Several more chapters appeared around the time he received the Nobel Prize for Literature in 1966, and he was actively at work on the book in the years before his death in 1970. On his deathbed, Agnon asked that *Shira* be published in its incomplete form; it appeared one year later, and in subsequent editions, carrying alternative endings, one of which indicated a direction the novel might have taken but did not.

For the reader this unrealized aspiration is no cause for lament. In the English translation what one has of the novel is equal to the best of Agnon and takes his writing into new thematic territory; that is no small thing. The workmanlike translation of Zeva Shapiro tends to be overly faithful to the singular patterns of Agnon's style, which has the advantage of suggesting what the Hebrew might be like, although it fails to recast Agnon as an author whose writing attains an independent embodiment in English.

Shira is set in Jerusalem in the late 1930s and centers on the figure of Manfred Herbst, a lecturer in Byzantine studies at the newly created Hebrew University. A scholar of considerable erudition and integrity, Herbst has bogged down his career after the success of his first book; a new work, a monograph of the burial customs of the poor of Byzantium, lies scattered on innumerable index cards and shows few signs of ever being written and securing him his professorship.

Herbst's comfortable life—he has a protective and affectionate wife and two grown daughters—is disrupted when his wife becomes pregnant and gives birth to a new daughter. In the maternity ward of the hospital, Herbst meets a nurse named Shira and begins an affair with her on the very day of his wife's delivery. Although he sleeps with her only a few times and she herself disappears midway through the novel, Herbst becomes obsessed with Shira. His work grinds to a halt; his family life becomes intolerable to him; and his psyche is delivered over to grotesque sadomasochistic dreams.

The main body of the novel in its present state leaves Herbst sucked into the downward spiral of obsession. The unfinished portion was apparently intended to leap up to the fragmentary concluding chapter

Agnon attached to the manuscript in which Shira is discovered to have contracted leprosy and to be living in a leprosarium. Herbst joins her there; embracing and kissing her, he willingly becomes infected with her disease to be with her always.

Adultery has been a staple of the novel since *Madame Bovary* and *Anna Karenina*; for Agnon it serves less as an erotic theme than as a device for portraying the breakdown of a worldview—the liberal German Jewish culture embodied in Manfred Herbst. Jerusalem of the 1930s as it is depicted in *Shira* is awash in German Jews—scholars, physicians, daughters of good families—who have fled Nazism only to find themselves at loose ends in an unfamiliar Zion. Their displacement is emblematized by many rare volumes and first editions of German classics that have come into the hands of Jerusalem booksellers as the impoverished refugees sell off their libraries to keep body and soul together. Although Herbst himself came earlier, before the rise of Hitler, out of vaguely Zionist motives and on the strength of an offer of a post at the new Jerusalem university, and although he has learned Hebrew and feels at home in Palestine, he remains very much the creation of German Jewish culture.

This is nowhere more evident that in Herbst's commitment to the vocation of scientific humanism as expressed in his scholarship. His researches into early Byzantine church history are impelled by the conviction that the path to truth lies through the careful and dispassionate investigation of past events, no matter how seemingly removed from the exigencies of the present. This pursuit is undertaken in the esteemed and cherished company not of persons but of books, which become eroticized objects. (The novel abounds in vignettes of bibliomania and bibliophilia.) Yet Herbst's soul has nothing of the arid pedantry of George Eliot's Casaubon in *Middlemarch*. His mind is steeped in German romantic poetry, and he makes notes toward the writing of a dramatic tragedy of his own. Politically, his liberalism extends to an identification with the Brit Shalom group, which in the Palestine of those days favored a binational accommodation with the Arabs. Even the family circle partakes of the German-Jewish ethos: an intelligent and solicitous wife who insulates her scholar-husband from the nuisances of domestic life and a strong-willed daughter raised to be useful and independent.

For all its attractiveness, however, this blossoming of late bourgeois intellectual culture curiously displaced to Jerusalem is presented in the novel as being ripe for destruction. It is being obliterated at its source as the forces of nonrationality triumph in Germany. Herbst's wife, Henrietta, wanders among the offices of the British Mandate bureaucracy in a vain search for immigration certificates for her relatives at home. The Arab attacks against Jews, which intensified in 1936, come uncomfortably close to the Herbsts' house in an Arab neighborhood of Jerusalem. Unbeknownst to Herbst, his daughter Tamara has become a member of an underground group set upon evicting the British by force. Even the world of the Hebrew University, with its largely German or German-trained professoriate, is less bent on the discovery of truth, however rarefied, than it is preoccupied with jealousies of rank and reputation. The utter secularity of Herbst's world, its radical and complacent alienation from the sources of Jewish faith, is underscored obliquely by the novel's intrusive narrator, who observed his subjects from a point of view much closer to the religious tradition.

The agent who precipitated the disintegration of this worldview is unlikely indeed. The nurse Shira, the object of Herbst's obsession, is neither young nor conventionally appealing. What attracts Herbst about her seems to be the mannishness of her sexuality, its freedom and nihilism. She is disdainful of religion and finds her only fulfillment in caring for the sick and suffering. In contrast to Herbst's German civility, she, who comes from Eastern Europe, fascinates him with an account of her flight naked into the Polish snows escaping from her lover on their wedding night.

As a character, Shira is both overdetermined and underrealized. This touches directly on what makes *Shira* a problem novel and on what makes the novel as a genre a problem for Agnon. The reader knows little about the nurse. Herbst's contact with her is very limited, and midway through the novel, as I have mentioned, she disappears altogether. (The frecklelike protuberances on her skin, noticed in the first chapter, turn out to be the early signs of leprosy.) Yet the temptation to underestimate her role in the novel, to see her as, in essence, merely the exotic catalyst of Herbst's undoing, is contradicted by Agnon's naming the novel for her, by the narrator's insistence that his story is as much about her as about Herbst, and by the fragmentary conclusion in which the two are united in a leprosarium. Shira is clearly very important to what Agnon wants to do in the novel, but the nature of that importance is never entirely demonstrated,

Most critics have sought to resolve this dilemma by invoking allegory as Robert Alter has done in his eloquently argued afterword to the new English translation. Thus, Shira, whose name means "poetry" in Hebrew, is understood as a figure for the subversive modernist fusion of eros and art; what circulated in Herbst's mind, then, is not the nineteenth-century poetry of sentiment but a Nietzschean melody fueled by the darker forces of life and death. It is exposure to this troubling power that pulls down the foundations of the world built by German-Jewish culture.

Such a reading of Agnon's novel, as with most allegorical solutions to literary puzzles, produces in the uninitiated reader a momentary thrill of recognition as the pieces suddenly appear to come together in a profound, overreaching scheme. But the *frisson* of comprehension soon dissipates when one attempts to analyze *how* the pieces fit together. Whatever the meaning of Shira's name, it is difficult to see how so perverse and sketchily rendered a character can bear the weight of such large designs.

Still, in the end the reader cannot do without allegory of some kind. In *Shira* one senses that the inherent limitations of Herbst's worldview are being exposed by Agnon not out of any pleasure in documenting its dissolution but out of a belief in the existence of some transcendent, alternative realm. The identity of that realm is never named, but its latent power is everywhere suggested. The transfiguring idea, call it what one may—art, eros, purity, spirituality—can simply not be accommodated by the this-worldly resources of the novel as a genre. For this reason I believe the novel could not be finished. Agnon's deathbed instruction to publish *Shira* in its incomplete state may, thus, have signaled his final acknowledgment and acceptance of that impasse.

One must be grateful, however, for his last-minute instruction, for there can be no other work of literature, however fully realized, that presents the contradictions of the modern Jewish imagination as powerfully as this incomplete masterpiece.

5

Between Holocaust and Homeland

Agnon's "The Sign" as Inauguration Story

ALTHOUGH BY MOST ACCOUNTS S. Y. Agnon is considered the greatest Jewish writer of the twentieth century, his work has little to say about the Holocaust. He wrote prolifically until his death in 1970, yet aside from a few shorter texts, his work does not directly engage what many regard as the transformative experience of the Jewish people in modern times.[1] It was long thought that, because Agnon's artistic world was shaped so much earlier and was influenced by the devastation of the first world war rather than the second, the Holocaust, although deeply felt, left little visible imprint on the body of his work. What Agnon had to say about the destruction of European Jewry, it was argued, was already said in his magisterial novel *A Guest for the Night*, which appeared in installments on the eve of World War II.

It was a case, as it turns out, of looking for something in the wrong place. If one hypostasizes the literary response to the Holocaust from the works of such writers as Elie Wiesel, Primo Levi, and Aharon Appelfeld, then, indeed, the Agnon corpus has little to say about the Holocaust. Agnon was interested in neither representing the horrors of the camps nor meditating on the breakdown of culture and belief nor exploring the problematics of theodicy nor examining the deformed inner lives of survivors. On the basis of the enormous amount of posthumous writing published in the 1970s and 1980s, it became clear that in the years after World War II Agnon was devoted to an enormous project that quite radically redefined what it means to respond to the Holocaust.

That project took shape in the works *'Ir Umelo'ah* (The city and fullness thereof) and *Korot Bateinu* (The beams of our house), in which Agnon undertook an epic retelling of the traditions associated with his Galician hometown Buczacz and with his family. Although none of the narratives in these hundreds of pages of texts refers to the Holocaust explicitly, I argue—following the lead of Dan Laor[2]—that Agnon mounted this effort as an alternative to forms of memorialization that brought destruction and loss to the forefront. For Agnon, the path was not lamentation, martyrology, theodicy, or conventional forms of consolation but the re-creation in words of what is lost in fact.

This epic re-creation is very special to Agnon, and it is a hybrid mixture of traditional and modernist elements that are very far from nostalgic ethnography. The term I use to describe it is the *imaginative chronicle*. On the one hand, Agnon is consciously drawing on the classical model of the *pinkas,* the communal register in which the public affairs of European Jewish communities were inscribed together with anomalous events and instances of deviance. (Mikhah Yosef Berdichevsky was a precursor also much attracted to the *pinkas* form.) On the other hand, playing against the grain of traditional authority is the full battery of ironic counterpoints and intertextual subversions that one knows from Agnon's earlier work. Nostalgia rubs shoulders with nightmare, hagiography comports with the grotesque, and the rule of divine providence is sometimes trumped by the absurd. The result is a magisterial achievement, that might be called "the epic story of one town."

Yet it is a achievement whose hybrid aesthetic is as yet understood very little. Cracking the code of *'Ir Umelo'ah* is not a technical academic exercise but a task of great cultural moment. What Agnon tried to accomplish in the posthumous volumes *'Ir Umelo'ah* and *Korot Bateinu* remains unique even at a time when the appreciation of the variegated responses to the Holocaust in the Yishuv and the state has vastly widened and deepened. One is in a position now to know something of how information was shaped in the media and what political leaders were thinking and doing, and one is beginning to understand something of the experience of the survivors in Israeli society. The responses of religious Jews are coming into focus more slowly, however. In the ultra-Orthodox world the impulse to replicate and amplify the culture of learning and its institutions is clear enough. The world of religious Zionism in which Agnon was located, however, is more complicated and more interesting because of the simultaneous identification with the religious culture that was destroyed and with the redemptive possibilities of the new state.

While one awaits a full critical account of Agnon's project of imaginative chronicling, one can profitably turn one's attention to a very special text from this corpus that reflects on the origins of the entire project. The long story "The Sign" can be taken as an inauguration story that puts forth Agnon's account of how he was called to become the chronicler of Buczacz after its destruction. "The Sign" is an autobiographical story in which the Agnon figure describes his response to the news of the destruction of Buczacz by the Germans on the eve of Shavuot in 1943 (the year is not mentioned explicitly) and then recounts a mystical experience occurring that same night in which the eleventh-century poet Solomon ibn Gabirol appeared to him and composed a piyyut (religious poem) to perpetuate the memory of Buczacz. The poem's alphabetical acrostic bearing the town's name is the "sign" of the story's title.

"The Sign" first appeared in its entirety in the 1962 collection *Ha'esh Veha'etsim* (The fire and the wood); it was reprinted as the concluding story of *'Ir Umelo'ah*. It was the interpretive intuition of Agnon's daughter and executrix Emuna Yaron, who edited and shaped the posthumous volume, that this story of the destruction of Buczacz provided the proper tragic coda for the epic collection. The reading of "The Sign" I am proposing does not quarrel with Emuna Yaron's placement of the story, which is brilliant and powerful in its own way, but privileges another moment in the text. By placing the story at the end of the cycle, Emuna Yaron stresses its function as a tragic elegy for Buczacz; in my view, the revelation of Ibn Gabirol and the poem he inscribes are key elements that stress the story's role in initiating a process of memorialization rather than bringing it to closure. If I were disassembling and reassembling *'Ir Umelo'ah,* I would, therefore, put "The Sign" in the first position.

Admittedly, my position is an interpretation as well. It is nowhere explicitly indicated in the text that Ibn Gabirol's poem is meant to serve as an example of the kind of memorializing creativity that the Agnon figure is expected, or authorized, to carry forward now in his own idiom. Yet, as I demonstrate, strong internal evidence pointing in this direction rests on an identification of the narrator both with the old hazzan (cantor) in Buczacz and Ibn Gabirol and with the entire institution of piyyut as the authentic figure for Jewish religious art. Support comes also from the publishing history of the text. The publication of the story in 1962 with its forty-two chapters was preceded eighteen years earlier by the publication in *Moznayim* (Iyyar/Sivan [May] 1944, 104) of a one-page text, also called "The Sign," whose matter corresponds to the last chapters (35–37 and 40–42) of the present story.

1

In a briefer format the 1944 text describes the revelation of the Ibn Gabirol figure to the narrator, an exchange about the neglect of piyyut, the narrator's grief over the destruction of his city, and the enunciation of the poem with the Buczacz acrostic.

Ordinarily, one might view such an earlier fragment as a sketch or a *jeu d'esprit* that the writer intended to return to and develop some day. The content of the fragment, however, makes much larger claims. In describing the revelation of Ibn Gabirol to him, the narrator takes pains to state that this was an event that actually took place. It is not a literary artifice or a sketch for a story or the retelling of a wonder tale or a neo-hasidic folktale. It is, rather, the transcription of a mystical experience that transpired at a particular time and place. What the modern reader is to make of it and which reading procedures and intellectual frameworks are to be drawn upon to process the event are serious questions deferred until later. For now one can say that the 1944 fragment is presented as the description of a profound and true autobiographical experience, a kind of privileged generative kernel, around which the story "The Sign" grew up and, by virtue of its placement at the end of the story, in which it was consummated. The essence of this experience is not grief and mourning but transcendence and poetic creativity. The 1944 fragment, in sum, gives strong support to a notion of the text not as an elegy but as an inauguration story in which a calling is confirmed.

2

If it can be said, then, that Agnon "grew" the story backward from its transcendental conclusion, one can clearly see how Agnon grew it in two parts. He first made the manifestation of Ibn Gabirol one of several different kinds of visionary events that the narrator experiences when he is alone in the synagogue on the night of Shavuot. He then provided the events of that night with a prehistory that unfolds on the eve of the holiday and lays out the set of seemingly irreconcilable oppositions that will be resolved, or at least mitigated, at the narrative's conclusion. This section comprises chapters 1–24; the events that transpire that night comprise the remaining eighteen.

The first half of "The Sign" is dominated by a stark and seemingly unyielding set of oppositions (Shavuot vs. Destruction and Talpiyyot vs. Buczacz), whereas the second half moves a mediating term (piyyut as a figure for sacred art) from the margins to the center of the story that is finally proposed as a transcendental resolution.

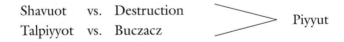

Shavuot   vs.   Destruction
Talpiyyot   vs.   Buczacz   Piyyut

Whether one is persuaded by this resolution, however stirringly it is presented, is ultimately a matter of the metaphysical world from which a reader responds to the text. Yet when it comes to the binary tensions, there can be no doubt that Agnon has unflinchingly thematized the central problems of religious Zionism after the Holocaust.

This is nowhere more apparent then in the juxtaposition—and a willed juxtaposition it surely is—of Shavuot with the news of the destruction of Buczacz. The destruction of Buczacz was not accomplished in one stroke—it was briefly taken by the Red Army before being reconquered by the Germans—and the terrible news was surely not received in one stroke.³ Agnon's staging of this intersection between the claims of the holiday and the force of the news is a deliberate effort to sharpen the contradictions and to place the autobiographical narrator between the horns of a seemingly implacable dilemma.

On one side there is Shavuot both as a joyful festival and as a celebration of the giving of the Torah. The holiday joy *(simhat yom tov)* is formalized through a series of prescribed behaviors, and the narrator presents himself as a kind of "halakhic man" whose affective life is shaped by religious duty. After midday on the eve of a festival the law prohibits a person who has lost a child or a parent from mourning, that is from performing the various behaviors attendant upon being a mourner. So, too, the narrator of the story, having received the news of his city's destruction after midday, self-consciously enjoins himself from any expressions of grief. He registers the news and puts it away while he turns his efforts to the preparations for the holiday. One then hears much about the new summer clothes he dons in honor of the holiday, the decoration of the house and the synagogue with branches and greenery, his attendance at festival prayers, the holiday family meal with special dairy dishes, and, later, his return to the synagogue for the *tiqqun leil shavuot,* the all-night study vigil.

Counterposed to the holiday is the crushing enormity of the reported catastrophe.⁴ In the words of the narrator in the opening chapter: "Tens of thousands of Israel, none of whom the enemy was worthy even to touch, were killed and strangled and buried alive; among them my brothers and friends and family, who went through all kinds of great sufferings in their lives and in their deaths."⁵ The subject is not the destruction of European Jewry as a whole but the destruction of that one community that had been his whole world until he left for Eretz Yisrael at the age of eighteen and had continued long afterward to serve as the font of his imagination. Surely he would have been only human had calamity of such unprecedented proportions and personal meaning cast some pall on the holiday festivities. Even "halakhic man" might be forgiven in this instance for a perfunctory observance of the commandment to rejoice that meets the letter but not the spirit of the law.

Yet the narrator is militant in his refusal to give sorrow any quarter.

> I made no lament for my city and did not call for tears or for mourning over the congregation of God whom the enemy had wiped out. The days when we heard the news of the city and its dead was the afternoon before Shavuot, so I put aside my mourning for the dead because of the joy of the season when our Torah was given. It seemed to me that the two things came together, to show me that in God's love for His people, He still gives us some of that same power which He gave us as we stood before Sinai and received the Torah and commandments: it was that power which stood up within me so that I could pass off my sorrow over the dead of my city for the happiness of the holiday of Shavuot, when the Torah was given to us, and not to our blasphemers and desecrators who kill us because of it. (Chap. 2)

The rhetoric of intentionality is striking. Where one might have expected the straining of fierce emotion against the strictures of the law or, at least, the grappling with a powerful ambivalence, there is single-minded assertiveness and a proud, if not prideful, sense of his capacity to put aside (he'evarti) sorrow for the mandated happiness of the day. Although he acted without hesitation, his achievement required strength and resolve (koah), and it is through this quality of power that he interprets the deeper meaning of the arrival of the terrible news on the eve of Shavuot. God gave the Israelites the strength to stand before Him and receive the Torah at Sinai, and it is that same store of strength, the power to sustain revelation, from which the narrator draws his capacity to put aside his sorrow. Thus, a metaphysical loop is created that links the Revelation with the Holocaust: because of the Torah that God gave at Sinai, Israel are killed by the enemy, and also because of the event at Sinai, the narrator is vouchsafed the strength to defer his mourning over that killing.

Strength in its various guises is a key motif. In addition to designating the narrator's control over his mourning, it recurs over and over again in the description of the settling of Talpiyyot, Agnon's new neighborhood south of the Old City, and in the response to the Arab disturbances in the late twenties and thirties. It is stressed again in the narrator's ability to sustain his parlous encounter with the shade of Solomon ibn Gabirol. In the early sections of the story, however, how one is to take his assertions, especially as they become more and more assertive, is not at all certain. When the narrator returns home from the synagogue to begin the festive meal with the blessing on the wine, he remarks, "This says a lot for a man; his city is wiped out of the world, and he doesn't even dilute his drink with tears" (chap. 8).[6] This kind of self-flattery begs the question and opens the possibility of an ironic reading of the narrator's renunciations. Does he put aside his grief in favor of the joyous rituals of the holiday because this indeed "says a lot" for a man's spiritual strength, or does he do so because he is overwhelmed by the enormity of the tragedy and seeks to escape into the familiar rituals at hand? Religious fortitude or psychological denial?

This is not necessarily an either/or determination. One might, for instance, invoke a model of conscious and unconscious behavior. At the same time as the narrator affirms his allegiance to the authority of commandment over calamity, he is in the throes of inner turmoil and disbelief. This simultaneity of outward faith and inner shock would explain why the narrator interpolates mentions of the loss of his city and the depravity of the enemy at almost every turn as he goes about the rituals celebrating the giving of the Torah.[7] Another approach would focus on the readers' response to the text. Seasoned Agnon readers trained on the tales in *Sefer Hama'asim* (The book of deeds) and on the novel *A Guest for the Night* coming across this late text would likely be alert to the evasions of the autobiographical persona and its advertisements for itself. Although on a first reading of the story such readers might be moved by the narrator's high resolve, during a second reading they would surely be attentive to the dynamics of denial and inner cleavage.

3

The second thematic opposition in "The Sign" juxtaposes Talpiyyot with Buczacz. If the opposition between Shavuot and the destruction, with its encounter between the eternality of revelation and the finality of the Holocaust, centered on time, this second contrast centers on space, symbolic and real. The great figure in Agnon's autobiographical myth is the movement *mibayit levayit*—from the home of his parents in Buczacz in the heart of the millennium-long settlement of Jews in Eastern Europe to the house he built and rebuilt in Talpiyyot, a neighborhood in the new Zionist settlement outside the Old City of Jerusalem at the center of the Land of Israel. In between was the long sojourn in Germany, wandering from one temporary domicile to another. And so the body of Agnon's work, its monuments great and small, array themselves around these poles. Within that corpus "The Sign" is singular in its insistence in making these two spaces encounter one another in an hour of extremity when they can no longer be cultivated by the imagination separately.

In the progression of the narrative, Buczacz and Talpiyyot are related to one another in a kind of envelope structure. (It should be noted that the name Talpiyyot is never used in the story; the place is always referred to as *hashekhunah* [the neighborhood]. The name Buczacz is mentioned, but only twice, being referred to as *'iri* [my city] throughout. The story effaces proper names—this applies to the narrator as well—in favor of archetypal signifiers with the exception of Solomon ibn Gabirol, whose name bears special status.) The story begins with the description of the present Shavuot in Talpiyyot (chaps. 1–10); it then incorporates an account of Shavuot in Buczacz (chaps. 11–16), and then returns to tell the history of the neighborhood from the turn of the twentieth century to the present. In the enclosure of the envelope, the narrator's childhood discovery of Ibn Gabirol's poetry is recounted, and this becomes the bridge to the mediating and even redemptive role of sacred poetry that further connects and transcends the narrator's two homes, one destroyed and the other being built.

The assertion that Talpiyyot is now his home is unequivocal. The celebration of this particular Shavuot is presented, in fact, as a kind of final arrival. "In all the days I had lived in the Land of Israel, our home had never been decorated so nicely as it was that day. All the flaws in the house had vanished, and not a crack was to be seen, either in the ceiling or in the walls. From the places where the cracks in the house used to gape with open mouths and laugh at the builders, there came instead the pleasant smell of branches and shrubs" (chap. 3). Later in the story the narrator relates that his apartment was ransacked in the Arab riots of 1929 and that he returned to the neighborhood to build a house there. The present moment of the story marks the completion of that process of "settling" that had been begun long before. All human dwellings are imperfect, the narrator implies, and their imperfections mock the intentions of their builders. But on this Shavuot, whether because the cracks have been repaired or are merely being camouflaged by the branches and shrubs, the narrator sits in his house with his family around the holiday table in an act of proprietary consummation.

The house and its natural surroundings are presented in pastoral, even Edenic terms. Like the rivers that watered the original Eden, the neighborhood is refreshed by special winds that blow from different directions. The house "stands in the midst of a garden where there grow cypresses, and pines, and, at their feet, lilies, dahlias, onychas, snapdragons, dandelions, chrysanthemums, and violets." The fruits and vegetables that grace the holiday table in abundance are brought from near rather than afar. The neighborhood is its own locale but it is situated overlooking the site of the destroyed Temple. More-than-natural conditions obtain in this garden as a reward for the hard work, self-sacrifice, and vigilance of its planters. "It is the way of pines and cypresses not to let even grass grow between them, but the trees in our garden looked with favor upon our flowers and lived side by side with them, for they remembered how hard we had worked when they were first beginning to grow" (chap. 9). The overflowing responsiveness of nature to human efforts reverses the curse on Adam after the sin in the Garden, according to which, toil will have no reliable issue. It reverses, too, the terms of the usual disheartening comparisons in Hebrew literature between the verdant lushness of the East European landscape with the arid intractability of the Land of Israel *(mashber hanof)*. Stressed above all is the ownership of the land as represented by this house and this garden. In Buczacz the greens that bedecked the synagogue had to be obtained from gentile gardens. In Talpiyyot, in contrast, the situation is described with the utmost proprietary concision—*ani migani sheli laqahti* (from my very own garden I have taken).

When the narrator returns to relate the history of the neighborhood (chaps. 19–24) after describing Shavuot in Buczacz, the tone is very different. The language of mythic overdeterminacy is exchanged for the more practical voice of the chronicler. These lengthy chapters form a distinct expository block that is interpolated within the present narrative. The section tells of the Turkish Jewish veterinarian who first took an interest in the area, the devastation of World War I, the manipulations of land speculators and absentee owners, the outbreaks of Arab violence, and, finally, the cooperative resolve of four chief families who succeeded in domesticating the wildness of the place and creating the garden suburb that is now the narrator's proud bower. At the center of this narrative, despite the usual acknowledgments of God's grace and God's help, is a very this-worldly story that returns the reader to the theme of power. It is not Zionist functionaries who settled the neighborhood but determined individuals who were motivated by attachment to the place rather than by ideological schemes. They dug in and stood up for themselves against their adversaries, and the narrator counts himself squarely among them.

4

Enfolded between the pastoral account of Talpiyyot and the political one is the Buczacz narrative, which is presented as an oral communication from the narrator to the members of his family (who remain anonymous and featureless) at the holiday table. The narrative is marked by a pronounced shift in focus. It begins with an ethnographic portrait of the community as a whole (chap. 11),[8] then proceeds to narrow the focus to the experience of the children (chap. 12), and, finally (chaps. 13–15), concentrates on the particular case of the narrator's own artistic stirrings as a child and his discovery of the poetry of Ibn Gabirol. This movement is experienced by the reader not as a considered exposition that passes from the general to the particular but as a shift that is compelled by an inner emotional urgency. Pausing before homing in on himself, the narrator says, *Harbeh harbeh harbeh yesh li lesapper ʻal otam hayamin. Kʾan lʾo asapper elaʾ meʾinyano shel yom* (I have so very much to tell about those times—but here I'll tell only things that concern this day) (chap. 13). But the narrator has, in fact, been speaking about matters relating exclusively to Shavuot. So whence the need to redirect himself? It would seem that, despite his intention to paint a broadly informative picture of holiday observances in Buczacz, he feels that he has not yet succeeded in recounting the real *ʻinyan* (the real "thing") (in the singular in the Hebrew) of the day. The epic story of Buczacz and its religious life is another project, a massive commitment to which this story bears a special relationship, but not the exigent matter at hand. So when the narrator resumes his story and approaches the account of his artistic beginnings, he has managed to refocus himself and proceed in the direction in which he must go.

What the narrator tells his wife and children about this matter is less important than what he keeps from them. He tells them that in honor of the holiday he would gather leaves and branches from the forest and fashion them with cord into the shape of a Star of David and that the old men of the *kloyz* (prayer house), who were known for their reticence, would enthusiastically praise his work with the words "Fine. Fine. The work of an artist, the work of an artist." What he "purposely" (*meḥokhmah*) does not tell his family concerns his first—and ostensibly naive, sentimental, and jejune—attempts to write poetry in the aftermath of the holiday: "When I saw the faded leaves falling from the Star of David I would be overcome by sadness, and I would compose sad poems."[9] The coy embarrassment over his juvenile efforts at poetry writing only calls attention to their role in laying down the connection between the narrator, as both child and man, and the consummate religious artist Solomon ibn Gabirol. It is significant that this connection, which becomes a defining empathic identification, is presented (in chaps. 14 and 15) only after the narrator has finished regaling his family with tales of Buczacz. He has arrived at the "thing" itself, and it is too fraught to be part of a round of nostalgic reminiscences.

The figure of Ibn Gabirol enters the story because it is the narrator's longstanding custom on the night of Shavuot to read that poet's azharot (a long sacred poem that versifies the 613 commandments of the Torah). (This practice is idiosyncratic, if not exactly deviant, because a canonical anthology of readings exists for the Shavuot vigil that he is declining to use in favor of Ibn Gabirol's poetry.) The recollections of the narrator's childhood discovery of Ibn Gabirol are organized around several common themes that become central in the story's final moment: power, empathic imagination, and poetry as advocacy. The narrator encountered the poetry for the first time when as a child he came across the following line of Ibn Gabirol's at the beginning of the morning service in a new prayer book given him by his father: *Shaḥar avakeshkha tsuri umisgavi / lifnei gedulatkha e'emod va'ebahel* (At dawn I seek Thee, my rock and tower / Before Thy greatness I stand and am confounded).[10] The boy presciently grasps that the poet seeks God because he cannot easily find Him and that, once he does, the experience of God's presence is far from beatific. But it is not the theological paradox the boy ponders but the romantic agony of the figure of the poet. "As I lie down at night I see this saint rising from his bed on a stormy windblown night. The cold engulfs him and enters into his bones, and a cold wind slaps at his face, ripping his cloak and struggling with its fringes. The zaddik [Hasidic spiritual leader] strengthens himself to call for God. When he finds him, terror falls upon him out of fear of God and the majesty of his presence" (chap. 14). The poet's fortitude in the face of adversity prefigures the courage the narrator will later be called upon to display, just as it resonates both with the stoic strength he has already revealed and with the iron resolve shown by the settlers of Talpiyyot.

The boy's capacity for empathic imagination is evinced on a later occasion when he hears the old hazzan intone a geulah (a piyyut based on the blessing for redemption after the *Shema* in the morning service), which begins: *Shiviyah 'aniyah bi'erets nokhriah* (Poor captive in a foreign land).[11] In the literalizing imagination of the boy, the *shiviyah* is not a figure for the people Israel but a "poor captive girl who must have been in great trouble," and he does not understand why neither God nor the people of his city takes action to deliver her and the poor old hazzan as well, "who stood, his head bowed, begging and praying for her." Sometime afterward, when the boy is thumbing through the big siddur (prayer book) in his grandfather's house, he comes across the same geulah, and joyfully he grasps visually what he could not have grasped aurally. The alphabetical acrostic composed by the first letter of each line marks this, too, as a poem by Ibn Gabirol.

Despite its juvenile expression, the image of Ibn Gabirol the boy constructs in his mind is of the utmost consequence for one's interpretive options at the conclusion of the story. Feeling sorry for the poet, he remarks, "As though he didn't have enough troubles himself, searching for God and standing in confusion before Him, he also had to feel the sorrow of this captive girl who was taken as a slave to a foreign country" (chap. 15). The poet's greatness, then, consists in his capacity both to sustain the vissicitudes of his own search for God and also to feel the suffering of others and to advocate for their needs. Such is the model of the poet-advocate, which incorporates, with variations and transformations, the linked figures of Ibn Gabirol, the old hazzan, and the narrator himself.

In wondering why the plight of the poor captive girl is not alleviated by God or the people of his town, the boy reins in the disturbing logic of his thoughts by simply saying *qetsat qasheh* (it is a little difficult [to understand]). The term, which is used in three other contexts later in the story (chaps. 26, 33, and 37), grows with each repetition from a barely noticeable tic to a theologically laden gesture. The term *qetsat qasheh* is drawn from the dialectical lexicon of the Tosafists who use it to introduce a contradiction in the text of the Talmud that needs to be resolved. Agnon is appropriating the term from its legal context and is deploying it theologically as an expression of intentional radical understatement. Take, for example, this passage from the conclusion of chapter 26, "The Eternal had a great thought in mind when He chose us from all peoples and gave us his Torah of life; it is, nevertheless, a bit difficult [*qetsat qasheh*] to see why He created, as opposed to us, the kinds of people who take away our lives because we keep His Torah." A more pointed formulation of the problem of collective theodicy cannot be imagined. Both facts are true: God chose Israel, and God created those whom the narrator earlier calls "our blasphemers and our desecrators, a filthy people, blasphemers of God, whose wickedness had not been matched since man was placed upon the earth" (chap. 1). Yet after forthrightly acknowledging the problem of evil, the narrator, as it were, walks away from it by allowing the mystery to dispose itself under the sign of the term *qestat qasheh.*

Is Agnon through his narrator playing the naif? To the contrary, I argue. His use of euphemism and understatement signal a considered decision to decline engaging the issue of theodicy in favor of alternative responses to the catastrophe. Trying to probe the ways of God's justice, it is implied, is a fool's game from which no gain can be gotten. Agnon pushes the discussion away from the theological crisis created by the catastrophe and toward the relationship with the lost object—his city and all it represents. How to use the imagination to remember the lost object is exactly the lesson the narrator has modeled for him by Ibn Gabirol at the story's conclusion.

5

Is the narrator himself vouchsafed a revelation as he sits alone in the synagogue on the night of Shavuot, the night during which Israel prepared itself for the awesome revelation the next day and the night ordained by kabbalists for a solemn vigil and the opening up of the heavens? The answer is yes, but it is not a divine revelation and it comes only after other forms of vision have been attempted and exhausted. This last major section of the story (chaps. 25–42) has a distinct three-plus-one structure. The narrator experiences in sequence three different forms of imaginative experience before the singular revelation of Ibn Gabirol takes place at the end: reverie, memory, and nightmare. They represent different options, some voluntary and some involuntary, for mounting a response to the destruction of Buczacz. Each in a sense is tested and found inadequate. The answer eventually comes from elsewhere.

In the first of these sequences, the narrator closes his eyes and systematically conjures up in his mind the entire male population of Buczacz according to their fixed places in the city's synagogues. He acknowledges avoidance and fantasy as motives for doing so. It is becoming increasingly difficult for him to maintain the partition between the holiday and his shock over the obliteration of Buczacz, and he shuts his eyes "so that I would not see the deaths of . . . my town and its slain, how they are tortured in the hands of their tormentors, the cruel and harsh deaths they suffer" (chap. 27)." The other motive is more fantasy-laden: "When I close my eyes I become, as it were, master of the world, and I see only that which I desire to see." In response to a threatened loss of control, the narrator has recourse to a technique of infantile regression. He shuts out the world and creates a space over which he has mastery.

What he does with this self-assumed mastery is to fashion a simulacrum of the lost city according to an ideal of sacred order. In this version of Buczacz—and there are many others in Agnon's work—the city is imagined as a *qehilah qedoshah* (a holy community) that exists by virtue of its synagogues in which each household has its appointed place. After summoning up each of his townsmen and, literally, putting him in his place, the narrator experiences something of the joy that he associates with the future resurrection. "I felt a taste of that day as I stood among my brothers and townspeople who have gone to another world, and they stood about me, along with the synagogues and the Houses of Study in my town." Best of all, the people of his town look at him "without a trace of condemnation in their glances" (chap. 28). Despite their suffering expressions, there is even one smiling old man whose expression seemed to say, in accordance with an anecdote in the writings of Nahman of Bratslav, *"Ariber geshprungen,"* that is, " 'we have jumped over' and left the world of sorrows."

What the Agnonian narrator first experiences sitting alone this night in the synagogue is recognizable as a reverie. It is not a dream; he is awake as his mind expands in a bubble of imaginative fantasy. The motive for the fantasy is the pain of separation and the inability to admit the enormity and finality of the loss. The people of his town are not murdered but resurrected, and he, their belated offspring who left long ago for Eretz Yisrael, stands firmly among them welcomed without reproach for his survival. That this is also a reality of his own making, a resurrection brought about by the force of his imagination, testifies to the source of infantile narcissistic omnipotence that energizes this scene. But the energy of denial soon fades, and "bit by bit the people of my town began to disappear and go away," like lights going out as a battery drains. Shaken out of the reveries, the narrator does not try to "run after them," for he now acknowledges that "a man's thoughts cannot reach the place where they were going" (chap. 29).

The second moment is memory. The narrator stays with the image of Buczacz as a liturgical community, but now in a willed act of remembering he focuses on the exemplar of that dimension of the town's religious life: the old hazzan as he intoned the geulah "Sheviyah 'aniyah." This is a re-remembering of the childhood encounter with the poetry of Ibn Gabirol related in chapter 15, and it will recur with a different emphasis in chapter 39. In the earlier recollection the emphasis was on Ibn Gabirol, the author of the poem, and on the boy's empathy with both him and the poor captive described in the poem. Here the focus is the old hazzan as a mediating figure who performs the ancient sacred songs as a means of pleading Israel's case for redemption before God. He does not compose the texts he intones; he is not a creator. It is his gift for expressivity that distinguishes him and also sets up a contrast between his tear-stained *tallit* (prayer shawl) and the narrator's dry eyes. Like the poor captive of the poem, the hazzan was once imprisoned by the Czarist authorities, but, unlike the poor captive, he was redeemed. The governor could not abide the implacable sad singing that came from the hazzan's cell and set him free.

The second part of the memory concerns the morning (the first sabbath after Passover), when as a young boy the narrator first heard Ibn Gabirol's geulah chanted by the hazzan. He wakes up, dresses, and, uncharacteristically unnoticed, leaves the house. "Even my mother and father, who never took their eyes off me, didn't see me go out" (chap. 31). Outside he is also entirely alone. After the birds have finished singing, he is drawn by the sound of the well. " 'I'll go hear the water talking.' For I had not yet seen the waters as they talked." He goes to the well where the water is running, "but there was no one there to drink," fills his palms with waters, recites the blessing, drinks, and goes off to the Great Synagogue (as opposed to the *kloyz* or the old *beit midrash* [study house] that were his regular places of prayer) and hears the old hazzan reciting the "O Poor Captive" hymn for the first time.

The innocence of this moment would seem to jar with the meditations on death and destruction that surround it. Yet Agnon is asking the reader to see this childhood experience in its relationship to the immediate crisis of the adult narrator. The aloneness of the boy as he stands apart from his parents and the community on that sabbath morning parallels the aloneness of the narrator as he sits by himself in the synagogue on this night of revelation and destruction. The animate, talking well is a figure for the abundance of the world and its natural poetry as they are present to the receptive sensitive mind. Like Moses turning to investigate the burning bush, the boy seeks this special source and drinks deeply from it. And it is but a few steps from the talking well to the hazzan's imploring melody. The boy engages the plenitude of the world at the same time as he feels empathic stirrings for the poor captive, whose unredeemed suffering, both metaphysical and historical, he does not yet know through his own experience. Now, at a time after innocence and in the midst of catastrophe, the adult narrator is faced, utterly alone, with unredeemed suffering that is not a poetic trope but a horrid reality. Can the words of Ibn Gabirol and the tears of the old hazzan avail him now?

Yet before Ibn Gabirol's ghostly intervention, a third experience overtakes the narrator—nightmare. Studying alone late at night, he dozes off and dreams. What is cast up by the unconscious is very different from the gratifying reassurances offered by the reverie. For readers of Agnon who know *Ore'aḥ Natah Lalun, 'Ad Henah* or any of the stories in *Sefer Hama'asim*, this is familiar ground. In the dream logic the narrator suddenly finds himself in Buczacz, the place "which my soul longs to see" (chap. 32), yet it is a Buczacz that is vastly different from the one he has recently repopulated in his mind's eye with each man re-installed in his rightful place. Now the old study house is abandoned ex-cept for two old timers who respond to the astonished narrator's questions by explaining that "[a]fter the first destruction a few Jews were left; after the last destruction not a man from Israel was left." After he realizes that he has been speaking to the dead, he goes off and next encounters a group of the sick and afflicted who are crying out to a rebbe (a Hasidic rabbi) about the persecutions of Israel and the failure of redemption. The rebbe, who the narrator knows left for the Land of Israel six or seven generations ago, responds by offering a distinctly Zionist/post-Holocaust exegesis of the verse from Psalms (29:11), "May God give strength to His people; may God bless His people with peace." "[B]efore God will bless His people with peace," explains the rebbe, "He must give strength to His people, so that the Gentiles will be afraid of them, and not make any more war upon them, because of that fear" (chap. 33).

The nightmare measures the depths of the narrator's denial of the catastrophe. That Jewish life in Buczacz was decimated after World War I (the "first destruction") was difficult enough to accept; to admit that it was utterly obliterated after the "last destruction" is impossible. Worst of all is the narrator's being excluded from the world of Buczacz both by his denial and by the grim reality of the destruction. He stands on the outside while the shades of the dead of his town laugh at him.

6

The revelatory experience recounted in the last chapters (35–42) of "The Sign" is unique in modern Hebrew literature. The manifesta-tion of Solomon ibn Gabirol to the Agnonian narrator belongs squarely in the tradition of mystical testimonies, and it goes far beyond anything the lexicon of modern fiction has to offer by way of epiphanies or heightened moments of realization. The narrator takes pains to as-sert over and over again that this is not a literary conceit but that it is re-ally happening. "It could not have been a dream," the narrator avers, "because he specifically [*beferush*] asked me what I was doing here alone at night" (chap. 37). What the modern reader does with this assertion is another matter, but there is no escaping the claim the text is making for an ontological status that is something different from "story" or "literature."

What the reader is told of this experience is easy enough to summarize. Ibn Gabirol appears to the narrator from between the staves of the Torah scrolls of the Holy Ark and communicates with him through a kind of special telepathy in which the poet's words are imprinted in his mind. The poet asks him, "What are you doing here alone at night?" and the narrator explains that it is the eve of Shavuot and that he is reciting the *Azharot* of Rabbi Solomon ibn Gabirol. A lull of uncertain duration ensues, and the narrator recalls the sorrow he had felt as a child for this poet who had bravely sought God only to stand confounded in His presence. He begins to sing the geulah about the poor captive in the melody he learned from the old hazzan, and he remembers the Sabbath morning when he was first struck by its beauty. But his voice chokes and he breaks down in tears. The poet asks, "Why are you crying?" and the narrator answers, "I cry for my city and all the Jews in it who have been killed." The poet draws close to him and takes the sorrow of the city upon himself. He says that he will make a sign *(siman)* so that he will not forget the name of the city, so he proceeds to compose a poem in rhymed verse whose strophes begin with the letters of the city's name. If it were not for the power of this poem, the narrator avers, his own soul would have been extinguished like those of his townsmen.[12]

The narrator's breakdown is the key moment because it sets in motion the exchange of empathy that results in the composition of the poem. The entire story is founded on an increasingly extreme and insupportable tension between the horror of Buczacz's extinction and the refusal to violate the protocols of the holiday. Finally, the tension snaps and the narrator weeps. The catalyst for this breakthrough is complex and overdetermined, but what it is *not* is also significant. It is not the unburied corpses and the murdered loved ones or any of the imagery of atrocity. It is, rather, a nexus between the narrator's own childhood and the powerful beauty of piyyut. The memory returns to him of the sorrow he felt for Rabbi Solomon ibn Gabirol who had to seek God so courageously and who, in turn, had to bear the sorrow of "that poor captive girl." He summons his strength to say to the poet who now appears before him: " 'In our town, wherever they prayed in the Ashkenazic rite, they used to say a lot of piyyutim. The beauty of each piyyut has stayed in my heart, and especially this "Poor Captive," which was the first geulah I heard in my youth.' I remembered that Sabbath morning when I had stood in the Great Synagogue in our city, which was now laid waste. My throat became stopped up and my voice choked, and I broke out in tears" (chap. 39). The world in which piyyutim are said has been laid waste, and their beauty remains only in his heart and not in the home he has built for himself in the new Zionist polity. Piyyutim, as a figure for the artistic vocation of Jewish religious life, were created by the great religious bards of the Middle Ages and kept alive in the integral liturgies of communities such as Buczacz so that a boy like Agnon could have the kind of transformative experience he had on that Sabbath morning long ago. It is the shattering of this axis that overcomes the narrator's denial and opens the floodgate of tears.

It also overcomes some of the spiritual boasting inherent in the prideful claims that he could go about the business of observing the holiday despite the awful news. The narrator bows his head, lowers his eyes, and says to the poet, "In my sorrow and in my humility, I am not worthy, I am not the man in whom the greatness of our city can be seen" (chap. 39). This time the gesture is sincere and free from posturing. Fully admitting the enormity of the loss for the first time, he feels puny and cut off from what has been the source of his imaginative and spiritual power. It is only once the poem has been composed and recited that the true proportions of the crisis are exposed.

> The hairs on my flesh stood on end and my heart melted as I left my own being and I was as though I was not. Were it not for remembering the poem, I would have been like all my townsfolk, who were lost, who had died at the hand of a despicable people, who trampled my

people until they were no longer a nation. But it was because of the power of the poem that my soul went out of me. And if my town has been wiped out of the world, it remains alive in the poem that the poet wrote as a sign for my city. And if I don't remember the words of the poem, for my soul left me because of its greatness, the poem sings itself in the heavens above, among the poems of the holy poets, the beloved of God. (Chap. 41)

The narrator's reflection on the significance of what transpires is presented as a recessive series of conditional clauses ("If not this, then this"). It is only the poem and its power, to begin with, that stand between the narrator's capacity to endure and his becoming "lost" like the people of his town. The crisis, which has been slowly gathering beneath the cover of his denials and now threatens to destroy him, has been averted by the production of the poem. Unlike the narrator, it is too late for the city. Nevertheless, the city acquires a kind of virtual existence, for although effaced (*nikhhedah*) from the earth, it exists in the poem with the special sign.

The problem is retrieval. The story and the ordeals it describes are not magically resolved by this Jewish version of deus ex machina with its revelation from between the Torah scrolls. True, the magisterial eleventh-century poet has descended from the heavens and composed a poem that saves the life of the narrator by offering his city a kind of reprieve from being forgotten. But where is the poem now? "Because of the greatness of the poem" (*mehamat gevurat hashir*), the narrator was too agitated to remember the words.

The poem is lodged in the heavens "among the poems of the holy poets" where it sings itself before God. The concluding chapter of "The Sign" stresses the inaccessibility of the poem and the burden that rests upon those who are left down below.

Now to whom shall I turn who can tell me the words of the song? To the old hazzan who knew all the hymns of the holy poets?—I am all that is left of their tears [*hareni kaparat dim'atam*]. The old hazzan rests in the shadow of the holy poets, who recite their hymns in the Great Synagogue of our city. And if he answers me, his voice will be as pleasant as it was when our city was yet alive, and all of its people were also still in life. But here—here there is only a song of mourning, lamentation and wailing for the city and its dead. (Chap. 42)

Like the exile of the *Shekhinah,* piyyut has been removed to the heavens to the *heikhal hashir,* which is the abode of the holy poets and their sublime poems. What is left on earth is a very different kind of poetry that, in the exigency of the present moment, is charged with the task of lamentation and mourning.

The holy poets and the old hazzan may be gone, but the narrator remains, and his relationship to these precursors is not accidental. In stating *hareni kapart dim'atam,* he is not belittling his own belatedness but acknowledging the responsibility that comes with his filiation. Being a kaparah means being a sacrificial replacement for someone. Being a kaparah for the *tears* of others is Agnon's own special construction. In this story the tears of the poets do not refer to wailing and lamentation as much as to the empathic advocacy of sacred art as evinced by the old hazzan's tear-stained tallit and Ibn Gabirol's signature poem. This is the mantle that Agnon through his narrator now assumes as he turns late in his career to compose not in poetry but in prose the imaginative chronicle of his city.

PART THREE

REWRITING THE ZIONIST NARRATIVE

Introduction

LIKE A. B. YEHOSHUA, Aharon Appelfeld belongs to the New Wave writers who came of age after the State of Israel was established and who began publishing in the 1960s. But unlike Yehoshua and other Israeli writers of his generation, Appelfeld came to Israel in his teenage years as a survivor of the Holocaust. The decision to conduct all of his writing during his prolific career under the sign of the Holocaust sets him apart from other Israeli writers but, I argue, makes him more of a Zionist writer than most, even if he does not set most of his work within the contemporary Israeli milieu. All of Appelfeld's fiction, whether it is set in capitals of the waning Hapsburg empire or in the villages and woods of Eastern Europe, is a meditation on the impossibility of assimilation. The Jewish identity of the Jews, so Appelfeld's fiction implies, is a fateful existential reality that cannot be escaped by becoming a cosmopolitan European or, for that matter, an Israeli sabra.

Appelfeld became well known to American readers after the English publication in 1980 of his first novella *Badenheim 1939*, a fablelike narrative set in an Austrian summer spa frequented by Viennese Jews. A succession of short novels followed *(Age of Wonders, Katerina, To the Land of the Cattails, The Healer,* and others), most of which are set in Europe on the eve of the great destruction. What is not available to American readers is the first fifteen years of Appelfeld's career as a writer during which he published five volumes of short stories and wrote many more that remain uncollected. These stories differ from the novellas in several ways. They tell the story of Jews who hid in the forests and sub-

133

sisted in bunkers and disguised themselves as gentile peasants during the war and what happened to them in the displaced person (DP) camps immediately after the liberation. There are also many stories that are set ten and twenty years later in Tel Aviv and Jerusalem among the shopkeepers and petty underworld characters who survived the war and live a marginal life of functional repression. And there are other stories that imagine the ancestral world of Eastern Europe already under the sign of destruction.

These stories, many of which are wonderful creations, differ from the novellas in many ways, yet they set up the entire thematic of identity that becomes so prominent later on. Appelfeld, the most translated Israeli writer, has chosen not to have the stories appear in translation for reasons that are his own. My discussion of these stories, which originally appeared in a study of responses to catastrophe in Hebrew literature, provides the English reader with an opportunity to grasp the fascinating beginnings of Appelfeld's distinguished career. This is, for self-evident reasons, the only chapter in the volume in which I discuss works that have not been translated into English.

In the case of Yehoshua, another writer who began with short fiction and then decisively moved to the novel, the availability of the early work in translation enables readers to appreciate the successive transformations of his fictional career. The densely existential and psychological early stories gave way after the Sixty-Seven War to narratives that were deeply engaged in political actualities of Israeli life. Yehoshua's first novel *The Lover* (1977) formed a turning point in his novelistic practice. The obsessive, narcissistic consciousness of his early character opens up into an interplay of voices as each character speaks in turn and speaks again. In addition to the many other things it does, Yehoshua's brilliant 1989 novel *Mr. Mani* plays with the idea of the dialogue by prizing apart the dialectic between listener and speaker and giving readers one side only. *Mr. Mani* also participates in the wider trends discussed in chapter 3 of part 1 in the breaking up of the master Zionist narrative. Although Yehoshua comes from a line of Sephardic families living in the Land of Israel for many generations, "Sephardic identity" was not a conspicuous component of Yehoshua's persona as a writer nor of his fictional world until later in his career. When Yehoshua addresses the issue of Sephardism in *Mr. Mani*, he offers readers complexity and many-sidedness rather than a stable and commodified meaning. *Journey to the End of the Millennium* (Masah 'el tom ha'elef), Yehoshua's more recent novel, continues this anatomy in a fascinating way that both idealizes and mourns a related but different construct of Sephardism.

Yehoshua's desire to destabilize received meanings allies him with a younger generation of Israeli writers who are at home with the practices of magic realism and postmodernism. David Grossman's *See Under: Love* is the most important and most ambitious treatment of the Holocaust in Israeli literature by a native-born writer. Grossman's Holocaust novel is not a text that informs readers about historical events but raises larger issues about the Holocaust's impact on the imagination and about the capacity of the storytelling imagination to reimagine and even transform the past. My chapter on this novel and on Grossman's other major novel, *The Book of Intimate Grammar*, focuses on the strengths and weaknesses of using the adolescent mind and juvenile literature as a lens for examining the dilemmas of the self under the shadow of great evil.

Meir Shalev's *The Blue Mountain* applies a similar eagerness for storytelling to the generation of the founding fathers of the State of Israel. The failed revolutionary Jewish youth who settled in the Galilee before World War I to live in Tolstoyan communes and who conceived a powerful attachment to the earth there became the stuff of legend for later generations. How the pioneers were themselves consumed by these fierce passions even as they enfeebled and brought injury upon those who came after them is a story that has been often told in Israeli fiction, especially by Amos Oz and writers of his generation. What Shalev has done is to break through the humorlessness of the Oedipal antagonism between fathers and sons and to shift the conflict onto the level of the recycled materials of storytelling with a restrained and tactical borrowing of magic realism.

Taken together, in these discussions I make the case for the importance and vitality of Israeli fiction not only as a source of imaginative pleasure in its own right but also as a privileged mode of understanding the enterprise of modern Israel.

6

The Unknown Appelfeld

Only with the appearance of Aharon Appelfeld at the end of the fifties did
Holocaust literature begin to acquire depth and direction. He brought it out
of the ghetto where Hebrew literature had placed it. I remember Appelfeld
reading us his first stories in his little room in Jerusalem. Instantly we all felt
that here is a new artistic code that lets us grasp this experience through its
own creative merit. We need not make allowances for it; it stands up to artistic
criteria like any other true work of creation.

—A. B. Yehoshua, *Yediyot Aharonot,* November 2, 1979

THE DISCOVERY OF APPELFELD'S VOICE was indeed a dramatic
moment for Yehoshua and other native-born Israeli writers who were
to become the literary forces of their generation. For many reasons they
were wary of the Holocaust as a subject, and what they had encountered of it until that time had not persuaded them that it could ever be
treated as art rather than kitsch. Appelfeld's early stories made them pay
attention and change their minds.

Yet despite the recognition given him by his contemporaries and by
the critics, Appelfeld's voice has remained a lonely one within the cho-
rus of contemporary Israeli literature. The silence surrounding the
Holocaust has been broken in individual works by a number of Israeli
writers, including Haim Gouri, David Grossman, Itamar Levy, Yitshak

An earlier version of this chapter was published as "The Appelfeld World" in Alan
L. Mintz, *Hurban: Responses to Catastrophe in Hebrew Literature* (Syracuse, N.Y.: Syracuse Univ. Press, 1996).

Ben-Ner, and Dorit Peleg. But Appelfeld remains the only major figure whose entire fictional production is located within a world transformed and recreated by the Holocaust so that even events and situations that have no ostensible connection to the Holocaust unfold under the unmistakable sign of that event. This creative monomania has earned Appelfeld the respect of critics and an elite audience in Israel, but he has not enjoyed the same measure of success—either in terms of sales and fame—as some other serious writers. The restraint of Appelfeld's writing and his principled avoidance of melodrama are responsible in part for the absence of a mass audience. His inalienable subject also plays a role. Although there is much more openness to the Holocaust in Israel than there once was, the fund of interest is not unlimited.

America is another story. The preoccupation, even fascination, with the Holocaust is substantial; it should not be surprising, therefore, that American readers have given Appelfeld's works in translation a warm reception. There is still no question of a truly mass audience, but Appelfeld's prolific output—something like a novel or novella per year—has always found good publishers and attracted a wide spectrum of favorable critical notices. If Oz, Yehoshua, Grossman, and Shalev are best-sellers in Israel and Appelfeld less so, in America the disproportion is evened out if not reversed. One can even go so far as to say that many American readers distinctly prefer the shadows of Middle and Eastern Europe on the eve of destruction—the setting for many of Appelfeld's works—to the sun-drenched actuality of Israel society.

The Appelfeld that American readers know, however, is not all the Appelfeld there is to know. The first work of Appelfeld's to be published in America was *Badenheim 1939;* it appeared in translation in 1980. *Age of Wonders* (Tor hapela'ot) appeared the next year, and the flow of short novels followed after that. From the late 1950s through the 1960s and the early 1970s Appelfeld published five collections of short stories, and many other stories remain uncollected.[1] Why these stories have never been translated is not entirely clear. To be sure, short stories are viewed by publishers as not being as commercially viable as novels. Given Appelfeld's success in America, however, it is difficult to imagine that a publisher could not be persuaded to bring out at least a selection of stories in translation. There seems to be responsible, then, more than a little of Appelfeld's own ambivalence about his early work. He may view the stories as jejune efforts belonging to a literary apprenticeship that came to an end when he turned to longer forms of fiction.

Appelfeld need not have these self-doubts, I believe. The stories contain some wonderful writing. Moreover, they give fictional treatment to experiences that cannot be found in the novels. The ordeal of Jews who escaped into the forests and subsisted in underground bunkers is given vivid and affecting expression here. The first moments after liberation and the reawakening of the body and the mind in the displaced persons camps are also powerfully represented. The evocation of the lost ancestral world, already under the sign of destruction, is also to be found here. In addition to the material that is new to the readers of the later Appelfeld, there are many stories in which the concerns that animate the novels are adumbrated, announced, and experimented with. These five collections of stories, in sum, constitute the first major stage in Appelfeld's career as a writer.

By offering a reading of Appelfeld's stories in the present essay, I hope to restore the "prehistory" of the Appelfeld readers have come to know in English.

♦ ♦ ♦

Appelfeld was born in 1932 in Chernowitz to a German-speaking assimilated Jewish family. The war years coincided with his boyhood between the ages of eight and fourteen. He was a prisoner in camps and escaped and knew the insides of monasteries as temporary refuges. Most of these years were spent in flight and in hiding in the forest of the Carpathians. Toward the end of the war Appelfeld served as a mess boy for Russian units and eventually found his way to the DP transit camps on the Italian coast and from there to Palestine in 1946. In an important sense Appelfeld's rescue was a failure. As an orphan survivor, the boy was educated within the institutions of Youth Aliyah and the youth movements; the ideological indoctrination these adolescents received encouraged them to disassociate themselves from the past, to forget it entirely, and to make themselves over as Jews and as men in the image of the sabra (the native Israeli). That Appelfeld resisted these pressures—at what cost one can only begin to calculate—was evinced by the fact that in 1962, after military service and a university literature degree, he published his first collection of short stories, whose theme was the subject he was supposed to have put out of mind. That the stories were written in Hebrew is itself something of a wonder. Although raised in German, Appelfeld was cut off from it in the years of hiding, during which he absorbed smatterings of Russian, Yiddish, and Czech. When he arrived in Palestine, he essentially had no developed language; the acquisition of Hebrew was entirely an act of will.

The significance of Appelfeld's short fiction for Hebrew literature and for the literature of catastrophe generally can be epitomized by the following formula: Appelfeld's stories succeed in creating the aura of a credible fictional world. Although this can be said of a number of writers—fewer than one thinks, really—when it is the reality of the Holocaust that must be made credible, then such an achievement is rare if not singular. By fictional world I do not mean the system of relation and difference set up by any text, but "world" in the extensive sense of the epic lineage of the novel form. The fact that the Appelfeld world is made of many short texts indicates that it exists at an even further remove from epic totality than the novel. It is the ghost of that totality, or its demoniac mirror image, that makes this multiplicity of discrete fictional gestures, ranging in setting from the forest and villages and monasteries to the Italian coast to small shopkeepers and their society in Jerusalem and Tel Aviv, all part of a recognizable and undisplaceable world; this is a world, moreover, given coherence not just by shared atmospherics but by the rule of certain laws that are as fixed as nature's. Because these laws derive from the Holocaust, the human actions they authorized are almost always unattractive: accusations, evasions, and betrayals being chief among them. The agents of these actions in Appelfeld's stories are presented in such a way that the distance of judgment that would ordinarily intervene between character and reader is neutralized. This is the credible quality of Appelfeld's fictional world, credible not just in the sense of believable but more in the sense of acceptable. The fact that one accepts the plausibility of these characters with neither censure nor sentimentality means that the boundaries of one's experience as a reader are stretched or, at least, become a bit more permeable. Although identification with the Appelfeld world can scarcely be spoken of, there is, indeed, a quality of connection that the texts make possible. Finally, in stressing the aura of a credible fictional world, I borrow with caution a term from parapsychology that designates an invisible field of force that surrounds the body and, like the whorls of a fingerprint, carries a pattern unique to each person. The reference in Appelfeld is to a quality of strangeness in the texture of the stories produced by the repetition of many small motifs, the recurrence of cognate roots, and the employment of a peculiar literary language that amounts to an idiolect.

Indeed, the question of technique, how Appelfeld achieves these effects, raises important issues for criticism. How is the illusion of world created in the fictional text, especially in postnovelistic forms? How is credibility established in the representation of ignoble behavior? These are questions that require sustained inquiry. In the case of Appelfeld it is clear that much of his success stems from an extremely fundamental choice about what not to represent. Everything having to do with what the French call the concentrationary universe—the transports, the camps, the *Einsatzgruppen,* the fascination with the Nazis and the paraphernalia of evil, that is to say, the entire stock-in-trade of conventional Holocaust literature—all this is left out. Before, after, parallel to—yes, anything but the thing itself. After, especially, as if to say that a catastrophe can be known only through its survivors and its survivals. Like Renaissance perspective paintings, the lines of sight in Appelfeld's fictions all recede to one organizing point, which is an origin assumed and necessary but never visible. But unlike the ideal geometry of the Renaissance, the origin here is a point of negative transcendence, a kind of black hole that sucks in representation the closer one approaches. Appelfeld's is a method of radical metonymy, a necessary stance of adjacency and obliqueness. In this choice there is also no small measure of cunning. Appelfeld assumes a kind of literary competence on a reader's part, a familiarity with the particulars of the concentrationary universe as supplied by documentary materials and films and by the more vulgar practitioners of the fiction of atrocity and even of the pornography of atrocity. Depending upon one's knowledge of what is at the center, Appelfeld can avoid the impossible task of attempting to deal with it and, instead, can stake out a position along the margins where the literary imagination has the chance to maneuver.

What this means in practice can be seen in the several thematic nodes around which the Appelfeld world organizes itself. Each node is a particular time relative to the war and is characterized by a special set of conditions that define experience. In the short stories, this time-experience continuum is divided into four principal segments. The first segment is set in the indefinite past and evokes the ancestral order of Jewish life in Eastern Europe as a time of disintegration and incipient apocalypse. These tales are largely collected in *Kefor ʿAl Haʾarets* (Frost on the earth) (1965). The second is roughly parallel in time to the war; it treats of metamorphoses of identity and of the tenuousness of repression. The characters are Jews who have sought to be absorbed into the peasant life of gentile villages and Jewish children raised in convents and monasteries—*Beqomat Haqarqaʾ* (On the ground floor) (1968). The third segment is the liberation—the first emergence from the camps, bunkers, and forests and the first months of rehabilitation in the Italian transit camps—*ʿAshan* (Smoke) (1962) and *Bagaiʾ Haporeh* (In the fertile valley) (1963). The fourth and largest segment is set in the Jerusalem and Tel Aviv of the sixties and deals with the unwanted persistence of the past in the lives of East European survivors from the petite-bourgeoisie and the underworld, with a glance at German Jews from the professional classes: *Adenei Hanahar* (Foundations of the river) (1971). (Appelfeld's more recent fiction, the novellas of the seventies, has gone back to the period of the eve of the Holocaust in assimilated, German-speaking Jewry, and then ahead to the late forties, the years of adolescence and adaptation in Palestine.)

Appelfeld's development as a writer has involved the progressive appropriation of new segments of the time-experience continuum. His mind works through and explores the conditions of existence determined by each circumstance, and then moves on. This progress, however, is not chronological. The publication dates of the major work or works for each segment do not correspond to a chronological arrangement. (This is a generalized structure; there are stories here and there that would seem to belong more properly to other collections.) The sequence according to the time of writing would be in terms of the ordering above: 3, 1, 2, 4. Liberation, ancestral past, metamorphoses of identity, new life in Israel. Appelfeld works by stages, but this lack of correlation tells one that his is not the way of chronology but of the subjective logic of memory. To follow his work in his order, therefore, is to learn that logic and to track memory as it unburdens itself of feeling, unfreezes as it were, and simultaneously arms itself with the structures of expression.

"*Aviv Qar*" (Cold spring) in *Smoke* (49–60) belongs to the second segment of the continuum. The story opens as the delayed news of the liberation reaches a group of Jews who have survived the war by holing up in an underground bunker in the forests. There are five of them: an adult woman, Tseitl; an adult male, Reb Isaac; an older boy, Berl; and two children, Hershl and the unnamed narrator. When the bunker is first opened, they do not know what to do. Reb Isaac goes bounding off across the fields, shouting a woman's name, "Sonia! Sonia!" and never returns. The others huddle in the recesses of the bunker until the melting snows of the new spring flood their home and force them out. As they wander about aimlessly, the peasants point them out as Jews who are searching for their relatives. A monastery rebuffs their request for refuge. Berl breaks away from the group, only later to be found wounded. In caring for him the group experiences something of the exalted solidarity it once had in the bunker. A peasant woman takes them in for the night, but the price is the sexual possessing of Berl; they move on without him the next day, shamed but incapable of protesting. The three who are left—Tseitl, Hershl, and the narrator—are ushered into the presence of a gentile holy man, a magus, who reveals in conjured images the faces of those relations who have died in the war. Seeing the truth, Tseitl, who throughout has striven to enforce the fiction of a surrogate family in which she played the role of mother, loses her grip. The story ends with her nostalgic utterance: "All I ask is to be together again as we were in the bunker with Reb Isaac and Berl with us; then I'd be ready to march from one end of the world to the other" (58).

The meaning of "Cold Spring" is generated by the opposed movement of two ineluctable and simultaneous processes: the return to normalcy in the gentile countryside signaled by the liberation and the disintegration and dismemberment of the ersatz family after the emergence from the bunker. Appelfeld is not one of those writers for whom the very signature of the cosmos has been rewritten by the Holocaust. In the order of gentile time, life goes on. Many of Appelfeld's stories are founded on a topos of the changes of seasons from winter to spring, signifying the world's forgetfulness; this is the eternal return of nature from which the gentile peasants are scarcely differentiated. The world's wounds scab over and heal, but the Jews inhabit a different order of time whose movement is as inevitable but whose direction is opposite. The community of the bunker is made up of individuals who are each the last survivor of a family; how their families perished and how they survived are the sorts of uneasy questions that, in Appelfeld, are always left to the reader's competent imagination. In the bunker they have constituted a substitute family with the roles of mother and father and children, and they have worked to sustain each other in their survival underground. Like gas molecules escaping from an unstoppered bottle, the artificial family begins to disband the moment the bunker's door is unsealed. The liberation is the beginning of the end. The functioning illusion of family had been predicated upon the suspension of memory. With the liberation comes the return of speech and consciousness; the reactivation of memory, the real catastrophe in this text, means that the illusion of restored or reconstituted family must give way to the knowledge of previous loss and ultimate aloneness. When Berl falls ill and is tended by the others, there is an imagined moment of grace, a return to the solidarity of the bunker, but the moment fades before the reality of loss, making possible only the denial and derangement of nostalgia for the bunker. This is as good an example as any of Appelfeld's strategy: nostalgia for the bunker—a small sadness, a modest redemption, but one which, in suggesting unspeakable matters, opens up a receding vista of loss.

There is an affecting moment in "Cold Spring" when the group comes to a fork in the road and has to choose between the way to Radicz and to Tolcz. Hershl cries out: "Radicz? No Radicz for me. They'll never see my face again!" (56). The sudden association has the effect of the firing of isolated synapses. It is one of the two or three moments in the story, before the concluding revelation, when a connection is made to the past. What happened in Radicz? Was it during the war years or before? The reader knows only that it is a source of pain, whether shame for something he did or hatred for something done to him. Hershl's fleeting association is a sign of the first stirrings of memory after the functional amnesia of the years of hiding. The feelings evoked form one of the major themes in Appelfeld's fiction—the ineluctable relationship between remembering and suffering. Suffering has two faces. Loss is the subject of "Cold Spring," loss of loved ones, whether family or those who have become like family. Shame and accusation are the darker side of suffering; this is the subject of another story from the liberation period, "Bagovah Haqar" (The cold heights) in *In the Fertile Valley* (135–53).

The story is set in a former fortress and monastery perched on an isolated promontory on the Italian coast, which has been mobilized as a temporary recovery station for a group of survivors. Now that the discipline and vigilance of concealment and escape are no longer necessary, they collapse into the pain that until now could not be indulged. Ravenous hunger struggles with nausea and shrunken intestines; mute and sedated, the survivors take to bed, each huddled in the ordeal of his own pain. Bone knitting bone, the process of convalescence slowly proceeds. Wounds heal, bits of speech return, sensations of beauty and pleasure are rediscovered, and practical plans for the future begin to be discussed. Like the return of spring to the gentile countryside in "Cold Spring," the progress of physical healing is matched by a countervailing process of darker import. A man and his niece, Spillman and Liuba, who had survived by joining a gentile troupe of traveling clowns, hold themselves aloof from the general clamor of plan making. The silence is suddenly broken by a terrible shriek of pain by Spillman. Swiftly he drags Liuba along the veranda by her hair and hurls her over the cliff.

The act explodes the busy hopefulness that had begun to establish itself. There are demands for Spillman's imprisonment, indictments of Liuba for fornicating with the gentile circus troupers, and defenses of her purity and immaculate lineage. These violent forces had been there all along; yet "until then everything had been pent up behind a barrier which only Spillman's tough body could smash" (147).

Spillman regains control of himself, Liuba recovers, and the group pulls itself together in preparation for departure. But the costs have been great and irreversible. Uncle and niece have become wasted in spirit and vitality, and the other survivors know that they must now go about reconstructing their lives with no expectation of solidarity. The consequences of remembering, it is implied, cannot be otherwise. To survive is to have done terrible things or at least to suspect others of having done them. When memory comes, it decimates because, for the survivor, the only contents of memory can be shame and accusation, real or imagined. Now, the return of memory is not inescapable. The way out is never to let it surface or to force it back underground by clinging tenaciously to a state of present-mindedness. This is not the ideal here-and-now of contemporary psychologies, the unimpeded availability to emotion, but the opposite—the present as a medium of incessant short-term calculation aimed at keeping emotion at bay. In Appelfeld this stance is expressed in the commercial ethos of the minor entrepreneurs, small merchants, and loan sharks who populate Jerusalem and Tel Aviv of the later stories.

The disingenuous origins of this ethos are the subject of such stories from the time of the liberation as "'Al Yad Haḥof" (Along the shore) in *Smoke* (163–80), and in *In the Fertile Valley* (116–34), which begins: "Immediately after the war, a world of opportunities opened up; the trains rushed to the ports, to the blue gates which now opened toward the world. A few succeeded in boarding ships; the rest remained here, onshore, near the small huts left by the army, near the waves. A bustle of activity ensued; there were even those who removed their clothes and offered them up for sale; the more enterprising set up stands." Berl sets out a suitcase and does a brisk trade in nylons and army clothes. Together with Fishl he gives himself over to the frenzy of petty transactions and grander schemes for emigration and business deals. Ostensibly, Berl and Fishl have avoided the burnt-out fate of Spillman and Liuba by suppressing the forces of inner subversion and deflecting them into the untiring energies of enterprise. Yet despite themselves something remains that binds them to the past. The requisite for success in the newly opened world of opportunities is mobility. A man must be ready to travel quickly and travel light to seize his chance, and Berl has an encumbrance to get rid of before the world is his. Her name is Gitl. She had been nine years old when Berl had found her in the snow and brought her into the bunker. He had abandoned her twice in the past. Once, in the forest, he had gone back to get her. At the end of the war she had found him. Dazed and feeble, she clings to him, and he to her, appearing to the others "like lovers doomed to friendship by a supreme decree" *(Smoke,* 171). But as the frenzy of expectations mounts, the renewed bond loosens. Berl and Fishl cannot resist the call to set out for the south and the opportunities that await them there. To gain freedom of movement they hand over Gitl to a convent, earnestly assuring her and themselves that she will be in good hands and will learn French there. Outwitting the debilitating forces of memory, Berl and Fishl make their escape; yet the costs are clear, and they extend beyond those suffered by Gitl. For Berl the repetition of his betrayal means that he has abandoned himself to a world so devoid of trust that the circle of betraying and being betrayed can never be broken. By eluding memory he has fallen into the clutches of the past.

Does Berl, after all, have a choice? The alternatives are the madness of Tseitl, the lobotomized gaze of Spillman, the repeated victimizing of Gitl, and even these can scarcely be said to be choices as much as outcomes. This is the great and simple secret of the Appelfeld world: there is no freedom. With one or two exceptions in the later stories, the lives of survivors bend to the shape imposed by iron laws of destiny. This shape is inevitably the same—a journey of evasion that is forced back to the ground of truth as if repossessed by a gravitational force that can never be broken. At the apogee of denial at the center of most of the stories hovers a moment of grace in which the characters repose into a belief in the restoration of what has been lost or at least a hope for cessation of the process of disintegration and denouement. In "Cold Spring" this is the moment of Berl's unexplained wound, which makes him dependent upon the ministrations of others and briefly allows the group to reexperience itself as a family. In "The Cold Heights" it is the moment before Spillman's eruption when the survivors are busy making plans for the future and hoping to keep together as a group. In "Along the Shore" it is the interval of reunion with Gitl when even Berl believes that he will never again abandon her. These moments always pass, yet there is no apparent causality; no one does anything to tip the balance. There is no need for explanations. The moment of grace has merely been a reprieve, an interruption in the unfolding of a process that admits of no ultimate alteration.

In a world shaped by predetermined forces, heroic action is scarcely thinkable. Nor does Appelfeld allow even the existential dignity of the symbolic protest of the condemned man. This is a dour vision in any climate; in a national literature forged by the Bialik of "Be'ir Haharegah" (In the city of slaughter) and carried on by the writer warriors of the Palmah generation, it amounts to a kind of sedition.[2] Deeply shamed by the supposed reality behind the slogan "like sheep to the slaughter," the leaders of the young state sought to deflect attention away from the morally compromised survivor and to highlight counterexamples of uprising and resistance. The Day of Holocaust and Bravery *(Yom hasho'ah vehagevurah)*, established in the 1950s, left no doubt in practice which of the two was the privileged term. Now Appelfeld would have obliged this national sentiment if he had made the reader feel the ugliness of what, on the part of his characters, are indeed ugly acts. But he declines to do so. Nor does his refusal take the opposite tack so common in contemporary Western literature—the glorification of the survivor as the heroic figure of the new world of persecution and absurdity, or more radically, the aestheticization of evil through an entry into a Genet-like world of redemption through transgression.

Appelfeld's is a middle course, yet one that never leads to the blandness of clinical presentation. It is a question not of neutrality but of neutralization. The writing works to defuse the norms of judgment that govern the representation of survival in Hebrew literature and to establish in their place a stance of understanding. Understanding is not forgiveness, which implies a cordon of purity from across which remission is offered. To understand means to accept that such is the nature of things, that to survive in a world in which the Holocaust happened means to have done certain things and to be a certain way. Appelfeld's goal is our knowledge of that world; he wants the reader to accept the reality of it against instincts of evasion every bit as strong as those of his characters. To the extent that Appelfeld succeeds in rendering this given and determined world fictionally plausible, to that extent he manages to purchase the reader's acceptance of his characters' humanity. And this is the paradox: this humanity is attained precisely because they have no freedom.

In Appelfeld's project of rendering his world fictionally plausible, there would seem to be an inherent limitation. If this is a world of implacable laws, how can it be interesting? The answer is that although the ultimate reality is fixed, the proximate means of evasion are manifold. The conditions and climes, the stages of life and of history, the differences of class and temperament are variegated; although the points of departure and arrival are always the same, the voyage of bad faith is different each time. It is this space in between, so briefly given and so hedged in from both sides that is the zone of these characters' humanity—what is left of their freedom—and they people it densely and variously. Appelfeld's world is monochromatic, but the intensity of contrasts he forces one to discover within his limited part of the spectrum has the effect—indeed the presumption—of suggesting that the part be taken for the whole.

Instead of taking its characters forward in time from the forests and the transit camps, Appelfeld's fiction of the early sixties—as collected in *Frost on the Earth*—moves backward. The themes are taken from the life of East European Jewry in a world that ostensibly knows nothing of the destruction to come: the pilgrimage of a group of Hasidim to their rebbe; the memoirs of a skeptical rabbinical court beadle; the declining power of the last in a family of shtadlanim (community representatives); the confessions of a businessman stuck for the winter in a distant trading post; the weariness of commercial travelers and Zionist lecturers in their rounds of distant villages; the failed preparations of a town to emigrate to America. One might expect that Appelfeld is probing for origins, searching for structures of consciousness and behavior that would explain what came later. In fact, the opposite is true. Instead of attempting to reconstruct the past, Appelfeld intentionally and systematically commits the fallacy of projecting onto the past a knowledge of later events. It is as if the ancestral order, as a world suffused with despair, entropy, and disintegration, were always already under the star of the Holocaust.[3] Here is the same condemned destiny of human life, the same implacable laws, the same temptation to evasion—although, of course, the strategies of evasion are particular to time and place. This sameness of conditions is a way for Appelfeld to assert that the nature of existence is one and that it matters little if one writes of survivors, who have gone through the event, or of their predecessors, those who later, at best, may have the chance to become survivors. "There is no earlier and later *(ein muqdam ume'uhar),* only the burning present," says one of Appelfeld's narrators, echoing the rabbis' counsel against seeking a sequential order of events in biblical narrative. It is in these tales that Appelfeld most closely approaches the canons of a mythic scripture. Indeterminate journeys, faraway capitals from which laws are issued but which can never be reached, isolated and nameless monologists, powerlessness in the face of encroaching forces—this is an ambience that suggests nothing so much as the wanderings of Israel in the desert as retold by the Kafka of *The Castle.* For the reader of Hebrew literature steeped in Abramowitsch, Berkowitch, and Agnon, Appelfeld's reworking of the long-used thematics of the shtetl has the force of a successful defamiliarization.

"Hagerush" (The expulsion) (56–65), one of the most accomplished stories in this series, literalizes evasion in the form of an actual journey and shows how finely textured the representation of this idea can be. The story concerns a community of Hasidim who are banished from their town and make the long trip to the provincial capital en masse in open wagons. The circumstance of the expulsion edict, the machinations of the gentiles, the failed intercessions and bribes—of all this there is nothing, implying that such information is beside the point.

Expulsion is inscribed in the cosmos; as in Appelfeld generally, such a fate is a defining condition of existence rather than a product of history. The truth that is evaded is simply put: their journey is coerced, not elected; what awaits them in the capital is further rejection and dispossession; this is the beginning of a decline that will stop only in destruction and death.

When they first take to the road, the Hasidim are exhilarated; they experience their leaving as a liberation. All these long years their lives have been ground down by the threats and harassments of the gentiles. Nor have they been left in peace by their fellow Jews; the Westernizers and half-breeds have persecuted them and ridiculed their faith. The unrelenting press of business and livelihood has dulled their spirituality. Now, as they move through the open fields, they shed their diffidence and abandon themselves to the vast openness of the heavens. The beauty of the countryside seems revealed for the first time, and they give themselves over to intoning the niggunim (Hasidic melodies) from whose spiritual strength they have long been cut off. Their progress evokes a nostalgia for the festival pilgrimage journeys to their rebbe's court in happier times.

The women are less exhilarated than agitated. The small-mindedness enforced by years of haggling in the market make them resist the abandonment of the men and stick closer to the details of the journey. In the past they have trod the road to the capital not for pilgrimages but to transport merchandise; they know how very long the journey is and how dear the price of housing there. It is they who have intimations that this expulsion is not a periodic annoyance but a permanent uprooting, and they are frantic because a hasty departure prevented them from taking leave from the graves of their ancestors. From their everyday intercourse with the gentiles, the women know them better than the men and can less easily shake off their anxieties.

The women's reservations remain unvoiced because articulation is against the principles of the community. They are known as the Mute Hasidim. Their strength lies in their restraint. In the welter of questions and calculations about the journey—how long? how many? where to?—they see the devil working to undermine the stance of faith. They know the art of silence and await the Redeeming Word. When the silence is at last broken, however, it is not by a redemptive utterance. One of their number, Reb Hershl, steps in front of the caravan and shouts: "Halt! Where are the horses taking us?" (59). Although it fails to stop them, Hershl's cry reverberates subversively. It implies that neither they nor a higher providence controls their movements; they are led by their horses. More than violating the silence, Hershl's provocation lies in its explicitly joining a name and a thing. Precisely what name to give to the kind of movement the group is embarked upon is a critical point: journey (*mas'a*)? wandering (*nedidah*)? expulsion (*gerush*)? The nominative potential of language is what is feared: to speak is to name; to name is to interpret; to interpret is to admit the possibility of alternative interpretations, which welcomes doubt and saps the will of the faithful.

That the question of language and truth is central to the story is underscored by the encounter of the Hasidim with a traveling troupe of mummers. The mummers are Jews who, in exchange for taking a solemn vow to renounce family, property, and their Jewishness, have been given an aptitude for comic imitation and mimicry. The mummers and the Hasidim are presented as each other's double. Both are covenantal communities endowed with special gifts, traveling the countryside detached from home and hearth. Yet for the mummers, their dispossession and their wandering are elected and acknowledged for what they are. If the Hasidim protect (or evade) a sacred truth by silence, the mummers ridicule corrupt truths by overarticulation. In their stage parody of a rich man's attempts forcibly to marry off his daughters, what is conspicuous about their speech is its loudness and inflection; they speak "so that each word should be heard and each rhyme sounded, and so that this Reb Shmuel on the stage should seem the most miserly of misers, the most fanatical of fanatics" (63). Their language tells too much of the truth; it exaggerates what is already extreme. The plasticity of their expression, its mimicking disguises, its very volubility disclose no truth worth protecting. The Faustian relinquishing of their Jewishness has made their wanderings truly aimless. Unlike the Hasidim they lack even a longing for a lost center—or the illusion of still having one.

Whereas the mummers cheapen reality, the Hasidim are in danger of making it into something much more than it is. The practical men among them seek to enforce the discipline of an operative illusion: their movement is a journey to a goal which will alleviate their plight. Required are moderation of behavior, attentiveness to the road, avoidance of speculation, confident faith on the model of the old pilgrimages. This restraint is opposed and overtaken as the narrative progresses by an apocalyptic and mythicizing tendency. There are the "soaring conjectures" *(hirhurim muflagim)* of those who would interpret their present afflictions as an opportunity "to be tested, as it were [*kivyakhol*], by the same trials to which the Patriarchs were submitted" (60). Their journey resembles the descent into Egypt; the capital is a necessary Pithom and Ramses to be endured before a greater redemption. The typological restraint represented by the "as it were" is soon abandoned. In the Sabbath observance, which corresponds to the moment of grace in most of the tales, there is a will to project existence onto the plane of already redeemed time. There were those who, "in their desire to exalt the hour, later told that this was a Sabbath as it was first given [*kenetinatah*]; even the smell of the sacrifices wafted to their nostrils" (64).

"The innocent would not corroborate this," the text continues immediately afterward, "because they are wary of any making of comparisons or parables" (64). This perspective of innocence, by which the variegated evasions of others are revealed, is the possession of an orphan from whose point of view "The Expulsion" is narrated.[4] Unprecocious, the child's mind is uncluttered by acquired knowledge; not yet knowing what to fear, he is untempted by the need to interpret reality and unpracticed in the art of interpretation. The boy's orphanhood gives him both an independence from human bonds and the special protection of the community. His unique place is lodged "between rumor and astonishment" *(bein hashemu'ah vehapeli'ah,* 56) where he can mediate between what people say about events and what he himself observes. (The noninterpretive amazement of the child later becomes the basis for the novella *Age of Wonders,* 1979.)

The issue is sight versus interpretation, and Appelfeld clearly puts forward the figure of the orphan as standing for the possibility of a fictional discourse that registers rather than construes, observes rather than interprets, and ultimately suppresses the urge toward imaginative transfiguration. It is not far-fetched to see in this defense something of the claims Appelfeld would make for his own writing:

> [The orphan's] eyes registered each sight, so that when the time would come he would be able to relate them in his own language, though he did not know then that only he would be the faithful witness. The depredation of time had effaced in them, without their knowing it, all expressions of glory. Only he, in his innocent attentiveness, could piece together image to image. Perhaps the practical men even understood that with his wondering gaze only he could grasp the moment; and they therefore allowed him to move among them so that no detail should escape his eyes. (61)

This self-reflexive meditation is one that Appelfeld seems to allow himself only within the mythic ambience of the ancestral tales. Although much of Appelfeld's fiction may be said to be broadly autobiographical, it is impersonally autobiographical, and there are few passages that reflect on the role of perception and writing. This passage stresses a quality of fateful prescience; there is a shadowy grasping of the orphan's future role not just as survivor but as teller. What is passively and wordlessly witnessed now will at some future time be transposed into language, and not just language but his own language. This hindsight/foresight framework presents the experience of the writer as coming in two stages. As a child young enough to be unburdened by grids of interpretation and dull enough to be free of precocious learning, his mind was the perfect blank film upon which images could record themselves—serially, comprehensively, without patterning. Later, after the events, when he gains language—and this is by no means merely a matter of age—he effects the transposition into words and arranges the images in meaningful configurations. Appelfeld's particular conceit is the claim that for him the writerly second stage carries over something of the photographic innocence of the first. His project of neutralizing judgment, his refusal to demonize or sentimentalize, is born out of a desire to be "the faithful witness," the one who eludes the pressure of later historical meanings and attempts to articulate images as they were grasped by the "wondering gaze" of the child.

"We must make a simplistic distinction between those who saw suffering through to the end, exhausted, as it were, and between those who escaped to the forests, disguised themselves as farmers and circus performers, and, so carrying death within them, wandered from place to place," declares the narrator of "The Cold Heights" *(In the Fertile Valley,* 135–53). Appelfeld's work—concentrated in his fourth book of stories, *On the Ground Floor* (1968)—represents a choice clearly taken. During the actual years of the war, it is the world parallel to the organized torture of the concentrationary universe that is explorable terrain. This is the world of Jews who, because of their constitution, their will, and their resourcefulness, succeeded in effacing all signs of their Jewishness, imitating the conduct and manner of the gentiles, and fading into the rural countryside as farmers, itinerant peddlers, and performers. This disguised life offers rich fictional opportunities for the anatomy of the curious type of the non-Jewish Jew or for an obscene picaresque in the manner of Jerzy Kosinsky's *The Painted Bird.* Yet for Appelfeld it is not the perversity of this situation that interests but its typicality. The peculiar figure of the Jew-turned-gentile serves as an occasion for raising large questions about the nature of Jewishness, the possibility of becoming an other, the encounter between the self and its double. These are questions that arise, in part, out of the separate experience of the Holocaust Kingdom, but just as much out of the mind's quandaries in the fables of identity of modernist fiction.

Again, Kafka is the bridge. The thesis story in *On the Ground Floor* (55–62) concerns a Jewish man and a Jewish woman who, pursued into the forest, suddenly discover that in body and gesture they have changed into gentile peasants. The story's title, "Hahishtanut," translates as "The Transformation" or "The Metamorphosis," and the allusion, perhaps the homage, is unmistakable. Like its precursor, the effect of Appelfeld's text is created by the interchangeability of disparate orders of things, as this confusion is rendered plausible by the matter-of-factness of naturalistic detail. Appelfeld's nameless protagonists awake after their months of flight to find that their skin has coarsened and hair grows on their hands. They find themselves able to swim, scale rocks, climb down into caves, fish in the streams. They make for themselves coats of pelts and tar-sealed boots and converse with the farmers in the local dialect. As in Kafka, too, the sudden thereness of the transformation is comically absurd. The text has the quality of time lapse photography: the male character is giddy from the rapidity of the change as if he were watching his skin toughen and hair sprout before his very eyes. For the reader it is a parody of evolution in which the gradually acquired adaptive traits in the long struggle for survival are compressed into a few moments. Finally, like Gregor Samsa's fate, the suddenly altered state of Appelfeld's characters probes a critical ambiguity about the nature of the link between before and after. Is the metamorphosis a fate visited by the decree of unspeakable events beyond their control? Or is it a chosen destiny, the certain consequences of willed evasion, or even the accelerated culmination of tendencies already latent?

For a while the couple's transformation is a fortunate fall into the lap of nature. They live a primitive life by a river: bathing and drying themselves in the sun, learning to cure fish and dry fruits, reading the signs of the wind and the clouds. In nearly every Appelfeld story, especially the tales of the liberation and the countryside, seasonal change serves as both the setting for the action and its clock, and it is always the circuit from early spring through summer. It is the metronome, set at different tempos, which is always ticking in the background of the text. Nowhere are the workings of this master trope as conspicuous as in "The Metamorphosis." The unalterable movement of nature through the seasonal cycle parallels the implacability of the laws that govern the destinies of the refugees and survivors. The parallel, however, is only a mimicking. Nature has its perennial rebirths, and the peasants, although at times scarcely differentiated from the earth, have shelter enough to survive the dying flux of the seasons. The Jews, however, move along another track. The beneficent warm months, which suggest the arrival of safety, turn out to be a false promise, merely a momentary coinciding.

This moment of grace is represented in "The Metamorphosis" as a still point between two movements: the memory of Jewishness has been effaced and the full naturalization into gentileness has not yet taken place. But things change with summer's end. On Sundays she goes with the other women to church to light a candle; when she returns, he is drunk. Sometimes he flies into a jealous rage and beats her, and she runs away weeping. Other times he weeps "the way grown gentiles weep beside a stone or a religious statue or when the lord raises his whip over them" (60). When their garden bower freezes over, there is no one to take them in. She would have them indenture themselves to the farmers in exchange for shelter; he refuses, convinced that this is a ruse to give vent to her adulterous desires. On the morning of the first snow, he awakes to find her gone, and his frostbitten feet prevent pursuit. Clutching his knife, as the story ends, he "realizes that now everything is ice: the garments, the river, even he. But when the spring thaw comes, he will bring her back and tie her down [*veya'akod otah*] here" (62).

This use of a rare word that can summon up only the Akedah in Genesis 22 is a subtle effect. The purpose is less to urge a closely observed comparison between the two contexts than to strike a concluding semantic chord of dissonant complexity. The man's bloodthirsty desire has nothing of Jewishness about it, certainly none of the high faith of Abraham and Isaac. It is the gentile brutality that has taken him over. Yet Appelfeld's insistence on the root *'akod* for this most non-Jewish of urges suggests the impossibility of the separations the story would at first seem to propose. The effacement of Jewishness is a state that can be approached but never arrived at absolutely. An unwished-for yet irreducible residue of consciousness remains that subverts the consummation. The Jew has forgotten enough to acquire the gentile's earthy brutishness but not enough to be allowed (or to trust in) the primitive shelter of gentile society. The restraints on human nature have been removed, and so have the protections. The frozen legs, savage thoughts, and Jewish words—these are the markers of the story's final image of arrested metamorphosis.

What would happen if the transformation, in fact, succeeded? Appelfeld locates the nameless hero of *"Haberihah"* (The escape) in *On the Ground Floor* (5–20) at a considerably advanced point along the path to gentileness. When the enemy rounded up the Jews of his region, he happened to be on the road. He bought himself a fur coat and a horse and set about assuming the identity of an itinerant gentile peddler. Within a month's time the ruse had been brought off to perfection. The features of his face rearranged themselves; he strode with the gait of a man familiar with the forest trails; his body exuded the smell of farmers; he learned to bless and to curse at the right times and to comport himself in the proper manner with landowners and priests. Within the year he was established in the countryside, not an isolate shunning human habitation but a relied upon supplier of small necessaries, a man respected and called by name. As in "The Metamorphosis," the transformation takes place with an almost miraculous effortlessness, and this astonishing change in individual identity finds an ironic correspondence in the fate of the Jews of the region as a community. Just as the peddler has succeeded quickly and cleanly in replacing the Jewishness within him, so the countryside as a whole, once the Jews have been removed, has easily managed to forget their existence. Grass grows over the Jews' houses; their valuables "soon find their place in the farmers' houses, lose their Jewish color, and bloom on the commodes" (7). A few Jewish words are left in the local speech; more than that, nothing at all.

The displaced candlesticks and wine goblets, although in themselves inert, represent the trace that is inevitably left by any change, no matter how seemingly total. Although the peddler's manner never faltered in his transaction with gentiles, when alone in the woods he sometimes becomes afraid and finds himself murmuring broken verses from the prayer book. "His Jewishness," observes the narrator, "lay beside him like the fallen leaves beside the trees in the fall. It decomposed beside him and within him" (7). Although the tenor of this image chiefly underscores the separableness and dispensability of the former identity, the vehicle permits other implications. The leaves, now shed, were once organically part of the trees, which will again put forth leaves, and even what has been discarded rots not just externally but within as well, a cankerous presence. Soon the text reveals that the eradicated Jewish community has also left traces that are not just inanimate objects.

Rustling sounds in the forest betray the presence of several other Jews who, like the peddler, survived by accident but, unlike him, have remained visibly Jewish and, therefore, must hide. The discovery of these mortified creatures is the fulcrum of the story; the peddler's response to them tests the nature of his transformation.

Self or other? At first he views them with fascination and disgust. Cringing, ragtag, they crawl through the high grass of summer, steering clear of the villages. They appear to him like grotesquely magnified insects flushed from their lairs. He regards them as a hunter regards an unworthy prey that he could cut down with one swoop if he so troubled himself. Soon the Jews' presence in the forest becomes something more than an annoyance. He feels his life invaded and infested; if he fails to reveal his identity to them, he fears "they will swarm over him like desperate summer roaches, storm him with the last of their anger, and bite into his alien flesh" (11). The peddler's fears neatly recapitulate the hysterias and demonologies that traditionally flourish in the absence of real contact with Jews. It is not until such an encounter that his alienness is disturbed.

The irritants come in the form of two boys and an old man, whose presence is given away by the audible strains of their singsong *ḥumash un taytsh* (the elementary school chanting of the biblical text). They are stuck in the high grass because their feet froze in the winter and they cannot move far; it was their immobility that saved them when the area was combed for unapprehended Jews. The plaintiveness of their Jewish voices has stirred something inside the peddler, and when they inquire, he tells them the story of his own accidental escape. The two boys are struck with amazement. The figure who stands before them is gentile in every detail; "How is it possible," they naively wonder, "for a man to change so much?" (18). The old man is less credulous and converses with the peddler with the cautiousness of a man used to the wiles of the world. The invitation to tell his story, the boys' astonishment, and the old man's suspiciousness combine for the first time to tamper with the complete externalization of self the peddler has achieved. The sensation of having his memory pricked involves beholding a self before his present one and, like the boys, wondering at the vastness of the change. "He was caught now in his own enigma" (18).

As the sun sets, the Jews draw off to themselves to pray, and the peddler is left standing by himself like an accused man *(kine'esham)*. Struggling to say something to them in Yiddish, he comes up with the foreign words that are now all the language he has. Although he offers them clothing and a horse and urges them to begin trading in the villages, they have become afraid of him and slip away in the darkness. Their rejection is a judgment: he may or may not once have been Jewish, but now he is one of *them*. The peddler, who began by feeling superior to and separate from these despicable and puny creatures, ends by finding himself "imprisoned by their gaze" (17). They have unmanned him by making him aware of his alienness. Yet paradoxically and tragically, the metamorphosis has been too successful; he has crossed over, and there is no way to come back. The encounter with the Jews has robbed him of his obliviousness and left him stranded in the middle, a survivor just beginning to realize the costs of his survival.

It is worth emphasizing that the agents of the peddler's undoing are Jews. Although one might have expected some unreconstructed bit of behavior to give away the disguise, the peasants and the farmers in all the stories on this theme entertain no suspicions, and there is not one scene of discovery. By making these unmaskings come from the stirrings of memory in the self or from the encounter with the other-as-Jew, Appelfeld is fashioning conundrums of identity and staging Jewish dramas that remain unconditionally internal. But he is doing something less than that as well. What he is keeping out is as significant as what he is keeping in. Excluded is the face of the enemy: peasants, farmers, landowner, local collaborators, and most of all, Nazis. This absence is the rule not just in these tales of the forest and countryside but up and down the line in all of Appelfeld's stories. The representation of gentile existence is undertaken only in the case of Jews who have entered into a gentile identity. This exclusion is the result, in part, of Appelfeld's rigorous aesthetic discipline, which calls for the avoidance of melodrama and gross effects. One senses in Appelfeld a moral stance as well. The fascination with evil is a highly appetitive faculty, and Appelfeld knows that the reader would prefer to have it fed than to be forced to concentrate on the threadbare and pitiable ordeals of the victims of evil, especially survivors. To represent the figure of the enemy in the medium of narrative prose fiction, moreover, means to understand and humanize it, and this is a project that leads in its own direction and carries its own responsibilities.

Removed from the context of the Holocaust, Appelfeld's choice is striking for its continuity with the precedents of the Hebrew literary imagination. The poets of lamentations, the rabbis of the midrash, and the *payyetanim* (the liturgical poets) of the crusader massacres are joined in keeping the enemy in the background lest the destruction fail to be grasped as an issue of the covenant between God and Israel. Bialik kept the perpetrators of the Kishniev pogrom out of his poem to check evasion of responsibility for Jewish self-defense. Elusive of theological and ideological goals, Appelfeld cannot be said to have such programmatic motives, and the metaphysics of his fictional world make no provision for a commanding, covenant-forming God. Nevertheless, the choice is the same, and so is the effect. The force of Appelfeld's fiction is centripetal, drawing readers' consciousness inward toward the Jewish people, toward the lives of survivors, toward the human heart. It is a writing of self confrontation that offers no outlets.

Appelfeld's strongest stories are largely contemporaneous with the time of their writing. These are the tales of new life in *Foundations of the River*—perhaps a play on *Streets of the River* [Reḥovot hanahar]). Set in Jerusalem and Tel Aviv of the 1960s, they concern survivors who have reestablished lives as merchants, restaurant proprietors, and loan sharks. It is just because this milieu seems so unpromising as fictional material that Appelfeld is able to exert the maximum control over his medium. In the earlier stories the narrative voice had to work against the grain of the narrative situations. Appelfeld's understated and minimalist mode of telling was in tension with feelings and events that were inherently overwhelming and melodramatic. This was a tension creatively exploited but uneasily maintained; the polarity was sometimes schematic and jarring. With the bunkers, forests, and displaced person

(DP) camps behind them by fifteen or twenty years and now settled into occupations roughly continuous with their lives before the war, Appelfeld's people present a reality that is tractably drab. Although this ordinariness is only evasion in another guise—the sign of a past more deeply buried—the layers and the surface provide an opportunity for more subtle texturing and for a narrative language that need be less on guard. Appelfeld's Hebrew style changes as well. Lush, difficult, and outré, the language of the early collections is a style whose artificiality contributes to the aura of strangeness in those tales. During the sixties Appelfeld's Hebrew undergoes a process of naturalization. It becomes more like standard literary Hebrew and less like—in the tradition of Gnessin—a replication in Hebrew of European literary diction. The style is still recognizably Appelfeld's; like his characters, it is far from assimilated into the new milieu, but it is at least more at home there.

Appelfeld's retreat from strangeness is scarcely a failure of nerve. Just the opposite. While he restricted his fiction to faraway settings and spoke in a difficult tongue about deformed creatures, his work could be respected as occupying a separate, perhaps sacred, niche within Hebrew literature. The later stories, with their new setting and new style, presume to claim a place within the mainland of the national literature and to leave behind the status of venerated anomaly. The positive heroes of the Palmah writers and the symbolic antiheroes of the younger writers who eclipsed them were drawn alike from the founders and sons of the New Yishuv. Kibbutz members, soldiers, teachers, writers—their lives took place within the institutional realities of the young state and were judged variously in reference to the faltering ideals of the socialist Zionist tradition. Appelfeld's shopkeepers and loan sharks stretch the scope of classes and types deserving of the attention of serious literary art. The main force of this move, however, is to take up for sympathetic study a population for whom the Zionist revolution and the founding of the state remain facts of consummate irrelevance. This indifference is not the result of ideological counterstatement or political illiteracy; the stories do not touch this level of consciousness. Rather, in the existence of the survivors the transforming event has happened long ago. That their lives were rehabilitated in the Land of Israel, whose creation as a modern state was thought by its founders to alter the framework of Jewish history, does not seem to touch them. They could be living just as well—probably much better—in New York or Buenos Aires. They remain unredeemed, their only deliverance coming, perhaps, from Appelfeld's writing about them. Nor can these characters be dismissed as a perverse selection, a collection of hard cases. The challenge of these stories to the values of Hebrew literature lies precisely in a normative claim: the state and all that it represents are, at some level, powerless in the face of other, prior realities.

There is, in fact, only one of these stories in which the State figures thematically. "Bronda," the first story in *Foundations of the River* (12–16), is set in Jerusalem on Independence Day in one of the years when the city was the scene of great military parades after the Six-Day War. Jerusalem in the story is alive with the swirl of gay crowds, bright dresses, and musical instruments as old and young join in a day of festive acclamation. The mood is summarized by a children's choir's singing the song "Yerushalayim shel ma'alah" (Jerusalem the heavenly). The title of the song, which is a fictional variant of the then-popular lyric "Jerusalem the Golden" (*Yerushalayim shel zahar*), implies the existence of a fallen double, a Jerusalem neither heavenly nor golden, which becomes the true setting for the narrative. For the inhabitants of this other Jerusalem the celebration is a day to stay away and stay inside. "How forlorn were the cafes! People huddled by the espresso machine, drawn into themselves, as if the secret of their impermanence had been revealed to them" (11). Among the gloomy company is Kandl, the loan shark, who is doubly dejected because of the death on the previous day of his lover, a blind woman named Bronda, to whom in the past he would repair for comfort on days like this.

The kind of comfort Kandl used to receive from Bronda was of a perverse kind. He needs to be comforted because his life of late has not been going well. Trained in the black market of occupied Germany, Kandl has transferred his profession of money lending with interest— with its methods of risk and intimidation—to life in Israel. But he has become a superannuated figure in the new environment; most merchants now use the banks, and those who owe him money feel little need to settle their accounts. He is caught between the world's contempt for him and his universal distrust of the world, emblemized by the savings sewn into the sleeves of his never-removed coat. What Bronda offered him was an explanation for his bad luck. She believed that his afflictions are a punishment for sins committed during the war, evasions and betrayals about which only he can know. Kandl is a man who has lived without God, she claimed, and until he seeks atonement he will have no rest. He, in turn, disdained her accusations and her talk about God and repentance. Try as he might, he could remember of his early life only that he had been born in Lodz, hidden by a gentile woman during the war, and afterward had escaped to Germany where he began his activities. Of parents, brothers, and sisters—nothing. Yet despite his protestations, Kandl cannot get free of the conviction that there is something rotten inside him, and each of Bronda's curses cuts him deeply. His memory is so deeply frozen by what he saw and what he did in those years that to thaw it would be to risk a pain much greater than what he endures now. Kandl and Bronda are bound together like sinner and confessor, with the difference that he can never name his sin and she can never supply absolution. He is like the figures of Lamentations, who bear the crushing conviction of sin without the knowledge of specific transgressions. He is unlike them in that he has no covenantal faith with which to console himself. He has only Bronda, and when she dies on the eve of Independence Day, the bond is severed. While the nation celebrates independence as freedom, Kandl experiences independence as abandonment and as the beginning of his end.

The bond between two survivors is the principal social unit in the Appelfeld world. In the fables of identity, like "The Escape," the bond exists between the Jew-become-gentile and a more visibly identified Jewish double. In most of the stories the bond is between two people, often unrelated by family, whose relationship was forged by the cooperation necessary for survival during the war—and sometimes by the betrayals as well. Like most things in the Appelfeld world, this relationship is less elected than given; the two people are forcibly and permanently "bonded together" by the necessity of events. In the narrative space of the stories that necessity has already become psychological and spiritual. Appelfeld never shows readers the crucible of brute, physical necessity in which the bond was formed. In the tales of the forest and the gentile countryside, the originating events are only in the recent past (e.g., the pursuit of the couple in "The Metamorphosis"). The stories in *Foundations of the River* study the fate of the bond after fifteen or twenty years. What emerges strikingly from this examination is, after so much time and such different circumstances, how little has changed: the nature of the bond remains stamped by its origins in need and suspicion. The need now has become a need for companionship with someone who has been through the same ordeals, who knows what things were like, who shares the past, and concomitantly there is a need for protection, unspoken and conspiratorial, from the contingencies of the world. Now, what unfortunately works against the functional success of this companionship is the fact that mutual suspicion was as integral to the beginnings of the bond as mutual support. The necessary habit of constant distrust of one's surroundings was internalized forever; and danger could be expected not only from the enemy but from internal betrayals as well.

The bond, then, is actually an equilibrium between the pushes and pulls of two contradictory—and, each in its way, absolute—forces: the need for the protection of others and the distrust of others. The fragility of this balance is the subject of one of Appelfeld's most affecting stories, "Hilufei Mishmarot" (Changing the watch) in *Foundations of the River* (54–59). The bond in this case is between Simha and Baruch, partners in a store who also share a room together. So often are they in each other's company that the residents of their pension call them "the couple." Yet despite this constant companionship each man maintains a separate business life of small private deals; they are forever borrowing and lending—with interest—between each other, and each is convinced that it is the fixed intention of the other to outsmart him. "Twenty years of hidden struggle. Yet the struggle had always balanced out. Over the years they had exchanged coins, gold, dollars, and pounds, and even these exchanges balanced out" (56–57).

The tipping of the balance finally comes one Yom Kippur when their private ritual of observance is interrupted. Each year on that day they would lay in a store of vodka and tinned foods, close the shutters, get into pajamas, and sleep through the night and the day, arising occasionally to nibble and drink. Their ritual seems to be both a symbolic reenactment of an ordeal of concealment during the war, perhaps years in a bunker, besides a strategy for avoiding the questions of sin, atonement, and judgment insisted on by the awesome holy day. And it is, of course, too, a withdrawal from the world into the security of their own bond. This year, with all the preparations made, Simha fails to come home, and as Baruch lies in the dark, he becomes seized by the painful conviction that his partner, who had borrowed a sum of money from him earlier in the week, has bilked and betrayed him. Toward the end of the day Simha does return and explains that the borrowed money had been for doctors and that his absence was the result of a convulsion that had immobilized him all day. The explanations, however, put nothing back together again. The knot has been doubly undone: internally the malevolence of distrust has broken free of its restraints; from the outside, death, so long kept at bay, has also broken through. Although they would outwit it, Yom Kippur has rendered its judgment.

The functional survival of the bond has much to do with the vicissitudes of memory. Staying together depends on a delicate homeostasis between recollection and forgetfulness. An example is the survivors of a town called Soloczin in "Ha'akhsanya'" (The inn) (35–39). The few left assemble on holidays in the cellar restaurant of Shimon Singer, where Singer's wife, his second, whom he married after the war and who is not a native of Soloczin, serves them the dishes of the town she has learned to cook from her husband. Beyond the tastes of Soloczin and the very fact that they are natives of the town, they can remember very little else, not even the names they went by there nor their families and their lineages. Singer himself is a partial exception because he is visited by unexpected moments of recollection. On occasion he will lead them in the singing of a suddenly recaptured *niggun* special to Soloczin or be able to describe the upper and lower towns or recall to one amazed member of the group that as the genius son of the town rabbi he used to be called the Yanuka. The survivors of Soloczin are drawn to Singer because of these powers, and as they sit around his table on

Sukkot, Hannukah, and Passover, they resemble nothing so much as Hasidim at a rebbe's court brought together not by religious enthusiasm but by the promise of memory.

While memory remains a promise, the bonds of confraternity hold. At Hannukah, the midpoint of the year's cycle, the men of Soloczin enjoy the Appelfeldian moment of grace: "A spirit stirred in their eyes as if in their blind gropings they had sensed intimations" (37). When the intimations deepen into surges of memory, what is brought up from the past is not nostalgia for pleasant melodies and tasty dishes. Characteristically, readers are not given the content of these recollections and are left to imagine rivalries, betrayals, and losses as the plausible explanations for the behavior that follows. For by Passover they are at each other's throats. The card games erupt in quarrels; Singer has begun to suspect his wife of unspecified infidelities; the Yanuka is tormented for the unsuitability of the woman he has become engaged to marry; and they cease believing in the power of Singer's memory. By Sukkot and the winter the group has disbanded entirely; the last survivors of Soloczin, after all they have lost, have now lost even each other. "They had now drawn deep," the story concludes, "into their infinite forgetfulness" (39). The opening of memory had been only momentary, but it had been enough to snap the bond and to drive them so deeply into repression as to preclude even the consolations of their guarded companionability.

The message is clear: to remember means to jeopardize the arrangements of one's life. Appelfeld's Jerusalem and Tel Aviv are populated by men who have put their lives back together again after the war, merchants and shopkeepers who have made a go of it and who live lives of moderate habits and measured amusements. Although they are not happy in a conventional sense—they are withdrawn and bear a vague feeling of unworthiness and guilt—they have, nevertheless, done well for themselves and have control of their lives. Yet the constitution of the Appelfeld world does not permit its subjects to persevere in their evasions, no matter how long established and scrupulously maintained. Something inevitably happens to provoke the past into reasserting itself, not with the sweeping force of a purgation but with just enough pressure to bring down the foundations of the newly constructed life. The uninvited reassertion of the past can be so sudden and so catastrophic that Appelfeld resorts to the technique of the comic absurd to represent this moment. It comes about in "Aḥar Haḥatunah" (After the wedding) (141–47) when the story's nameless protagonist seeks to break out of his loneliness by marrying. His bride, Lisia, is an orphan who has wandered through many lands and has just now had the fact of her Jewishness revealed to her by distant relations. "The charm of her strangeness touched my forgetfulness. I fell in love," says the protagonist (43). Befitting a man marrying in his middle years, he has planned a quiet, private ceremony. But immediately after the *ḥupah* he looks around and discovers an immense throng of abandoned celebrants, a group of fiddlers and singers, including a large contingent brought from America by one rich man.

They are all, it turns out, survivors of the town of Rotzov, and according to them, he is the Rotzover, the son and heir to their deceased spiritual leader, the rabbi of Rotzov, and now the remnant of Rotzov has assembled from around the world to celebrate the marriage of their leader. Does he know that he is the Rotzover? At some level of consciousness the fact of his identity is known to him, but that is all. Rotzov itself and all it means lies in the oblivion over which he has constructed his new life. Passive and stunned, he is handed around from person to person and reminded of names and faces; he remembers no one. They, for their part, feel let down and are certain that he is dissimulating. In "After the Wedding" the betrayal that lurks in the past has to do not with moral transgressions of the war years but with a later abandonment of the leadership of a community. It is, circularly, this defection that has caused the loneliness and shame that this character seeks to escape by falling in love. But his marrying only triggers the exposure of his evasion. He is a man whose secret has been revealed, yet it is a secret that he has long since ceased being able to comprehend.

Even Appelfeld's law has its exceptions. From this bleak, determined world, which is constantly recapturing its escaped prisoners, there is only one way out. It is a path that seems barred to men and opened only to women because they bear a different relationship to memory. The issue is not just the willingness and the capacity to face the past but the question of which past and of the depth of the past: How much of personal history can memory be stretched to include? Appelfeld's men have devoted their best efforts to clinging to a precariously established new life; the past they labor to keep at bay is one-dimensional: the war years and the entailed range of experience between personal loss and personal turpitude. For the women, the past is much less constricted, and this makes the difference. There are several female characters in *Foundations of the River* who possess this breadth of memory; they are important figures because in this fictional domain they offer the only models of what it means not only to survive but to succeed in living.

Regina, in the story of that name (27–31), is the center of one of Appelfeld's surrogate families. There is her husband Zeitchik, who has a small restaurant, and his two waiters, his nephews Misha and Murba; they all went through the war together and continued on together in Israel. All of them are in decline: Regina is an invalid who more and more has had to take to her bed; the two waiters have grown sullen and dispirited under Zeitchik's petty tyranny; and Zeitchik himself is so devoted to Regina that his desperation has grown as her condition worsens. Yet from among them all Regina is an exception. Her decline is only physical; she remains interested in life, vital as a source of strength to the others.

The source of Regina's spiritual invulnerability can be discovered by comparing the divergent ways in which she and Zeitchik (the names are significant) remember the past. Here are his memories:

> When he first met Regina she was pretty as a frightened wildflower. They were already dulled and emptied out, with neither language nor love. Misha used to say, like you find everywhere. Murba did not behave well toward her. The evil winds of war, which had blasted everyone, had not skipped her. She had changed along with them, but already then he could see that she could not be humbled as other women. Who then could distinguish between pure and impure, be-

tween those who had their ancestors within them and those who go through this life without ancestors, lifeless? (29)

Zeitchik's rambling, fragmentary associations are as close as any Appelfeld character gets to a direct description of the experience of the war. Nevertheless, even these allusions are enough to evoke a time of universal degradation, dispossession, and cruelty. Although these forces worked on and affected Regina as well, she retained a fundamental dignity that could not be effaced. The basis of her perseverance is linked to her being one of those who have "their ancestors [*avot*] within them." *Avot* can mean fathers, parents, patriarchs, or ancestors, and having the *avot* within one implies possessing inner resources that derive from an incorporation within the self of the vitality and values of one's family and people. Zeitchik and the others share the fate of those not so endowed.

Zeitchik's recollections dramatize the limitations of his consciousness. His mind does not go back to before the war; he was "dulled and emptied out" in such a way that those earlier human bonds and experiences were lost to him. His life—his nonlife, in fact—dates from the war, and the only truly living content in his life lies outside of himself in the person of Regina. What she remembers as she approaches her death gives an indication of what else is possible:

Her memory became progressively more lucid. Many events flitted through her mind, faraway places and long-passed years. Her recall of names and places was astonishing, and Zeitchik, whose memory was as feeble as an ant's, stood beside her the way that peasants stand tongue-tied beside the post office. These were in fact delirious visions. Her ancestors would appear to her. She would talk with them. Laughing, she would ask questions and answer them. She knew that soon the train would come to a halt; the cars would bang against each other and she would return to the place that she had been cut off from long ago, without Zeitchik, without Murba, without Misha. All this went through her mind without pain. A kind of pity stirred in her for Zeitchik, who had changed without his transformation bringing him tranquillity. (30)

For others of Appelfeld's women remembering is less serene but still life giving. The capacity for true mourning is what distinguishes Rosa in "Shemesh shel ḥoref" (Winter sun) (149–57). A waitress in a restaurant, her inner dignity attracts the love of a well-off merchant, a bachelor of middle years, whose emotional life has been frozen since the war. The scene that consummates their love is an all-night vigil in the salon of her pension. Rosa shows him photographs of her lost family and for hours tells him about them, crying and telling. Although he himself can remember nothing, he is drawn to her capacity for memory and emotion as if to a source of his own salvation. The surrender to her love means the collapse of the carefully constructed mercantile ethos that until now has structured his life.

Strength of memory is not just a personal endowment but also a cultural fact. In "Hasoḥer Bartfus" (The merchant Bartfuss) (43–51) it is linked to the differences between East and West. Bartfuss is the scion of an upper-middle-class acculturated Austrian Jewish family who has reconstructed his life in Israel; he has put his excellent commercial instincts to work in building a large and successful retail operation. But like many of Appelfeld's men, he bears a symbolic wound of unspecified origin that seems to result from the shame of something done during the war; gradually he loses interest in the business and, sick and infirm, withdraws to his house. To take care of him the store dispatches Bronka, an ugly, Yiddish-speaking, middle-aged woman. She is the daughter of a *shoḥet* (a ritual slaughterer); she lost her brother and sisters in the war; and she had been left some time ago by her husband. Although at first Bartfuss is repelled by her appearance and *ostjud* manner, over time a reversal of power and desirability ensues. She is a kind woman with unstinting vitality, and to the waning merchant her presence is nearly restorative. Even her Yiddish, a language repugnant to him, comes to seem charmingly musical. "Compared to her speech, his Viennese German sounded artificial and hypocritical" (46). Most of all, the blows and losses she has suffered do not show on her; she manages

to live buoyantly in the rhythms of life. The secret of Bronka's indom-
inability lies in her remaining in touch, in her heart and her imagination, with her dead family, with their world, the world of her childhood.
In the stories she abundantly tells about life in her village, it is apparent
that in some sense her existence is still grounded there. The strength of
her prewar Jewishness, a matrix of family bonds and religious faith, has
much to do with the quality of her later life. "And if her present life does
not match what her father would have wished—well, it is only a temporary passage. In the future she will return to herself" (46).

In the portraits of Regina, Rosa, and Bronka, Appelfeld is clearly
making a statement about the capacity of some women to sustain great
love and great pain and, thus, to escape the need for evasion. As a mode
of response to catastrophe, the example is not limited to women nor to
individuals. Appelfeld is implying that a national culture is doomed to
be subverted from within unless it can do two things: acknowledge and
mourn fully and without shame or judgment what was lost and, at the
same time, maintain a living and affirmative conversation with the cultural world of those who were destroyed. This is a difficult confrontation indeed, and the great majority of Appelfeld's characters do not fear
it without reason, but their fates demonstrate how much more fright-
ening are the consequences of declining the encounter.

7

Constructing and Deconstructing the Mystique of Sephardism in Yehoshua's *Mr. Mani* and *Journey to the End of the Millennium*

1

FROM THE BEGINNING OF HIS CAREER, the dust jackets of A. B. Yehoshua's books have proudly identified him as the scion of a Sephardic family living in Jerusalem for five generations. Yet until recently this aristocratic heritage has not found much of an echo in his writings; there is little discernibly Sephardic about most of his characters or the settings in which they moved. The heroes of his stories are teachers, university lecturers, army officers, lawyers, writers, students, and other members of the professional classes who display no special signs of their ethnic origins. As a public figure, moreover, Yehoshua has been identified with—and assimilated into—an Ashkenazic intelligentsia who think of themselves as Israeli rather than anything else.

Yehoshua's reticence on this score has been remarkable for two reasons. The decade of the seventies, the time during which Yehoshua's authority in Israeli literature became firmly established, was the same period during which Sephardim and Oriental Jews—the terms are used

The section of this chapter on *Mr. Mani* was previously published in *New Republic*, June 29, 1992; reprinted by permission. The section on *Journey to the End of the Millennium* was previously published in *Commentary*, Sept. 1999, 84–89; reprinted by permission, all rights reserved.

interchangeably by some and differently by others—became a conspic-uous cultural and political force within Israeli society. Emerging during this time as a numerical majority newly alive to its interests as a group, Sephardim helped to throw Labor out and bring Menachem Begin in and were not timid about demanding recognition for the past glories of their culture.

Now if Yehoshua were an author who set his fiction at a historical remove from the present or who was concerned mainly with the inner life, then the failure to deal with this phenomenon would not call atten-tion to itself. But Yehoshua's profile as a writer is just the opposite. The fiction of this period is preoccupied with the actualities of Israeli soci-ety: the Seventy-Three War, the War of Attrition that preceded it, the great stock market speculations and the growing prosperity of the mid-dle classes, the restiveness of Israeli Arabs, and more. His stunning story "Early in the Summer of 1970," which was published in 1971, is typical of Yehoshua's desire both to ground his fictions in a precise mo-ment in the life of Israeli culture *and* to make that moment just yester-day. Yet in all this emphasis on social forces and present actualities, the rise of the Sephardim did not find much of a place. And this is not to mention both the public hoopla and the serious discussion around the commemoration of the five centuries since the expulsion of Spanish Jewry, whose "golden age" is the font of Sephardic pride.

This began to change several years ago when Yehoshua published *Five Seasons* (Molkho), a quietly beautiful novel about a Sephardic civil servant in the year after his German-born wife's death from cancer. Al-though the protagonist's Sephardic origin is not incidental to his iden-tity, the novel's focus lies elsewhere, largely on deeply psychic dramas of need and denial. Certainly little in that work prepares readers for the frontal assault on the mystique of Sephardism mounted by Yehoshua in his new novel *Mr. Mani*. It is as if Yehoshua has attempted in one stroke to make up for the cumulative inattention of the past. For this is a Sephardic novel par excellence. Playing with the conventions of the family saga, Yehoshua's novel devotes equal attention to five genera-tions of a family of Spanish exiles who emigrated from Salonika to Jerusalem in the middle of the nineteenth century. The cultural and historical description is thick, and the will to engage the meaning of Sephardism unmistakable. *Mr. Mani* has certainly struck a chord in Israel; it has been a runaway best-seller as well as an enviable critical success.

The motives for undertaking this project appear to be as much biographical as societal as can be seen at once from the surface likeness between the history of Yehoshua's own family and the family he describes in the novel. More explicitly, *Mr. Mani* carries a dedication to the author's father, "a man of Jerusalem and a lover of its past." A member of the fourth of the five generations of the Yehoshua family in Jerusalem, Yaakov Yehoshua was a professional orientalist and an amateur ethnologist who published a series of books affectionately chronicling the neighborhoods and folkways of the old Sephardic settlement in his native city. By his own account these compilations meant little to Yehoshua during his father's lifetime, and it was only after his death that the son was moved to explore what this exotic patrimony meant to him.

Yet as one would expect from a writer of Yehoshua's genius, the novel is no simple act of homage. The statement it has to make about Sephardism is equivocal and in the end rather slippery. On the one hand, Sephardim in this novel are portrayed as cosmopolitans whose worldliness has allowed them to remain free of the ravages of ideology and to glimpse options not seen by others at crucial turning points of history. Yet, on the other hand, they are prevented from making an impact on history—and their very survival is put in jeopardy—because of their abandonment to obsessional notions and obsessional desires. The novel is, in the best sense, something of a tease. Yehoshua is mixing up the basic stuff of modern Jewish history with the basic stuff of human nature and refusing on principle to underscore the presence of some grand design, although many suggestive, and sometimes contradictory, patterns seem to propose themselves readily and without stint.

For most readers, however, finding these coordinates will be secondary to the extraordinary pleasures *Mr. Mani* offers as a narrative experience. I suspect that this subordinating of historical schemata to the energies of reading is at the heart of what Yehoshua is doing in the novel in any case. For *Mr. Mani* is wonderfully knotted in ways that are both enthralling and challenging. Attention is required—and rewarded. This is not a conventionally constructed novel. It is composed of five "conversations" that take place between 1848 and 1982, but in each case Yehoshua has provided the speech of only one of the two interlocutors. The reader is thus required to infer the words of the other participant from the rejoinders, hesitations, and annoyances of the audible partner. Each of these dramatic half-conversations is preceded and followed by informative notes written in a dry journalistic style documenting the biographical events of the two partners before and after their exchange.

One can imagine the occasions for invention presented by a novel with five different speakers from five different historical periods. Add to this the fact that the original language of each conversation is supposedly different (Hebrew, German, English, Yiddish, and Ladino) and one gets a sense of the challenges Yehoshua has set for himself. Yehoshua is immensely successful in carrying this off in the Hebrew of *Mr. Mani*. He draws upon Hebrew's many layers of development to obtain the right degree of archaism for his different speakers; he uses untranslated idioms from the original language to create an atmosphere of linguistic authenticity, and he draws liberally upon the kinds of cultural speech habits that differentiate milieus and mentalities one from another, such as, for example, the world of a pious Ottoman Jewish merchant from the world of an enlightened Polish Jewish physician.

What is a formidable challenge for the author turns out, for the very same reasons, to be a golden opportunity for his translator Hillel Halkin. Because four of the five conversations are not conducted in Hebrew, Yehoshua and Halkin—in a certain peculiar sense—start from a common point of departure and move toward their respective languages. Halkin has as good a time rendering the clipped understatement of a British military lawyer during World War I as he does with the tendentious historical musings of a German officer in the next world war. In the many translations from Hebrew he has done over the years, Halkin has been at his best when his gifts for idiomatic usage could be released in the representation of speech. *Mr. Mani* allows him full scope, and he has achieved what seems to me to be his finest translation so far. Happily for the English reader, as Cynthia Ozick has remarked, Halkin's translation has "a brilliant and spooky life of its own."

Yehoshua's most radical tampering with the conventions of the novel—his debt to Faulkner is profound and long acknowledged—are manifest in two related acts of decentering. The novel is ostensibly about five generations of the Mani family, yet with the partial exception of the last conversation, the Manis are not the speakers but the ones spoken about. The participants in the conversations are outsiders whose lives intersect meaningfully but serendipitously in the affairs of the Manis. However powerfully dramatized, the Manis are viewed indirectly and through the eyes of others, and they are never allowed to be embodied in the marvelously vivid speech given to those who observe them. Perhaps the greatest dislocation is Yehoshua's decision to tell history backward. The first conversation in *Mr. Mani*—as the reader comes across it—is set on a kibbutz in the Negev in 1982; the second in 1944, then 1919, 1899 and finally 1848. For Yehoshua this "counterdirection" to history is not just a device but a major theme shot through the novel at every level.

Because Yehoshua winds his plot up backward, it needs to be unwound and laid out consecutively to appreciate its true strangeness. Here it goes from the beginning: In the 1840s a young man comes to Jerusalem from Salonika to marry and stays on in the Holy City, obsessed with the idea that the Arabs are really Jews who have forgotten their Jewishness. Concerned that the young couple have produced no children, the young man's father, Abraham Mani, journeys to Jerusalem only to discover that the marriage has not been consummated because of his son's homosexuality. Immediately after his son is killed, the father sleeps with his daughter-in-law, who gives birth to a son, Moshe. The boy grows up to be a gynecologist who establishes a lying-in hospital in which women from all the nationalities in Jerusalem come to give birth under enlightened conditions. Fascinated by the figure of Herzl, the doctor travels to Basel for the Zionist Congress of 1899 and there meets a well-to-do brother and sister from Galicia, who return with him to Jerusalem. He falls desperately in love with the young woman and commits suicide in the Beirut railway station as the brother and sister are about to return to Europe.

His orphaned son Yosef grows up among the polyglot of Christian, Jewish, and Arab groups that make up Jerusalem during the first decade of the century. The trauma of witnessing a woman giving birth in his father's old clinic transforms him into a self-described *homo politicus,* and he betakes himself to Beirut to study the laws of the many nations that will determine the fate of the Middle East. Having made himself an indispensable translator in Allenby's advancing army, he offers his services as a spy to the Turks in exchange for the opportunity to address gatherings of Arab villagers throughout the countryside. His message to his sleepy and uncomprehending listeners is that in the wake of the Balfour Declaration Palestine will be divided up among those wise enough to grasp the opportunity and that the Arabs will lose out unless they awake to the meaning of the hour. Yosef Mani's sedition is discovered, and he is sentenced by a British military court to banishment on the island of Crete. He dies of a heart attack when the German army invades the island in 1941, but not before instructing the paratrooper who has captured his family in the history of the Minoan ruins at Knosus where he has made a living as a tourist guide. His son Efrayim tries to convince his Nazi captor that he is no longer a Jew because he has willfully canceled his Jewishness and become, simply, a person; the attempt succeeds only in part. Although his wife and child manage to escape to Palestine, Efrayim Mani is deported and dies when his ship is blown up by British pilots.

The final act unfolds in Jerusalem in 1982 where Efrayim's son Gavriel serves as a judge in the district courts. His son Efi is a young university instructor who has an affair with one of his students, a women named Hagar from a Negev kibbutz, whose father had been killed during the Six-Day War. The son is called up to a resented reserve duty in the invasion of Lebanon at the same time as Hagar believes she has become pregnant from him. She journeys to Jerusalem on the pretext of delivering a message from the son only to find the father preparing to commit suicide. She stubbornly attaches herself to Judge Mani for several days, thinking all the while that she carries within her the seed of a new Mani. Hagar's pregnancy turns out to be illusory, but she later does, in fact, become pregnant and gives birth to Roni Mani, even though his father refuses to marry her.

Now one might think that the saga of the Manis is deliciously convoluted enough on its own terms without Yehoshua's trying to stuff the jack back in the box and tell the story in reverse. But he has decided to make this the structural principle upon which the novel stands or falls. Besides, as a reader, one does not have a choice. However interesting are Hagar's escapades in Jerusalem, too many motivations and references remain tantalizingly obscure unless one takes the plunge backward. The small apartment building owned by Judge Mani that was once a maternity clinic and the embroidered flannel nightgown from his mother who raised him in Crete are obvious teasers, but the unexplained reason for the judge's nocturnal experiments with suicide is a more significant provocation. Fortunately, the novel delivers; it gets progressively more interesting the further one goes back. The fifth and final conversation, set in the courtyards of a Jerusalem that still seems medieval, is positively breathtaking in the elemental dramas that unfold within it—although it is also maddeningly elusive when it comes to answers.

It is exactly the expectation of getting answers that is set up by Yehoshua's history-in-reverse method. *Mr. Mani* starts out in the moral confusion brought on by the invasion of Lebanon, the first Arab-Israeli conflict initiated by Israel, and then moves back, conversation by conversation, through the events and developments leading to the creation of the Jewish state: the Holocaust, the Balfour Declaration, the rise of political Zionism, and the emergence of modern nationalism following the Congress of Vienna. The novel, in short, peels away the layers of historical inevitability and rolls back the triumph of Western ideology as it moves one closer to a time before nations and national identities were finally consolidated. Provocatively and perversely, Yehoshua follows this line not into the recesses of the Ashkenazic Diaspora whence modern Zionism issued but into the world of Sephardic Jewry, which historically composed the largest segment of the continuous Jewish settlement in Jerusalem, though a smaller percentage of world Jewry. He gives readers Jerusalem *before* Zionism and places within it an hypostatized Sephardism whose growing entanglement with Western Zionism can be traced through stages of resistance and capitulation.

Just what, then, does this journey upstream into the heart of Sephardism reveal? The answer, as I have intimated above, goes in two directions. On their behalf, the novel makes claims for a superior worldliness of the Sephardim, a quality that enabled them to see alternatives to the ideology-driven march of Western history. Jews of Ottoman lands lived in closer and less conflictual contact with Muslim peoples than with the members of the other principal minority, the Christians. Their mercantile travels gave them an international perspective and a sensitivity to the relations among national groups.

In contrast to the Judaism of their East European coreligionists, the religious convictions of the Sephardim were deeply but less fanatically held and were less insulated from the world. When religious faith collapsed for a segment of Russian Jewry at the end of the nineteenth century, political Zionism was seized upon as a substitute for failed messianic beliefs and turned into an ideological movement. Sephardim chose a path of accommodation instead. Rather than rejecting religion and adopting secular replacements for it, they made room for elements of modernity alongside their family-centered piety. Zionism came to them naturally, not as a radical redefinition of the Jewish people but as an extension of a primordial attachment to both an ideal geography and a real place. (The novel, incidentally, excels in conveying the gritty dreaminess of Sephardic Jerusalem before the arrival of the Zionists. The attention given to the evocation of Jerusalem in this novel represents, literally, a reorientation for Yehoshua, whose previous writings have mostly been set in the secular "Labor" city of Haifa.)

In *Mr. Mani* this set of ascribed traits plays itself out in the peculiar "alternative" political notions placed in the minds of the earlier generations of the Manis. Young Yosef Mani, who comes to Jerusalem in the 1840s, is convinced that the native Ishmaelites are really Jews who refuse to remember that they are Jews and must be chastised for their forgetfulness. The clinic founded by his son, the gynecologist Moshe Mani, is described as "multiethnic, syncretistic, ecumenical." Women

from all communities of Jerusalem are drawn to give birth there because of the methods of natural childbirth instituted by Dr. Mani as if to
imply that the pain inscribed in nature can somehow be alleviated by
the commingled openness embodied by the clinic.

This vision receives its most articulate—and most transparent, one
may add—expression in the third generation with Yosef Mani's self-
ascribed calling as a *homo politicus*. To prepare himself for his role in life,
he drifts "among the identities of Jerusalem while working out his politics and acquiring languages as though they were a batch of keys to a
house with many doors."[1] The message he delivers to his hastily
rousted Arab village listeners is peculiarly prescient for 1918:

> "Who are ye? Awake, before it is too late and the world is changed be-
> yond recognition! Get ye an identity, and be quick!" And he takes
> Balfour's declaration from his pocket, translated into Arabic, and
> reads it without any explanation, and says: "This country is yours and
> it is ours; half for you and half for us." And he points toward
> Jerusalem, which they see shrouded in fog on the mountain, and he
> says, "The Englishman is there, the Turk is here; but all will depart
> and leave us; awake, sleep not!" (189)

He is tried and banished by the British more for the loss of canons his
espionage causes than for stirring the fellahin (peasantry) into a nationalist fervor, which he, of course, fails to do. In later generations this
catholic vision is muted and survives only in Judge Mani's fondness for
the old neighborhoods of his city and his son's opposition to the military adventure in Lebanon.

These notions are never fully explored and remain fuzzily idiosyncratic. (Yehoshua, by the way, has a lot to answer for in using ideas that
have little actual historical basis and that are rather transparent retrojec-
tions of his dovish politics, which, by any measure, approaches Zionism
from an aggressively ideological standpoint.) Nevertheless, the point
being made is that at crucial junctures of modern history (such as the
Balfour Declaration), the Manis, because of who they are and where
they come from, are able to glimpse options invisible to the majoritar-

ian Zionist movement. They contemplate an alternative path while the movement forecloses possibilities and lurches forward toward the consolidation of a uninational state condemned to unremitting tension with its neighbors and with a growing minority of its own citizens.

Now if this were all, then Yehoshua's Manis would simply be true heroes for those who see Israel as Yehoshua does. But the novel thankfully complicates things by giving them more interesting lives. The Manis—again the earlier generations—are presented as being grandiose, ineffectual, and obsessed in ways that work to undercut the legitimacy of their visionary politics. It all goes back to the first Yosef Mani, the one who believed that the Arabs are Jews who have forgotten their Jewishness. According to the account given by his father, who is an unreliable but insightful narrator, Yosef's ideas are the ultimate result—in ways too complicated and elusive to summarize here—of the boy having been seduced by the young wife of his elderly rabbi and teacher, which in turn led to his homosexuality and his death. The father calls the son's notions about the Arabs an *idée fixe,* and he journeys to Jerusalem from Salonika to try to ensure that the marriage "bears seed and not just *idées fixes.*" His failure to do so and his guilt over impregnating his daughter-in-law lead him later in life often to contemplate suicide. And so the urge to suicide, obscurely enacted by Judge Mani more than one century later, is imprinted in the genetic code of the Manis.

The novel makes a significant distinction between ideologies and *idées fixes.* Ideologies are what Russian Jews have; ideologies generate movements, which, in turn, exert enormous collective force upon the face of history. *Idées fixes* are what the Manis have; they are idiosyncratic notions held by the febrile minds of solitary men who endanger themselves on behalf of their ideas but who have little influence on the world. Because their notions come to naught their decision to pursue their ideas at the expense of the preservation of their species is doubly self-defeating. For faced with the choice to sow their seed or to sow their ideas, they consistently do the latter. In contrast to received notions of potent oriental patriarchs propagating vast clans, the Manis have to be tricked into reproducing. From the father who sleeps with his daughter-in-law at one end of the novel to the kibbutz student who gets Judge Mani an illegitimate grandson at the other, this is a family whose dynastic line hangs by a very tattered thread.

Mr. Mani is, in fact, as Arnold Band has pointed out, a rather unsparing send up of the very concept of the pure Sephardic, the *Sefaradi tahor*. It is the practice of some Jews who trace their lineage directly back to the exiles from Spain (as opposed to the mass of North African immigrants) to place two initials at the end of their names designating their distinguished ancestry. If Yehoshua's Manis are taken as standing in some paradigmatic relation to Sephardim as a group, then their lineage is anything but pure and unadulterated. Besides the homosexuality, incest, illegitimacy, suicide, and the various forms of surrogacy that reside in their past, there is also the fact that for at least two of the generations the mothers are not even Sephardim.

The either/or choice between sexuality and political consciousness, which resides at the heart of the novel, is most vividly expressed in the case of Yosef Mani, the treasonous translator and *homo politicus* of the third conversation. This is also the section of the book that drew wide attention when it was published in the *New Yorker*. Yosef Mani, the boy orphaned by his father's romantic suicide, grows up in the dilapidated Jerusalem maternity clinic, and there at the age of twelve he undergoes the transformative experience of his life. Left alone with a woman who unexpectedly gives birth, Yosef is transfixed by what he is forced to witness:

> Then he stood watching the birth canal heave open and listening to her moans; saw the baby's head appear slowly in a pool of blood; witnessed it all: the dreadful suffering, the screams; and was made to swear while standing helplessly in that cold room that he wouldn't leave her or lay down his knife before cutting the umbilical cord. And throughout all this he never shut his eyes. He looked now at the woman and now at the mirror . . . which is how, so he says, his intense political consciousness was born, gripping the knife in that cold room. (168–69)

The boy's traumatic solitary exposure to the female genitalia in their most fearsome aspect is a quintessentially Freudian moment, and it is the experience given as the reason for Yosef's turning away from women and devoting himself, is such a singularly futile way, to politics.

Now why he might be put off women is obvious enough, but why the alternative is politics is left unexplained. Readers are left to assume, I think, that in contrast to his father Yosef chooses to contemplate the birth of nations rather than the birth of children. The novel is preoccupied with the idea of the womb, not just as the birthing house of biological life but as a kind of primordial soup of latent possibilities from which national identities emerge. The fact that the action in *Mr. Mani* begins (and the story ends) in 1848, the year of nationalist rebellions, is no coincidence. This notion is given a gloss of pseudoscientific respectability by the speaker of the second conversation (and to my mind the weakest of the five), a young intellectual German soldier, one Egon Bruner, who is part of the police force occupying Crete during World War II. Recalling the account in Greek mythology of the birth of Europa in the waters of the island, Bruner regrets his country's appeal for legitimacy to Teutonic myths and bids it turn southward toward the restorative purity of Hellenic culture. Only by thrusting itself into this recumbent blue womb of civilization, he reasons, can the motherland renew itself.[2]

Coming across the Manis, the soldier is at first incensed that a "lot of beastly Jews" had gotten there first and sullied his adoptive ancient womb. He is mollified, however, by Efrayim Mani's assertion that he has "canceled" his Jewishness—another variation on the *idée fixe*—and, therefore, poses no threat. For if by an act of will the self can indeed be separated from culture, then it is good news for Germany, which could "return to the starting point and become *simply human again,* a new man who can cancel the scab of history that sticks to us like dandruff" (128).

Bruner's obsessions are as dangerously perverted as mainline Nazi racialist theory, but they ironically serve to point to what may be the final meaning of the Manis in Yehoshua's novel. They are identified with matters of the womb because they represent a body of latent possibility in modern Jewish life. Ideology-driven Jewish political nationalism has closed crucial doors as it has marched forward to the constricted present. The Manis, however, remain closer to the womb of culture in that their identity remains less differentiated and consolidated and more libidinally chaotic. This is a principle of polymorphousness that plays over both the construction of selves and the construction of societies. It is in the end a succession of identities rather than a secret single essence. This seems to be what Yehoshua was after when he gave his elusive fictional dynasty the name Mani. The name of neither a place nor a profession nor an attribute, Mani is presented as a kind of cipher that bears a seemingly endless series of midrashic associations: manic, maniac, money, manifold, Manichean, and others that work only in Hebrew.

In the end, although the Manis are vivid and fascinating figures, they remain vague and unknowably fantastic. They may make the stuff of a good story, but their presence alone cannot account for the arresting complexity of *Mr. Mani* as a novel. The dimension of novelistic depth is provided by the Manis' story being embedded in the conversations around which Yehoshua has built his book, and what wonderful inventions they are! To say that the Manis are embedded in these conversations is not to use a conceit. They literally exist as creatures in a discourse not their own. This sense of being owned by the speech of others, or at least being dependent upon others for their representation, nicely conveys the Manis' failure to make an impact on the world or even to propagate themselves.

It is scarcely arbitrary, then, that most of these speakers belong to groups that occupy positions of power during the periods in which the conversations take place. The tragedy of Dr. Mani, for example, is related in 1899 by Efrayim Shapiro, a Jewish physician from Galicia whose father (his interlocutor in the conversation) is a wealthy landowner and an important figure in the proto-Zionist movement that set the course for the development of a Jewish homeland. In the case of Yosef Mani the spy, the speakers are representatives of the imperial power that will control the affairs of Palestine for the decades to come.

Similarly, one has seen the Nazi soldier on Crete and his adoptive grandmother, the widow of a German naval hero, and then Hagar and her mother, the kibbutz stalwart, who represent the socialist Zionist ideology of the Ashkenazic founders of the state. To be sure, the sway of each of these regimes is eventually checked (some much sooner than others), yet in their moment they represent the mainstream upon which the notions of the Manis have little impact. The centrifugal movement *away* from the Manis, moreover, is reinforced by journalistic biographical notes about the speakers that begin and end each conversation.

Yet despite the Manis' historical marginality, their seductions remain palpable. The conversations come into being in the first place because each speaker has conceived an obsessional attachment to one of the Manis. This ranges from the incestuous erotic triangle of Efrayim Shapiro, his sister Linka, and Moshe Mani to the historiosophical compulsions of Egon Bruner. Each speaker speaks out of the need to disburden himself of the hold he has allowed a Mani to make on him. The need is so great that the speaker has to work very hard—cajoling and manipulating all the while—to maintain the attention of his interlocutor, who is sometimes, quite literally, made into a captive audience. Free of the speaker's obsession, the interlocutor, in turn, offers a very different take on the figure of the Manis. (Then there is the matter of the interlocutor's missing half of the conversation, which the reader must actively work to recoup from the dialogical repartee of the audible half.)

Indeed, Yehoshua has packed *Mr. Mani* with no small measure of games and devices, but there is rarely the sense—which one gets with some younger Israeli writers—that he has given himself over to postmodernist antics. The novel's implied invitation to the reader to participate in the production of its meaning seems to me to be meant quite sincerely. For despite the unmistakable political critiques and messages contained in the book, Yehoshua does not know in the end what to make of his elusive Manis. As a subject, they resemble what the psychoanalysts call primary material, and they possess the kind of fecund negative power that at once elicits and undoes the interpretations and constructions offered to account for them. The novel is as much about the intriguing challenges and pleasures of *reading* modern Jewish history as it is about modern Jewish history itself. Put another way, readers are lucky to have *Mr. Mani* and not just the Manis.

Yehoshua's novel is a welcome sign of the maturing of Israeli literature. It is a rare thing—a document of true cultural openness.

2

A. B. Yehoshua, who is widely regarded as Israel's greatest living writer, has recently made the claim that the record of his many previous works of fiction, all of which deal with the acute actuality of Israeli life, have given him the right to offer the public a historical novel, and a medieval novel at that. The spectacle of a prominent writer justifying himself in this way is astonishing, but it rings true. Unlike the literary scene in America, where one waits to be surprised by the latest idiosyncrasies of leading U.S. writers, Israeli readers make their writers accountable for holding up a mirror of the way they live now and interpreting the gyrations of a society whose sense of reality is constantly being remade by today's conflicts and tomorrow's headlines.

Israel's absorption in the overheated present is understandable on many grounds, but no less understandable is the writer's desire not to escape the present but at least to come at it from a different direction. This Yehoshua began to do in his remarkable 1989 novel *Mr. Mani,* which began in the middle of the nineteenth century and worked its way through a series of peculiar monologues to the present day. Yehoshua's new novel takes a much bigger leap backward, all the way to the year 999, the very verge of the thousandth year to Christ's birth, which in Christian Europe, where the story takes place, excited even more frenzy than the coming of the current millennium. The awareness of time in *A Journey to the End of the Millennium* is always acute and always cited in a triple notation: time from the birth of the Christian savior, time from the Prophet's Hegira, and time from the creation of the world in the Hebrew Scriptures. For although the novel's action unfolds in northern Europe on the banks of the Seine and the Rhine, its theme is a journey to the north by a group of Jews and Muslims from North Africa and the triangular encounter among these cultures.

The premise of the story, whose point of departure is the breakup of a mercantile partnership, is singular and nicely perverse. For ten years, a Jewish merchant from Tangier, Ben Attar, and his local Muslim partner have yearly transported a ship full of Mediterranean merchandise to northern Europe; there Ben Attar's nephew, Abulafia, an exile from Tangier, has sold the fragrant spices and colorful fabrics to Europeans who, as the millennium approaches, are increasingly hungry for goods redolent of their desert savior. The lucrative partnership is threatened with dissolution when the wealthy and large-hearted Ben Attar takes a second wife, a practice that was fully sanctioned by the religious norms of North African Jewry but unknown among Ashkenazic Jews where it was to be formally banned by rabbinic edict during the eleventh century.

The objection to this north-south partnership comes from Abulafia's new wife, Esther-Minna, the daughter of a distinguished Rhineland rabbinic family, who sees in the uncle's bigamy not only a moral scandal but also a threat to the exclusiveness of her own marriage. Stung by her repudiation, Ben Attar takes his two wives and journeys to the north to demonstrate by personal example and legal argument the sufficiency of his amorous solicitude for his expansive household. The novel's action tracks the merchant's quest for vindication as he travels by sea to Paris and then overland to the Rhineland city of Worms and back to Paris, from whence, after two rabbinic trials, one of which he wins and one of which he loses, and after the death of one of the wives, he returns to his Mediterranean home.

The journey in the novel's title is not only the Sephardic merchant's penetration into the heart of Ashkenaz but also the contemporary Israeli writer's journey into the depths of medieval Jewish history. Yehoshua's placement of his narrative in the last days of the first Christian millennium is not just a conceit of market timing but an evocation of a particular moment in the Jewish past. In the sphere of Mediterranean Jewry, it was a period of fruitful cultural collaboration between

Muslims and Jews, the joint inheritors in Arabic of the traditions of Greek philosophy, just before the eruption of the Almohade persecutions, a wave of Islamic fundamentalism that was to drive Maimonides's family into exile at the beginning of the twelfth century. In northern Europe it was the century before the Crusader massacres of Rhineland Jewish communities cast a pall of martyrdom over the next thousand years of Jewish-Christian relations in Europe. Jewish rabbinic dynasties, such as the Kolonomids (Esther-Minna's family), had been invited by the princes of the Holy Roman Empire to move from Italy and to settle in the Germanic lands, where they established colonies of great commercial success and enormous Talmudic erudition. Yehoshua's *Journey to the End of the Millennium* unfolds, in short, at a time when—in the face of many received notions about the age—the rage of the nations against the Jews was less the issue than the differences of the Jews among themselves.

The best part of Yehoshua's novel is, in fact, this evocation of the strangeness of a world that is not our own: the vivid colors of robes and veils of the southern visitors and their worldly piety, the marshy drabness of the Rhineland towns and the horn-shaped hats worn by its Jews, Paris as a small town with cows grazing its fields. Particularly fascinating is the way that Yehoshua handles the language issue. The southerners speak Arabic and the northerners speak Frankish or High German, the language which, admixed with Hebrew, will become Yiddish as Jews take it with them in their movement eastward into Poland and the Ukraine. The embroiled nature of these cultural relations is nicely reflected in the continual difficulties in the novel surrounding pragmatic communication and the variety of devices and impromptu translators mobilized to negotiate these differences.

The chief enabling vehicle is the Hebrew language itself. As a common possession of the male elites of Sephardic and Ashkenazic Jewry, Hebrew, like Latin, served in the Middle Ages as a lingua franca not just in commentaries and epistles but, as reflected in the novel, in spoken communications as well. Now *Journey to the End of the Millennium* is, of course, written in modern Hebrew, which is different from the medieval Hebrew that the characters would have used. Yet for the purposes of this novel Yehoshua has fashioned a literary language that reverberates with just enough of an antique inflection and a lush semantic richness to create an atmosphere of strangeness, and this has been successfully carried over in Nicholas De Lange's adept translation.

Yet despite the wonderfully exotic spell cast by Yehoshua's writing, readers are never unaware of the fact that this novel, like all historical novels, is, in the end, not about history, at least history of the dead and buried kind. The fraught identity politics of contemporary Israeli society is never far from readers' minds, and it allows them to see how much fun Yehoshua is having tweaking the noses of the European Jews who founded Israel and until recently dominated its political culture. Born into an old Sephardic family in Jerusalem, Yehoshua began to explore the mystique of Sephardism in such later works as *Five Seasons* and *Mr. Mani* after evincing little interest in his origins in the early stages of his career. *Journey to the End of the Millennium* is set during the apogee of a great Mediterranean civilization from whose vantage point the beleaguered northern settlements in the depth of European Christendom seem particularly pitiable. Through this lens, the religion of these northern Jews appears crabbed, parochial, legalistic, and defensive; it is a culture entirely shorn of the poetry of faith and delight in the created world that is the recognizable progenitor of the political and religious regime of ultra-Orthodoxy in Israel today.

The novel's tendency toward triumphalism, however, is checked by an acknowledgment of a fatal vulnerability at the heart of this seemingly resplendent civilization and, by implication, at the heart of present-day Sephardic identity. In the battle of wills that rages between the merchant from Tangier and his northern coreligionists, a battle marked by many reversals of fortune as the antagonists struggle to use the protocols of etiquette and Talmudic law to their advantage, it is the merchant who falters and undercuts his own cause. After being victorious in one disputation, he agrees to engage in another, whose disastrous outcome is foretold. His motives lie in a self-destructive need for vindication. It is not enough to win the reinstatement of his successful trading partnership; he desires the acknowledgment of these austere European rabbis for the legitimacy of his double marriage and the largeness of heart it represents. In the Israel of today, the novel implies, the gifts of Sephardism—vividness, vitality, and generosity of spirit—are vitiated by the need to be confirmed by the culture of what was once the North and is now the West.

Yehoshua is not issuing a call for the reinstituting of bigamy, but he does use the idea of dual marriage to form part of a deeper philosophical argument at the center of the novel. Ben Attar, the merchant from Tangier, demonstrates through his affectionate solicitude and passionate attention toward both his wives that love is not of necessity a limited human resource. Yet what Yehoshua builds upon this endearing character is a very large scaffolding indeed. He wishes to do nothing less than take Sephardic culture at the height of its classical vigor as the bearer of Eros and Ashkenazic culture in its incipient legal pietism as the bearer of Thanatos. The threat posed by bigamy is not so much the small-minded problems of jealousy and licentiousness as the seditious multiplication of desire, or, as framed in the fearful thoughts of one of the Ashkenazic judges hearing the Ben Attar case, the idea that "duplication inevitably leads to multiplication, and multiplication has no limits."[3] But these profound ideas are too profound and, in the end, too stale, amounting to a familiar mélange of Herbert Marcuse, Norman O. Brown, and assorted countercultural drivel. Riding this high horse, the novel runs the danger of breaking down into a kind of banal Cartesian geometry of desire. Undigested and thesis-laden big ideas are a problem that bedevils most of Yehoshua's fiction; fortunately, as is the case here, the characters and the situations are so fascinating and finely realized that the balance of success is not tipped.

For readers who have followed the work of this important writer since it first appeared in the 1960s, *Journey to the End of the Millennium* marks a new and intriguing set of alignments. The protagonists of the early fiction were unrelievedly alienated and impotent, and Yehoshua showed them little empathy; the world they inhabited was dissociated and indeterminate and of the present moment, and the Hebrew employed to describe their movements strove to expunge the nearly unexpungable historical nuances embedded in the language. With its exotic medieval setting, rich linguistic texture, and strongly individuated characters with their amorous couplings and religious observances, Yehoshua's new novel is clearly something else again. Having taken his leave to write about the past, Yehoshua, who is a prolific writer always making himself new, will likely return in his future fiction to the embroiled present of Israeli society. Yet having immersed himself so deeply and so pleasurably in historical waters, it will be interesting to see what sticks to his pen.

8

David Grossman's Postmodernist Ambitions

DAVID GROSSMAN, the rising star in the firmament of Israeli literature, has had a jumbled career in America. He first came to prominence
in 1988 when the *New Yorker* published a long piece of political re-
portage in which Grossman described encounters with Palestinians
during seven weeks of visits to villages and refugee camps in the Occupied Territories. Although the original Hebrew version had appeared
before the outbreak of the intifada in December 1987, the English
translation (published as *The Yellow Wind*) appeared afterward, and it
struck readers with the full force of a prophecy fulfilled. On the strength
of his political writings, Grossman was brought to America by Peace
Now and invited to address large and attentive audiences about the
moral horrors of the occupation.

All this took place before much was known here about Grossman
the novelist. Grossman's political reporting—he later published a book
about the Arab citizens of Israel titled *Sleeping on a Wire* (Nochahim nif
kadim)—is observant and sensitive and above all "writerly" in his use of
vignette and character sketch. But Grossman's political books do not
cover new ground even if they succeed in making the plight of their
subject affecting. They redouble the sense of tragedy without offering

The section of this chapter on *See Under: Love* was previously published in *Com-
mentary*, July 1989, 56–60; reprinted by permission, all rights reserved. The section on
The Book of Intimate Grammar was previously published as "Dark Passages" in *Partisan
Review* 63, no. 4 (1996).

much clearheaded thinking about difficult choices and modes of accommodation.

As a novelist, however, Grossman is a great innovator who has pushed his genre in productive postmodernist directions and who has not been afraid to engage big issues left untouched by other Israeli writers. Grossman's claim to greatness as a novelist rests chiefly on the achievement of his second novel, *See Under: Love,* a daring work about the Holocaust that was published in 1985 in Israel, *before The Yellow Wind* but brought out in translation in America in 1989, only after his political writing had established his reputation. To add to the confusion, Grossman's first novel, *Smile of the Lamb* (Hiuch ha-gedi), an only partially successful story about Jewish-Arab relations during the occupation of the West Bank, came out in the United States well after *See Under: Love* was already in the hands of American readers.

Setting the record straight on Grossman's publishing history is not as pedantic as it sounds. Grossman's reception in America was in a sense kidnapped by the success of *The Yellow Wind. The Yellow Wind* went down easily, much in the manner of the kind of *New Yorker* reporting that informs readers about distant afflictions while confirming their previously held moral convictions. Although Israeli readers knew that this was Grossman journalizing between novel projects, American readers were unprepared for the ambitiousness and difficulty of Grossman's big Holocaust novel when it was belatedly placed before them.

1. *See Under: Love* and the Fantasy of Story as Rescue

During the first fifteen years after World War II, the Holocaust did not figure as a major theme in serious works of Israeli literary art. (The great exception lay in the epic poetry of Uri Zvi Greenberg.) This absence, however, is not as surprising as it might appear. The young writers belonging to the group often called the Palmah generation were thrust to the forefront on the strength of the voice they gave to the War of Independence and the establishment of the new state. It was, indeed, in the death and sacrifice that accompanied the struggle for new national life that they located *their* response to the destruction of European Jewry. But their silence also bespoke a deep sense of shame over the spectacle of Jews going to death "like sheep to the slaughter" and, because of their socialist-Zionist training, a lack of connection to the Jews of the Diaspora.

This disengagement was later jarred by the Eichmann trial, and a number of writers belonging to the Palmah generation—Haim Gouri, Hanoch Bartov, Yehuda Amichai, Yoram Kaniuk—went on to write interesting works that grappled with the Holocaust, or at least with the unsettling challenges it presented to their identities. In the sixties and seventies younger writers such as Amos Oz and A. B. Yehoshua submitted the mystique of Israeli heroism to a withering critique, but the Holocaust still remained peripheral to their writing. For a serious engagement of these issues, one has to look to the work not of Israeli-born writers but of a small group of survivors: the fiction of Aharon Appelfeld and the poetry of Dan Pagis.

In light of this background the appearance in English of David Grossman's novel *See Under: Love*[1] must be counted as something of an event. This novel is the first important piece of writing on the Holocaust to be produced by this younger group, and quite apart from its extraordinary literary qualities, it may have things to tell readers about a generation that grew up not only at a different remove from those events but also within a society very different from the one that shaped earlier writers. The novel's appearance is all the more remarkable because Grossman is not a child of survivors and does not belong to the so-called phenomenon of the "Second Generation," writers and artists, such as Art Spiegelman in *Maus,* whose work is impelled by the need to work through a relationship with survivor parents. Yet despite (or, who knows, perhaps because of) this lack of personal connection, the first ninety pages of *See Under: Love* are the most stunning Holocaust literature I have read in any language.

See Under: Love commands attention on its own because of the very large ambitions that are most evident in the series of big ideas it seeks to float aloft. These ideas tend toward the metaphysical: Can the effects of the Holocaust on survivors and their children be undone? Can love survive under conditions of adversity? Is it possible so to be transformed as to see the world through the intelligence of another? Can the past be altered by being retold? Is evil susceptible to the powers of art?

The last is the crux of Grossman's undertaking. Throughout all of the stories-within-stories and multiple frames of reference in this complex and complicated work, one challenge is presented again and again, and it has to do with the attempt of the imagination—by which Grossman means the storytelling faculty of invention—to redeem the suffering of the past by, in a sense, rewriting it. The audacity if this challenge is patent, and one might be tempted to dismiss it out of hand were it not for Grossman's genuine achievement and the many pleasures afforded in the reading. That in the end the attempt is impossible perhaps goes without saying.

See Under: Love is made up of four discrete sections that, although interconnected, tell separate stories. There is a puzzle quality here. The connections are not always obvious, and, in the often annoying manner of postmodernist fables, the reader is obliged to participate in the game by searching for the elusive correlations. Grossman's most daring move is to make the difference among the stories hinge on style. Each of the four sections is written (à la Joyce in *Ulysses*) in a radically different Hebrew style, ranging from the stilted locutions of the nineteenth-century Haskalah (Enlightenment) to the spare pseudoprecision of modern scientific description. At times the chosen style is of a piece with the story being told, at other times ironically at odds with it—the point being that style is not merely surface texture but a mode of perceiving the world.

Grossman's manipulation of these varieties of discourse is brilliant although it often leaves the reader groping for a stable point of literary and even moral reference behind, or within, the play of voices. In any case, the emphasis on style, and on features of style highly peculiar to the history of modern Hebrew, poses significant problems of translation. Happily, Betsy Rosenberg has met these problems with flair and a virtuoso range of effects; to suggest the texture of the original, she has also wisely chosen to leave in her text bits and pieces of Hebrew and Yiddish.

The first section of *See Under: Love* is the most accessible, and in it the ratio of aspiration to achievement is the most satisfying. The section is named for Momik (a diminutive of Shlomo), the nine-year-old only child of two survivors, Gisella and Tuvia Neuman; the story, set in the mid-fifties, takes place over a period of five months in an immigrant neighborhood in Jerusalem. It is told from the perspective of Momik himself, a perspective captured not only in the lilt of childhood speech with its run-on sentences but also in the immigrant inflections of a child who speaks Yiddish at home and Hebrew at school.

Like many survivors, the Neumans say very little about their ordeal during the war. Momik knows that his life is different in a thousand ways from those of other children—he is not encouraged to have friends, he is not allowed to go on an overnight class trip, his father never says more than a few words to him—and he further knows that all these differences are the consequences of what happened "over there" (as his parents call it). Yet because of his parents' silence, precisely that which would explain his life is kept from him.

Being a boy of methodical intelligence and adventuresome spirit, Momik treats this blank as a mystery to be solved, or (as he quotes Sherlock Holmes), "what one man invents another can discover" (29). Arthur Conan Doyle, Jules Verne, *Emil and the Detectives* are, in fact, just some of the boyhood reading through which Momik absorbs his terms for understanding the world. For Grossman the fantasies expressed in juvenile adventure literature are not merely a passing point of reference; here and in the third and fourth sections of the novel they become the central vehicle for weightier explorations of redemptive capacities of art.

The literature of childhood adventure is embodied here and later in the novel in the figure of Anshel Wasserman, Momik's senile and demented great uncle. At the beginning of the century, Wasserman had been famous as the author of an immensely popular series of adventure tales written in Hebrew and translated into many European languages. Now, reduced by his experiences in the Nazi camps to mumbling the same few incomprehensible words, Wasserman has suddenly been deposited with the Neumans and is put in Momik's charge. It is Wasserman's arrival that sets off Momik's quest to solve the mystery of his parents' life by keeping secret "spy notebooks" in which he records clues unwittingly dropped by grownups—including the words his father screams in sleep at night—about life "over there." The passages reproducing his decoding of this mystery derive skewed pathos from the childish, almost comical innocence of Momik's approach to the macabre:

> [T]here was a war in that kingdom, and Papa was the Emperor and also the chief warrior, a commando fighter. One of his friends (his lieutenant?) was called Sondar. . . . They all lived in a big camp with a complicated name. . . . Also there were some trains around, but that part isn't clear. . . . And there were also these big campaigns in Papa's kingdom called Aktions, and sometimes (probably to make people feel proud) they would have really incredible parades, like we have in Independence Day. Left, right, left, right, Papa screams in his sleep. (29)

Like the heroes of all good mystery stories, Momik seems not only to put together the pieces of the puzzle but also to save the hapless victims of evil: "Who else can save Mama and Papa from their fear and silences and krechtzes?" (18) His rescue efforts revolve around the elliptical allusions his parents have often made to something called Nazi Beast, which he imagines literally as an actual creature imprisoning his parents. He sets out to find this creature, tame it, persuade it to change its ways and stop possessing his parents, and get it to tell him what happened Over There. But beyond this self-appointed mission, which takes the practical form of keeping a menagerie of captive animals in his basement, there is the sad fact that the person Momik most needs to rescue is himself, and the inevitable failure of his campaign leads to something more than a loss of innocence. It is too much for him; he collapses, defeated by the Beast.

The second section of *See Under: Love* is titled "Bruno," for the Polish-Jewish writer Bruno Schulz, and is the most difficult. The real Schulz was shot by a Gestapo officer on the streets of the Jewish quarter in his native Drohobycz, Poland, in November 1942. In Grossman's telling, however, he does not die; escaping to Danzig, he jumps into the sea, and instead of drowning he is embraced by the ocean and becomes a fish, developing fins and gills and learning to roam the oceans swept along by the currents with great shoals of sea creatures.

All these events are related in that surrealistic or "magic-realist" mode of familiar from the works of Günter Grass and Gabriel García Márquez and, of course, Bruno Schulz himself, in which the remarkable and fantastic, described in minute naturalistic detail, are made to seem part of the ordinary scheme of things. The Hebrew style Grossman adopts for this section evokes the lushly figurative diction of Avraham Shlonsky and Natan Alterman, the preeminent modernist poets of the Jewish community of Palestine between the two world wars, whose verse, characterized by musicality and a penchant for neologism, draws deeply upon French and Russian symbolism. Here, however, the novel's stylistic experimentalism is overextended; what may be evocative in conception turns out to be tedious in practice.

Not all is watery depths, fortunately. One meets Momik, now in his late twenties, as a published poet of "thin-lipped," ironic Hebrew verse. He has put aside his poetry to try to write, with little success, the story of Anshel Wasserman's experiences during the Holocaust, for he has been assailed by "visions of the old man locked inside the story for so long, a ghostly ship turned away at every port," while he, Momik, remains "his only hope of liberation, of salvaging his story" (105). It is not only Wasserman he is trying to rescue but, again, himself as well. Momik's life as an adult has not been a success. He has not been able to drive away the ghosts his parents brought from Europe; he can neither trust nor love nor extend empathy. After his long-barren wife, Ruth, gives birth to a son, he helplessly watches his anger begin to poison his offspring as well.

The way out comes via Schulz's *The Street of Crocodiles*, given to him as a parting gift by a woman, a kind of all-in-one Holocaust groupie and muse, with whom Momik has had an affair. The experience of reading Schulz is a revelation. The constriction of Momik's imagination is overcome by Schulz's passion for language, the "veritable stampede of panting, perspiring words." He becomes obsessed with Schulz, seeking not merely to write like him but to become him. He wants, in short, to submerge himself in Schulz, and it is this desire that provides the link to the oceanic passages here.

Going off to Poland to swim in the waters off contemporary Gdansk—which, he is certain, embraced and enveloped Schulz forty years earlier—Momik receives there reassuring news of Bruno through long conversations with the sea, personified as a knowing, world-weary vamp of marvelous and constantly changing polymorphous possibilities. What happens to Momik in the bosom of the ocean—it involves a vision of Bruno's messianic Age of Genius—cannot, as one might imagine, be easily summarized. Enough to say that the ocean serves as a mythic representation of the unconscious, a realm in which transformations are possible and one can push through to become another.

The prize Momik wins for his descent into the unconscious is the capacity to tell the story of his great-uncle Anshel Wasserman and the story told by Wasserman to a concentration-camp commandant by the name of Neigel. This tale-within-a-tale occupies the remainder of the novel (the "Wasserman" and "Kazik" sections), and it is more straightforward than what has come before—but no less fantastic.

Wasserman's wife and daughter have been shot upon arrival at the camp, but Wasserman is not allowed to die; by some degree of fate, he *cannot* die. It comes to the attention of the camp commander that Wasserman is the author of tales that he, Neigel, had hugely enjoyed as a child; he therefore installs Wasserman as his "house Jew" (much as Bruno Schulz in Drohobycz) with Scheherezade-like orders to amuse him when the day's work is done. Wasserman consents, but, in a reversal of the Scheherezade motif, on condition that Neigel shoot at him at the end of each evening's telling.

Even in this section of the book, Grossman does not permit Momik to break out of his solipsism. As the story is conceived, Momik is actually physically present in the camp—no one but Wasserman can see him, presumably—standing over Wasserman's shoulder and frequently being addressed by him. Not for a moment are readers allowed to forget that it is Momik who has brought Wasserman back to life—in every sense, reinventing him—and has given him a chance to live his life over again.

The figure of Wasserman moves the theme of juvenile literature to the center of *See Under: Love*. Although his children's stories were penned in the twentieth century, their ethos and style hark back to an earlier era, and Wasserman himself writes in the antique modern Hebrew of the Enlightenment—this is the style of the entire section. Furthermore, like the literature of the Haskalah his stories are deliberately universal and didactic in their concerns. They narrate the adventures of the Children of the Heart, a band of young people from different backgrounds and lands who join together to fight for right all over the globe and, through their trusty time machine, in earlier eras as well, rescuing a runaway American slave, assisting a scientist in his battle against cholera, lending support to Robin Hood, and so forth.

The twist comes with Wasserman's resurrection as a storyteller. What the Nazi commandant wants from him is more of the same—benevolent, childlike tales that will divert his overwrought mind. What Wasserman gives him instead is something very different. He again conjures up the Children of the Heart, but now, instead of the brave adolescents Neigel knew and loved as a child, they are forty years older, not broken exactly but ragged and disillusioned. He places them, furthermore, not in the eternal land of youth but squarely within the world the Nazis have made in Eastern Europe. Neigel complains bitterly; he is being cheated. But Wasserman invokes against him the sacred principle of the inviolability of art; a story, he avers, cannot depart from its own truth. Given his elaborate second chance, Wasserman succeeds in rising above juvenile fantasies and in placing his gift for invention within the constraints of historical actuality.

The final section of *See Under: Love,* no less exorbitantly inventive than those preceding, is titled "The Complete Encyclopedia of Kazik's Life." Kazik is a newborn baby discovered by the aging Children of the Heart in the abandoned Warsaw zoo. The baby is found to suffer from a rare disease that causes it to experience the entire human life cycle within the course of twenty-four hours. This miniaturized life provides the unique occasion for Momik, posing now as the voice of the complete editorial staff, "to compile an encyclopedia embracing most of the

events in the life of a single individual, as well as his distinctive psycho-somatic functions, orientation to his surroundings, desire, dreams, etc."
(303). The encyclopedia is, of course, organized alphabetically with nu-merous cross references, the title of the novel being one of them.

This section, preoccupied with definition and classification, is writ-ten in stiff and hyperrational social-sciencese, which plays in counter-point to the horrible irrationality of the fate that awaits Kazik. The key here is suggested in words used earlier about Bruno Schulz: "For him the Holocaust was a laboratory gone mad, accelerating and intensifying human processes a hundredfold" (98). Kazik represents the freak inten-sity of human experience under conditions of the greatest extremity. Al-though the Children of the Heart do their best to educate Kazik under these conditions and to guide him as he rapidly progresses through life, their efforts come to naught. Kazik requests to see the world beyond the zoo; what he is shown are the electrified barbed-wire fences of Neigel's concentration camp. Horrified, he commits suicide two hours short of his allotted twenty-four.

Yet Kazik's fate triggers Neigel's own suicide, and this death repre-sents a triumph of the storyteller's art. By locating his nightly tales in the present reality and by involving Neigel in the telling, Wasserman has managed to lure the commandant into an emotional identification with the victims of the persecution. The death of Kazik in a world he has helped to create—Neigel has by now ceased to distinguish between story and life—is too much for him—not that he has been morally re-generated, but the story has unmanned him, made him hateful to him-self, and the taking of his own life becomes the only way out. So *See Under: Love* is brought to a close.

Although the lengthy description I have offered may seem to tell too much, it fails to touch on dozens of this novel's motifs and charac-ters. For example, all of the deranged survivors Wasserman meets on the public benches of his neighborhood in the "Momik" section are in the "Kazik" section amplified into full-fledged characters with individual life histories. One wonders, indeed, whether the whole conception of an encyclopedia may have come into being as a brilliant "solution" for these many tangential narratives, which could thereby simply be filed as entries without being integrated into a narrative fabric. Here and in many other instances, at any rate, one yearns for a sober editorial hand.

But the problems of *See Under: Love* go deeper that what could have been solved by judicious pruning and disciplined restraint. Grossman is endowed with literary genius, but the particular models he has chosen to follow are precisely of the sort that fan the flames of his native extravagance rather than lend it structure and purpose.

The novel imitates two key features of the postmodernist sensibility in contemporary fiction: self-conscious literary borrowing and the solipsistic preoccupation with literary artifice. As to the first, it must be said that Grossman's decision to narrate each of the four sections in a different Hebrew style succeeds completely; in its own context, each style is consistently sustained and thematically supported. Yet within this canny architectonic design, Grossman has opened the door to a swarm of other influences. Reading through the novel is like making one's way down the halls of a museum: look, here's a Grass, there's a García Márquez! And, for the Hebrew reader, there is Sholem Aleichem, Mendele Mocher Seforim, Yoram Kaniuk, and many others. The possibility of total derivativeness is parodied in Wasserman's pulp adventure tales with their indebtedness to Karl May, Jack London, James Fenimore Cooper, et al.

Nice distinctions might be made here among literary concepts of allusion, homage, and imitation, but they are swept aside by the riveting, monumental figure of Bruno Schulz. Schulz has exerted a pull on other writers, especially Cynthia Ozick in *The Messiah of Stockholm,* and it would take a reader with intimate knowledge of Schulz's Polish-language stories to say just how Grossman has appropriated him. But the dominant impression is that, to adapt the oceanic metaphor of the "Bruno" section, Grossman has been sucked under by this material. If Momik, as the novel's narrator, seems to understand thematically the difference between being influenced by someone and *becoming* that person, for Grossman the novelist this boundary at times disappears altogether.

Which brings one to Grossman's preoccupation with the mechanics of storytelling. After the relatively "straight" description of Momik's boyhood, the focus of the novel shifts to the question of how one *writes* about the Holocaust. Readers are given an account of Momik's case of writer's block, then of his search for inspiration from Bruno Schulz; finally, there is the reinvention of Wasserman as a writer and, to cap it all, the completed encyclopedia. In the story of Wasserman and the Nazi commandant, Grossman puts together his most involved arrangement of Chinese boxes. It is Momik who has conjured up Wasserman, who, in turn, tells the story to Neigel, who, for his part, is not only morally overcome by the story—thus changing historical reality retroactively by means of fiction—but steals Wasserman's story and retells it to his wife as his own. All the while Momik, the conjurer, is present inside the frame and is addressed by Wasserman in direct discourse. The result is a constant cutting back and forth between narrative contexts as the devices by which the story is told are deliberately exposed to view.

The deep purpose of these games, one supposes, is to make a statement about the ineluctable interdependence of reality and illusion, event and story. Grossman's maneuvers, however, end by producing the opposite effect. Instead of becoming intertwined, the realms of art and life seem to proceed along separate and ever-diverging tracks. In *See Under: Love* the realm of "life," in the sense of reality represented fictively without magical transformation, is unrelievedly bleak: the deformed emotions of Momik's parents, the murder of Bruno Schulz in the streets of Drohobycz, the shooting of Wasserman's wife and daughter, Wasserman's own hard labor in the latrines and crematoria. This unbearable sadness is summed up in an aside Momik utters about his Aunt Idka, who came to his wedding with a Band-Aid over the number on her arm. "All evening I couldn't tear my eyes away from her arm. I felt as if under that clean little Band-Aid lay a deep abyss that was sucking us all in: the hall, the guests, the happy occasion, me."

Yet although this cosmetic bandage is occasionally removed in *See Under: Love* to reveal the horror beneath, most of the novel takes place in the realm of art and storytelling, a much happier place by far. Thus, not only is Bruno Schulz brought back to life, and Wasserman, too,

204 | *Rewriting the Zionist Narrative*

given a second chance, but, in an ultimate compliment to the power of art, an SS officer is conquered by the enchantments of story.

What is most startling about *See Under: Love* is the moral vision implicit in this divergence, most strikingly embodied in the tales Wasserman tells to snare his prey. Wasserman's own moral code is a direct transcription of the naive universal values that his children's tales were designed to inculcate. All men are brothers. Band together to work for the useful and the good. Be faithful and courageous in the face of evil. Amazingly, Wasserman's vision stands here unmolested and unreconstructed, as if to say that *this* is the truth of art, everywhere and always.

Through the figure of Momik, Grossman had an opportunity to project a subtler and deeper understanding of the links between his dissociated realms of art and life. Readers could have been shown, for instance, how Momik's life is affected by his success in telling Wasserman's story and in compiling his encyclopedia. What would it mean to return to the business of everyday life after writing about such horror? But Grossman, apparently unwilling to renounce the consolations of story, passes the opportunity by.

The limitations of this vision stem from a fantasy of rescue that Grossman seems not to want to relinquish. Integral to the juvenile literature invoked so extensively in the novel is the notion that the weak and defenseless can be saved by the courage and secret intelligence of others. For Grossman the magic ring is not action but language. As a child, Momik works to deliver his parents from the clutches of the Nazi Beast through the words in his spy notebooks. As an adult, he seeks salvation from terminal embitterment by submersion in Bruno Schulz, himself saved from death as a reward for his luminous prose. Wasserman is rescued from mediocrity as a literary hack and given the chance to practice true art, and it is that art that saves Neigel from his bestiality. Whereas in the early "Momik" section such fantasies of rescue are deployed to great ironic and pathetic effect, later the novel seems drawn to a disturbingly close identification with the figure of Wasserman, who, despite his marvelous vividness as a character, remains fixed in the adolescent world of his literary creations.

Does Grossman's work mark a new, third-generation response to the Holocaust in Israeli literature? It is, of course, too soon to say. But two issues that emerge from *See Under: Love* are worth bearing in mind in this connection. The first is the book's relationship to the Jewish past. Historically, the Jewish literature of response to catastrophe has consciously invoked the models of the Bible and midrashic legend and exegesis, even if in modern times the relationship has been one of parody and rebellion. In *See Under: Love* this literary tradition simply does not figure. Grossman's imagination is engaged by certain universal questions raised by Jewish suffering, and his literary modes are correspondingly alien to the Jewish canon.

A second, more delicate issue touches on what might be termed the uses of the Holocaust. What this novel has to teach one about the Holocaust itself, in any of its dimensions, is in the end quite limited. The description of Momik's childhood is an exception—a brilliant and genuine contribution to our understanding of the effects of the catastrophe on children of survivors. But after this initial point, *See Under: Love* moves off in another direction, becoming absorbed in the drama of the writer's soul, the virtuoso manipulation of narrative, the redemptive potentialities of art. The novel's ostensible subject is reduced to a backdrop on which the adventures of the artistic ego are projected.

The Holocaust presents a singular temptation to the artist: on the one hand, its bleakness as a subject acts as a discipline, giving little scope for grandiosity or revery; on the other hand, to the undisciplined or narcissistic imagination, that very bleakness may spur fantasy and ostentation without end. Grossman's daring novel may, indeed, thus betoken a disturbingly wider impatience with the intractability of the Holocaust as a subject—and by extension (as his more recent, "soft" political writings would suggest) with the tragic element in human conflict altogether.

2. *The Book of Intimate Grammar* and the Anorexia of the Spirit

The central problem with *See Under: Love,* as seen here, bears on the question of whether stories can redeem reality. At the center of each of the novel's many plots lies the ambition to rescue victims and survivors by constructing their stories and retelling them with a surplus of imaginative invention. The chance given by the narrator to his great uncle to redeem his artistic mediocrity by going back to the past and retelling a set of stories that will unman an SS officer is only one example of a pervasive fantasy of deliverance. Yet rather than firmly setting the fantasy in an ironic perspective, Grossman too often seems charmed by its spell, as if the fertile extravagance of his own storytelling capacity should by rights be able to count for more than it does and work against the unredeemable tragedy of its subject. Grossman's work ends up being caught between parallel convictions: an acceptance of the unyielding difficulty of reality and a belief in the transformative powers of art.

The problem of life and art as parallel lines remains a creative but unresolved tension in *The Book of Intimate Grammar*, Grossman's third novel, which appeared in Israel in 1991 and in English in 1994, again in a splendid translation by Betsy Rosenberg.[2] The novel is unreservedly and unrepentantly presented as a portrait of the artist as a (very) young man with the requisite gestures to Joyce and other practitioners of the genre. In composing this work of self-portraiture at this particular stage in his career, Grossman is laying claim to his status in Israeli literature as the major novelist of his generation. He is presenting himself as an artist whose realized and potential achievement brings with it the obligation to furnish an autobiographical myth and an account of origins. He is further seeking to widen the scope of his art and to establish the fact that he is not just a fabulist and a narrative pyrotechnician but a writer capable of mounting a realist engagement with the gritty Israeli reality that furnished the inhospitable soil for the growth of his artistic self.

The account of Grossman's origins is noteworthy because it describes a social location that is very different from that of the Israeli writers who preceded them. Whether it was the young veterans of the 1948 war such as Aharon Megged and S. Yizhar or the New Wave writers such as Amos Oz who came to prominence in the sixties and seventies, there was a background held in common, one that was rooted in the ideals of socialist Zionism and powerfully sustained by the solidarity of the youth movement. In contrast, Grossman has his autobiographical protagonist Aron Kleinman grow up in a world that is untouched by the passions of ideology and is as distant from the utopian ethos of the kibbutz as can be imagined. *The Book of Intimate Grammar* is set in Jerusalem in a *shikkun*, a block of workers' flats built around a central courtyard, the kind of housing familiar to travelers in East Block countries. The *shikkun* is inhabited by laborers, clerks, and shopkeepers who are recent immigrants to Israel from many lands and who, although they are eager fans of the new state's soccer teams and its armies, remain followers fixed in the small-mindedness of their domestic preoccupations. The world of the *shikkun* is a version of the world of the tenement, and the affinity underscores the fact that *The Book of Intimate Grammar* belongs more to an American and international literature of Jewish immigration—with a particular debt to Henry Roth's *Call It Sleep*—than it does to the traditions of Israeli writing.

Aron's parents, Hinda and Moshe, are at once monstrous and endearing. Raised in Poland, Moshe joined the Red Army out of a youthful enthusiasm for communism and ended up close to death in one of Stalin's arctic prison camps. The price paid for surviving life in the camp and later escaping across the vast reaches of frozen tundra was, simply, becoming an animal, and the gruesome story of what he did to come through is one that Hinda never allows her husband to tell, although it ends up coming out despite her. Hinda meets him when he makes his way to Palestine in 1946, an emaciated, traumatized shell of a human being. She is twenty-six at the time, an unmarried orphan, who is raising her five younger brothers and sisters alone. Hinda brings Moshe into her home, and, during the years of terrible privation brought on by the siege of Jerusalem and the austerity following independence, she slowly succeeds in bringing him back to life. She feeds him, teaches him Hebrew, socializes him, and finally marries him. When he sustains a minor injury after years of contented physical labor, Hinda conspires to get him a union desk job, thereby completing the project of his domestication.

In *See Under: Love,* Grossman's Holocaust novel, Momik's parents are survivors whose experiences in the camps have rendered them isolated and paranoid. Aron's parents in *The Book of Intimate Grammar* are also survivors, although survivors of less horrible circumstances. Yet in their case, the enormous energies necessary to come through have not been dissipated but trained on their children. Aron and his only sibling, his sister Yochi, become the victims of their mother's intrusive, suffocating, and controlling love. All-seeing and brilliantly manipulative, Hinda cajoles and pushes her children to become ideally successful and attractive young people in conformance to the social pressures that bore down upon Israeli society in the 1960s as unrelentingly as they did upon American Jewish society in the 1950s.

Yet, however seductive and determined his mother's will, it remains within Aron's power to deny her her victory. And this he does and in a special way that sets the terms of the novel as a whole. He refuses to grow. Aron is clever in school, popular among his friends, and generally obedient at home. But as he reaches the year of his bar mitzvah, he fails to develop beyond the diminutive frame of a nine-year-old, and he fails to reach puberty. While the boys in his class are developing sideburns and body hair and feeling the rush of hormones in their loins, Aron remains unchanged. His cognitive equipment races ahead, but his body stays in place. As in the case of Günter Grass's *The Tin Drum*, Aron's smallness is presented as a kind of magical given of the plot rather than as a medical mystery. The only real interpretation open to the reader is that, however unconsciously, Aron is simply refusing to grow.

His refusal is an anorexia of the spirit that aims to repulse the mother in the precise area of her most aggressive nurturance. But only in part. His refusal to grow is also a decision to decline entry into the world of adulthood represented not only by the parents and social horizon of the *shikkun* but also by Israeli society as a whole on the eve of the Six-Day War. What Aron finds so disturbing about the adult world he is expected to enter is the exact reflection of the means he uses to protest it: the body and its claims of dominance over culture. His rejection of puberty is his response to a society that is permeated at every level by a vulgar sexuality and a spirit-killing scatology.

This is not necessarily an unconvincing picture of Israeli society, but it is not one very familiar to readers from other Hebrew writers. Surely in the wider frame of coming-of-age novels generally—before *Catcher in the Rye* and afterward—the sensitive young man feels affronted by the crude sexuality he sees around him. But usually the debased sensuality of the adult world is contrasted with the adolescent's discovery of purer although no less sexual stirrings within himself. This is Aron's difference in *The Book of Intimate Grammar.* By refusing to make the passage from latency to adolescence, Aron stays on one side of the great dividing line. He observes the corrupted world of the flesh all around him; he is forcibly immersed in it. Yet he has no answering experience that would provide him with a way of crossing over on his own terms. He is left to find a way out that concedes nothing to the body and instead lays claim to the consolations of art. It is a way out that in the end leaves readers less than persuaded.

In the meantime, Grossman uses Aron's unmediated vision of the grown-up world as a technique of defamiliarization that results in some of the novel's sharpest writing. Take, for example, the story of Yochi's menarche as recalled by Aron at a time when he himself should be entering puberty. Aron is sitting with his older sister and parents at the dinner table as Yochi fends off her mother's attempts to stuff her with fat slices of bread smeared with butter and topped with matjes herring. Suddenly, they notice that the bathroom toilet is overflowing. Papa gets a pair of pliers and thrusts his arm into the "muck and filth."

> Finally he fishes out a glob of something that looked like a piece of meat, and he stood there gaping at it until Mama grabbed the pliers from him and waved the glob in front of Yochi's nose. Well, well, the princess has the curse, like a million other women, including her mother, and right on time, too, so why don't you just keep it to yourself, do you have to shout it from the rooftops, and she waved the pliers in front of her, like a triumphant surgeon, screaming at the top of her lungs; maybe that's when Yochi developed the whistling in her ears, and Yochi, nobody's lemaleh, sat perfectly still this time, red as blood, and after that she was always careful with the curse, and Aron too learned to be careful in the toilet, and Mama said, "Nu, Aron, are you going to stand there gaping all night, can't you see the table's set?" (25)

Welcome to puberty, Yochi! The fact that her humiliation takes place as an interruption of the evening meal (to which Aron is forced to return) is not accidental. The table and the kitchen indisputably belong to the mother, and she uses her power to create a system of total control over what the members of the family consume and what they eliminate. The bloody menstrual napkin that resembles a piece of meat nicely makes the connection between crude alimentary processes and the more intimate mysteries of sex and procreation; it also signals the mother's intention to extend her dominion over both. Although she screams at her daughter to keep the curse to herself, the real message is the inversion of any notion of privacy. Every bodily process, no matter how inward or intimate, cannot be shielded from the humiliating—and in Aron's case—castrating gaze of the mother. One can learn to be careful in the toilet but there is ultimately nowhere to hide.

Aron cannot escape the suffocating impress of his parents' bodies. After surprising them one day while they were having intercourse standing up, he learns to cough conspicuously before entering their room. Trips to the beach with other families are occasions for a painful exposure to the abundant unclothed flesh of his parents' friends as they cavort on the shore and teasingly pull down each other's trunks under the water. He sometimes finds girlie magazines around the house with the crosswords filled in in his mother's hand. Part of Aron's sentimental education comes from the discovery of a pack of pornographic playing cards in his father's sock drawer featuring "Alfonso, the whip-cracking dwarf, ringmaster of the Pussy Circus," and his slave, the lovely Roxana. Aron is disgusted and fascinated by his find but, alas, not aroused. The frequent inspection of the cards leads instead to an elaborate fantasy of rescue. Roxana, he imagines—and it does not take much to grasp his own identification with her—agreed to have "her picture taken to earn money because she was poor, and had innocently fallen into the clutches of that bastard Alfonso; if only he were older, if only he had power and money, he would dedicate his life to saving Roxana from Alfonso, because how long would she remain virtuous with so much corruption around her?" (41–42).

Now, Aron's parents and their friends are scarcely the same as

Alfonso's Pussy Circus. They may be crude, but there is nothing perverted about their crudeness. That is just the point. Their preoccupation with the body is simply part of the normal texture of working-class life, which hides no secret deviance beneath its surface. This is the kind of normative corruption that besets Aron, like the Roxana of his fantasy, and in the face of which he struggles to remain virtuous. The problem is that corruption is inscribed in the nature of things, and although Aron may resist it in himself, he cannot extirpate it in others. The point was brought home when once as a boy Aron lovingly raised a kitten from birth on a vegetarian diet until the kitten became a cat and escaped to roam the neighborhood. Aron painfully suffers his parents' taunts about the cat's native carnivorousness and its feasting on discarded chicken legs snatched from the garbage can in the alley. Sadistically, they prove their point by taking the cat indoors and placing before it a piece of raw liver. The parents roar hysterically as the cat gleefully devours the meat and growls menacingly at Aron, who had fed it milk from a dropper as a baby and who is now reduced to tears of humiliation and powerlessness.

Aron's powerlessness within the family is underscored by an extraordinary weekly ritual. Every Thursday night, while the women are doing a thorough house cleaning, the father takes a long bath and then, with his towel wrapped around his waist, he comes into the living room and lies face-down on the sofa. The women gather around him (this includes the grandmother, Moshe's mother) and scour his massive back for blackheads and whiteheads, which they fall upon with horror and rapture, squeezing with their fingernails and applying alcohol, and working in tune to the father's answering groans of submission and delight. As an evocation of Stone-Age rites, the scourging and grooming of the dominant male, with its not uncomplicated exchanges of pleasure and control, presents an revealing picture of gender relations in Israeli society of thirty years ago. It is a picture in which the son does not figure. Aron takes in the scene through the doorway of the kitchen where he sits on a low stool working on his assigned chores of peeling a mound of potatoes for the Sabbath cholent. Scrawny and underdeveloped, Aron is unlikely ever to accede to the prerogatives of the father's bearlike body, nor is he even permitted to participate in the collective female tribute to it. His response to his exclusion is to daydream while performing his repetitive scullery chores, and it is in these vivid reveries, undertaken as both denial and escape, that Grossman locates the origins of Aron's aesthetic consciousness and the seeds of his identity as an artist.

This is the beginning of the track that is laid down in *The Book of Intimate Grammar* as an alternative to the vulgar sensual life. But before discussing the claims of art, it is worth asking the obvious question of why this novel is so extravagantly preoccupied with the claims of the body. Beyond an undisputable pinch of idiosyncratic pathology, the answer lies, I believe, in Grossman's presentation of Israel as a society of immigrant survivors and in his analysis of the unseen but enormous costs of successful survival. In the conventional Zionist story the settlers of the country are not common immigrants but pioneers whose powerful spiritual longings enable them to endure privation and hostility. The truth, of course, is that the vast majority of Jews ended up in Israel because of historical circumstance rather than ideological motivation. The obstacles faced by these accidental immigrants—certainly as much after their arrival in Israel as before—were every bit as difficult as those faced by the more famous intentional immigrants, yet their struggles remained untransfigured and unmystified by a rhetoric of sacrifice and ideals. Grossman sees in this unspiritual survival a force that is at once vastly impressive and threatening.

There is a crucial difference between Aron Kleinman's parents and the parents of Momik in Grossman's Holocaust novel, *See Under: Love*. Although they remained alive, Momik's parents were sucked into the black hole of the camps and left fearful and enfeebled. Aron's parents, whose brush with twentieth-century Jewish history was gruesome but not so catastrophic, were not so impaired. They survived, each in his or her own way, precisely because of their enormous energies and appetites, which remain intact and unstilled. This kind of survival, Grossman implies, necessarily requires—and results from—living life within the orbit of the body with its pleasures, nourishments, and waste products. And for Aron's parents, it is enough. Yet through Aron's eyes,

Grossman shows readers that the price paid for life lived in this way is nothing less than the obliteration of culture itself. In his parents' home there are, simply, no books except for the Hebrew encyclopedia his father purchases by subscription through his union. His mother will not have books around because they collect dust, and in her eyes dust is an apt metaphor for the weight and utility of culture.

Aron ends up discovering the world beyond the body through an act of illicit breaking and entering. (He certainly does not find it in the public schools, which teach academic skills and statist ideology but little resembling culture.) In Aron's *shikkun* lives a forty-year-old single woman, a university graduate, named Edna Bloom, who owns a piano and plays classical music on it (it is the only instrument in the neighborhood) and who has decorated her flat with reproductions of modern art and with artistic bric-a-brac brought back from trips abroad. To the boys Aron hangs out with she is an object of ridicule and of some fascination as well. So, in an episode that takes place in the opening pages of the novel, they steal a passkey and slip into her flat while she is at work. For the rest of the boys, the strange surroundings they find inside are reason for redoubled derision; for Aron, who is as ready as they to mock the absurd distortions of "modern art," the experience is transformative. Standing before a copy of Picasso's *Guernica,* with its fractured bodies and tortured faces, Aron tries to maintain a contemptuous distance but ends up being staggered by the work's power.

> Aron went back to the painting. First he faced it, then he turned away, then he turned back to gape at it some more, shutting his eyes, surrendering with open arms, backing off with a little dance, meandering like a lost panther, like a spy colliding with his mirror image, scratching where his skin tingled, glancing over his shoulder, what if it came off the wall and started following him, and a flower blooms out of the sword in the dead man's hand, and suddenly you see eyes everywhere, run for your life. (7)

He is conquered by something that, although scarcely material and substantial, is more real than the embodied life of his parents' world.

The prowler has been kidnapped. For the other boys one visit is plenty, but Aron cannot stay away. He barters for the passkey and illicitly makes Edna Bloom's apartment the secret home of his spirit.

But even this safe haven cannot long stand before his parents' philestinism. In the end, the wolf is invited in through the front door. When Edna Bloom hires Aron's father Moshe to demolish the wall separating the bedroom from the salon, her purpose is not interior decoration or home improvement. Watching this muscular bear of a man hammer away at her wall in his sweaty undershirt, Edna lapses in and out of a tremorous autoerotic fantasy. After years of loneliness and exploitative affairs with married men, she has decided to give herself this gift. To prolong her rapture, she pays for another wall to be torn down after the first has been demolished, and then another and another, until her apartment has been gutted and all her savings depleted. In the end she is taken away by her parents to be institutionalized.

The destruction of Edna Bloom's apartment is one of the longest and most brilliant sections of the novel. The narrative breaks with the disciplined allegiance to Aron's mental and social world and approaches, as Robert Alter has pointed out, the magic realism of Grossman's earlier work. Transformations and symbolic exchanges abound. As Edna declines and her walls are torn down, Moshe is built up and turned into a larger-than-life figure, a kind of Vulcan in the netherworld world of the *shikkun*. After years of domestication and inactivity, the heavy work with the sledgehammer pumps him up and returns him to his outsized manliness. His vigor makes him newly attractive to his wife, and they surprisingly conceive a child who will presumably console them for the disappointment and embarrassment over Aron's failure to grow. The greatest liberation for the father comes with the release of his story. In the presence of Edna and Aron and in the absence of the mother, Moshe is freed to tell the long-forbidden story of his past. The chronicle of terrible suffering and astonishing survival tumbles out in fantastic cadences and becomes the boy's most tangible inheritance from his father.

The fall of Edna Bloom's house of culture is the critical counterpoint to Aron's nascent consciousness as an artist. Although Aron is stunned by his first encounter with high art, her flat can serve only as a site of initiation but not as a model of how to be in the world. The function of art in Edna Bloom's domestic space lies somewhere between decoration and self-improvement, and the collection of familiar reproductions and artistic travel souvenirs verges on kitsch. The pillars of her psyche are certainly not shored up by contact with the higher things in life, and when Moshe Kleinman demolishes the inner partitions of her self, the whole edifice collapses.

To become an artist Aron must supply the missing qualities of tenacious will and inner depth. Tenacity and cleverness pose no problem; he has them in abundance. He beguiles his friends with fabulous schemes and hilarious imitations and awes them with his Houdini-inspired escapes from impossible confinements, and he makes up for his smallness by being a scrappy wrestler and soccer player. The quality of inner imaginative power is more elusive. It is revealed in Aron's reveries, which begin as an escape from unpleasant realities (like his daydreaming while peeling potatoes on Thursday nights) and go on to become a zone of inner freedom and linguistic experimentation. These inner explorations are connected to one of Grossman's most inspired pieces of cleverness. Hebrew's tense system lacks the present continuous, and when, as a native Hebrew speaker, Aron learns of its existence in English class, he is enthralled, and he proceeds happily to add the English "-ing" suffix to Hebrew verbs. Through this discovery he can give a name to his particular mode of serious daydreaming; he calls it "Aroning."

As Aron's friends grow physically, he develops imaginatively. His reveries deepen in their function and content, at times leaving the orbit of his narcissism and attaining to an empathic vision of the inner experience of others. Language is the subject of many of these moments. He has favorite words that he plays with and caresses in his mind; for there, in his mind, materiality poses no threat, and it is permissible for words to be incarnated as "sensual beings." Whether sensual or precisely Cartesian, the rich linguistic code of Aron's inner life is what is being referred to as the "intimate grammar" of the novel's title.

It is in these passages that the debt to Joyce is most evident. Like Stephen Daedalus, Aron Kleinfeld aspires to be a priest of the imagination who, through the mystery of language, can transmute the gross bread of daily life into the wine of the spirit. The shaping allusions are drawn from different sources, of course. Aron's name refers to the eponymous high priest of the Hebrew Bible. The foundational text for him is chapter 6 of Isaiah, which he chants at his bar mitzvah—a ceremony meaningless in every other way—and which describes the prophet's call to his vocation. God touches Isaiah's lips with a glowing coal, and immediately his impurity is removed and his sin expiated. Yet where Aron's call emphasizes purification and the redemption of sensuality, Stephen's call underscores his embrace of the world and his readiness to sin and to fall over and over again in devotion to his art.

Grossman's turn toward art as an alternative to life rather than an engagement with it is evident in the ambiguous conclusion to the novel. Feeling betrayed by his friends and isolated amid the frenzy of a country on the brink of war, Aron climbs inside an abandoned refrigerator in an empty lot near his house and shuts the door. He intends to perform—for himself as the sole audience—the most audacious exploit of his young career as an escape artist. Well, whatever Aron's intentions may be, readers know what it means for depressed teenagers to climb into abandoned refrigerators and what happens to them when they do, and it is not an affirmation of art.

I read *The Book of Intimate Grammar* when it first came out in Hebrew with a number of friends in a reading group, and we were all convinced at the time that the novel ended with Aron's suicide. Since then we have had our doubts. In postpublication statements and interviews, Grossman has made it clear that he intended the refrigerator to serve as a chrysalis for Aron's rebirth as an artist. This intent can be given some plausibility by a second reading of the novel that is alert to the imaginative intensity of Aron's inner life. Yet, in the end, this transcendent interpretation can at most be felt as the pressure of an authorial intention that remains schematic.

This concluding equivocation is merely a sign of the failure of the novel's two tracks, the life of the body and the life of art, to meet. In shaping an autobiographical myth in fiction, Grossman has presented a wickedly brilliant account of the social milieu from which he emerged.

But this world has nothing to say to him and nothing to give him, and the implied next stage would be a successfully engineered escape that would catapult him into a different trajectory. The fabulistic inventiveness of *See Under: Love* indicates, retrospectively, where this flight path will take him, as does a recently published novel about the picaresque adventures of an adolescent hero. Although Grossman has taken on large issues such as the Holocaust and relations between Arabs and Jews, the ordinary construction of Israeli reality, with all its extraordinariness, seems to hold little interest for him. He is operating on a different plane.

9

Revising the Founders

Telling and Retelling in Meir Shalev's The Blue Mountain

BASHING THE ICONS of the founding fathers has long been a favorite pastime in Israeli culture. For more than a decade before the
Labor Party lost its hegemony in the seventies, the New Wave in Israeli
fiction led by Amos Oz had been embarked on an aggressive program
of demythologizing. The chief targets were the larger-than-life pioneers
who came to Palestine from Russia during the period between the failed
1905 Rebellion and World War I. Fueled by a powerful mix of Hebrew
nationalism and back-to-the-earth Russian populist idealism, the pioneering settlers labored to fashion the fundamental political and agricultural institutions of what was later to become the State of Israel.

Along with an aptitude for vision and hard work, the pioneers
brought with them a zeal for endless debates over nuances of principle
and, more chillingly, a readiness to impose ideology on life. Their actions were often conducted with an air of grandiose self-sacrifice and
theoretical self-importance that masked the actual submission to their
wills required of those around them. To be a wife or a son to one of
these giants meant not to escape unharmed.

Much of Oz's best early fiction *(Where Jackals Howl* and *Elsewhere,
Perhaps)* is an exercise in rapping vigorously on feet of clay. The job is

Portions of this chapter were previously published in *New Republic* 205 (Sept. 9,
1991). Reprinted by permission.

done with great artistic sophistication and with the best techniques in the modernist repertoire, but there is no disguising the fact that the encounter between father and son is not playacting but a struggle for survival in which the will of the father remains a potent force. And now a new chapter in the reckoning with the fathers has been opened up in *The Blue Mountain* an important and immensely entertaining first novel by the youngest Israeli writer, Meir Shalev.

The substance of the criticism put forward by Shalev is as damning as what one finds in Oz, but the judgment is intertwined with affection and humor in such a way as to take the confrontation between the generations to a new plane of engagement. Rather than demythologizing the pioneers, Shalev has taken the opposite tack. He treats the myths *as* myths and succeeds at a stroke not only in loosening their hold but also in making the myths serve his purposes as the stuff of stories. *The Blue Mountain* is a virtuoso storytelling performance at whose center stands the very act of converting myths into stories. In this quality Shalev's volume joins David Grossman's extraordinary novel of the Holocaust *See Under: Love,* which appeared in Hebrew some two years earlier. In both books the horrors of history (the travails of pioneers were horrible in their own way) are dissolved or decentered by the consolations of storytelling. Shalev goes about this differently from Grossman, but taken together their work points to the arrival of a postmodernist temper in Israeli fiction.

The blue mountain is the Carmel, which overlooks the Jezreel Valley in northern Israel and separates the settlements in its shadow from the sea and the worldly cities on its farther flank. The valley was one of the first areas settled by the pioneers, who drained its swamps and made it into some of the richest farmland in the country. The story is set in a village modeled on a famous moshav (cooperative settlement) named Nahalal. What distinguishes a moshav from a kibbutz is the private management of the small family-run leaseholds; the settlement is run as a cooperative, but there is scope for individual initiative, even competition. This distinction is important because Shalev's novel is about a group of people who are at once propelled by a collectivist ideology and possessed of romantic self-dramatizing egos. Despite their utter revolt against the benighted decadence of the diaspora Judaism, the village created by the pioneers resembles nothing more than an Eastern European shtetl: a small, intensely provincial community held together by a shared set of beliefs (there religion, here socialism) but torn apart by hatred, passion, and intrigue.

Like a shtetl, too, the village has its own foundation myth. In the hoary ancient days when the land was still in the hands of the colonists' agents and the effendis, three intrepid pioneers—Mirkin, Liberson, and Tsirkin—asked a young woman named Feyge Levin to join them in forming a peripatetic labor collective. They drew up protocols in which they solemnly committed themselves to sharing wages and chores equally and to "making no improper advances toward their female comrades." Formally constituted as the Feyge Levin Workingman's Circle, the four labored in the quarries, on the roads, and in the groves, fending off despair and malaria and snatching moments of playful high spirits. When they founded the village and settled down to become farmers, Mirkin married Feyge, who gave birth to the group's "first fruits," the first children born on the soil of the land.

The heroic and antic exploits of the founders find a devoted chronicler in the person of Baruch Shenhar, Mirkin's grandson and the narrator of the novel. Orphaned at the age of two, when his parents were killed in a terrorist attack, Baruch was taken in and lovingly raised by Mirkin, himself long a widower. The education that Baruch receives at the hands of his grandfather, a wizard in the cultivation of fruit trees, and Pinness, the village schoolmaster who is an expert in entomology, is peculiar. He learns nothing about relating to women and a great deal about crop rotation and the behavior of beetles. His chief source of nourishment is the rich flow of tales—alternatingly touching, grotesque, and comical—told to him by these two men about the Feyge Levin Workingman's Circle and the earlier years of the village.

The distinctly unheroic present in which Baruch retells these tales rests upon a hugely funny joke. The grandfather designs his death to serve as an act of revenge for the supposed banishment of his son Efrayim, who was disfigured as a commando in World War II and could not find a place for himself in the village when he returned home.

Mirkin instructs his grandson to bury him not in the village cemetery but in the soil of his own orchard, and Baruch does so. Because Mirkin was a revered figure in the movement, however, other pioneers want to be buried near him. Soon Baruch is receiving requests from old men and women from all parts of the world, especially America, who consider themselves veterans of the Second Aliyah even if they only spent a few months in Palestine before going on to become factory owners in California. (These far-flung comrades indeed made up the majority, for in point of fact only 10 percent of the "pioneers" who came to Palestine before World War I ended up staying, and even among those who stayed, many committed suicide.) The ex-pioneers from abroad pay large sums of cash for the privilege of being thus repatriated, and Mirkin's farm is quickly transformed into a cemetery called grandly Pioneer Home, and Mirkin's grandson becomes a rich undertaker.

The joke turns on the literalization of a metaphor. At the center of the pioneer vision stood the slogan: self-realization through a return to the earth. The necessary antidote to the sickly otherworldliness of diaspora Judaism and its *luftmenchlichkeit* was a rootedness in productive agricultural work in the Land of Israel from whose soil all manner of life-giving blessings would flow. Baruch's cemetery is a perfect send-up of all these solemn ideals. After so much bitter struggle against rabbinical beliefs and about the afterlife, the veteran pioneers unashamedly clamor to secure their immortality by being interred in the pioneer home. It is only in their burial that many of them are "ingathered from the Exile" and given to achieve the aspiration of returning to the soil of the land.

The village, of course, is outraged. Mirkin has made good on his threat to "get them where it hurts: the earth." Formally charged with violating the spirit of cooperative farming, Baruch's lawyer argues that just the opposite is true: "My client quite literally earns his livelihood from the earth. He supports himself by his own labor, considers himself a tiller of the soil, regards the mortuary profession as a branch of agriculture, and uses agricultural tools to excavate, plant, fertilize, and irrigate his prospering business." What most annoys the villagers is that Baruch makes more money at "farming" than they do.

This idea and its parody embody the double perspective that Shalev's novel offers on the achievement of the founding fathers. The romantic view is assiduously cultivated by the narrator, Baruch, the true offspring of Mirkin and the loyal pupil of Pinness. Raised on their stories, he preserves and weaves the tales of their exploits and their shenanigans into an epic narrative that makes myths out of key events and returns to them obsessively. What keeps Baruch's telling from becoming pure hagiography is the affectionate irony with which he treats his subjects and the contrast between the liveliness of his voice and other models of remembering represented in the novel. Meshullam, the son of another founder of the village, for instance, has devoted his life to creating a museum containing the early "artifacts" of the settlement. His relationship to the past is embodied in the prized object in his collection—the huge straw-stuffed hide of Hagit, the greatest milk-producing heifer of that generation. When some revisionist historians question whether there were ever any swamps in the Jezreel Valley, Meshullam loses his grip on his sanity and tries to flood the village fields to re-create the fabled bogs whose draining remains the cornerstone of the pioneer myth.

The antiromantic view is articulated by Levin, the brother of the eponymous member of the Feyge Levin Workingman's Circle. Levin was unsuited for physical work and made a career in the city. When Feyge died shortly after the birth of her third child, Levin left Tel Aviv to settle in the village as the manager of its shop and to help raise his niece and nephews. The escapades of the early pioneers hold no charm for him. From his perspective, the Feyge Levin Workingman's Circle, renowned for its pathbreaking equal treatment of women, was based on a fraud. Mirkin's marriage to Feyge came about as a result of a lottery, unbeknownst to Feyge, held among the three men. For reasons of ideological amour propre, the men could not bear the idea that she would become another's, even though none of them was in love with her. (Mirkin was in love with a woman who remained in Russia and who finally came to Israel when he was an old man.) The further pressure to give birth to the village's "first fruits" forces Feyge, depleted by years of wandering and hard labor, to an early grave.

For Levin the glorious old days can be summarized pithily: "They humiliated me and killed my sister." Of these two acts, the humiliation of Levin, although less melodramatic, is arguably the more significant. The taunting and the teasing of Levin for not being a laborer continues even after he throws in his lot with the pioneers and settles in the village. An old hard-working donkey brought from Russia called Zeitser is coddled and showered with all the honor due a true hero of the working classes while the devoted and diligent Levin is shown no respect.

Levin's resentment speaks for the true majority of the founders of the Jewish state, who were not farming pioneers but industrious and self-sacrificing men and women who furthered the national cause in many other ways. Yet the ideological prestige of the return-to-the-soil banner was so powerful that anyone associated with it was enviably thrust onto center stage. The theatrical image is just to the point: Levin shouts at Pinness

> [Y]ou people never had any appreciation of plain ordinary work. You were too busy acting in your great Theater of Redemption and Rebirth. Every plowing was a return to the earth, every chicken laid the first Jewish egg after 2,000 years of exile. Ordinary potatoes, the same *kartoffelakh* you ate in Russia, became *taphuchei adamah,* "earth apples," to show how you were one with Nature. You had your pictures taken with rifles and hoes, you talked to the toads and the mules, you dressed as Arabs, you thought you could fly through the air.

To be sure, Levin's is the animus of the virtuous man left out of the picture, but this analysis is right on the mark. The mystique of the founding pioneers was made up of only one part hard work and many parts of self-invention, self-dramatization, and self-promotion. The socialist Zionist conviction that the New Jew would be reborn from working the land gave powerful authority—and a near monopoly on arrogance—to the few who realized the ideal and relegated the many who toiled in less "correct" callings to an ancillary status.

Although he is the keeper of the flame, the narrator, Baruch, is the best evidence for the unromantic legacy of the members of a generation who comported themselves as if they were characters in a Russian novel. (*A Russian Novel* was the title of the Hebrew original.) As a boy raised by his grandfather, Baruch is the direct creation of the elder pioneers; yet apart from his oxlike stamina and stubbornness, he has inherited none of their passion and their vitality. The present time (the early 1980s) in which Baruch tells the story is flaccid and played out. He has nothing better to do with himself than tend his cemetery and tell his stories, and like many native sons he has moved away from the village. Around him the surviving pioneers decline into blindness, enfeeblement, and dementia.

And tragically, it is only they whom he can love. Baruch is incapable of knowing love for women, or, for that matter, of forming bonds with anyone of his own generation. His sterility is a recoil from the absence of a mother and from the messy misalliances he has observed among the pioneers; his cousin Uri reacts in the opposite way by compulsively seducing most of the married women of the village. Both are responses to something fundamentally amiss in the lives of the great pioneers. *Their* grand passions were ideas and the earth, and they loved women, badly, only as reflection and handmaidens of these first loves. How else could Feyge have been given to Mirkin by lottery?

The Blue Mountain, in sum, juxtaposes the romance of the pioneers with an antiromantic view of motives and consequences. Yet what Shalev does with this opposition is something very different from what one would expect from Oz and the other New Wave writers; Shalev declines to embark on the enterprise of demythologizing. He approaches the conflict between generational values not as a dialectic to be resolved but as material to be woven into story. This is a rich book, but it is not a deep one. The characters are vivid and memorable, rather than complex, and the ideational framework holds no surprises.

But can Shalev tell a story! He spins his yarn very adroitly, alternately pulling the threat taut and letting it play out. There is a mesmerizing and Scheherezade-like quality to the narrative, suggesting a world in which the tale and the telling go on forever. The story is moved forward through an accretion of episodes that are repeated and returned to through the perspective of different characters. Baruch's bovine quality makes him the perfect narrator for this kind of story: unhurried, loyal, observant, and rather stupid. He receives and replays all the stories he has been told by his grandfather and by others but does not—indeed, cannot—comment on them. The commentary is provided by the stories themselves; the inclusive jumble of the narration means that the ideological rhetoric of the pioneers is forced to rub shoulders with the anecdotal reality of their lived lives. Baruch is certainly not an intentionally comic narrator, but his very earnestness makes the stories run the gamut from wryly ironic to the unabashedly hilarious.

The many amazing things that happen in this novel are related with an utter absence of amazement as if they were simply inscribed in the being of the world. The disfigured Efrayim, Baruch's uncle, walks around the village with a 2,900-pound bull on his shoulders. Zeitser, the veteran pioneer donkey, is treated by the narrative as a person rather than an animal, and his views are often quoted. Shifris is a pioneer who left Russia with others at the beginning of the twentieth century but decided to walk overland; his arrival is still expected daily. When *The Blue Mountain* appeared in Hebrew, much was made of Shalev's debt to the "magical realism" of García Márquez. The borrowing is real, but to Shalev's credit the technique is kept to the soft edges of the novel, and it is fully domesticated within the Israeli world of which he writes. Besides, it is not so very strange that elements of nature—trees, livestock, fields—should be alive in the experience of a generation that gave itself up so fully to a return to the land.

The urge to fantasy is kept in check by a concomitant fascination with the shapes and the surfaces of the material world. Shalev writes a noun-saturated prose filled with references to the realia and the arcana of entomology and agronomy. This is a novel that keeps its ear, quite literally, close to the ground, and it is in picking up this mute language of rustling and murmuring, besides the louder ideological noises above ground, that Hillel Halkin's translation demonstrates its superb grasp of idiom and nuance.

In the end it is the fusion with the land that remains the most vivid experience in Shalev's novel. The pioneers may have theatrically cooked up the romance of the land, but they succumbed to its spell in a way no one could have predicted. Their attachment was not to the soil in general, or even to the Land of Israel as a whole, but in a radically parochial way to the land of their valley, their village. *The Blue Mountain* is a regional novel in the true sense. Most of the characters never venture beyond the shadow of the mountain of the title, nor do they feel any need to do so. They move in a world that is similarly separated from the great wars and scandals from which Israeli history is usually constructed. There is not a mention in this book of the establishment of the state and the War of Independence.

Shalev's novel, in the end, is about a kind of attachment to Israel that one hears little of in contemporary journalism. This is not the messianic commitment of the adherents of Gush Emunim to redeem all the land promised by God in the Bible, nor is it the political nationalism capped by the establishment of a sovereign entity with its own army, flag, and diplomatic corps. It is, for want of a better term, an autochthonous attachment, a mythic pre-Judaic connection that derives from the earth and is rooted in the soil of a particular place. Before the politicization of Palestine nationalism, one used to hear, quite plausibly, much about the primary attachment of Palestinians to the fields and springs of their particular village or town rather than to some larger entity. The Jewish settlers may have come later, but as Shalev's wonderful novel illustrates, the force of their return engendered no less fierce and no less embroiled an attachment to the land.

Concluding Theological Meditation

Hebrew Literature as a Source of Modern Jewish Thought

ONCE THE WORLD WAS CONTAINED by Torah; now the Torah is contained by the world. Once the life of a Jew was regulated by the rhythm of chosen days and appointed times; now the flux of experience is shaped by different forces. Once Zion was an other-worldly ideal; now it is an exigent and complex actuality. Once the soul of the individual Jew was bound up in the collective life of the people; now the space of the self, subject to perpetual analysis, recedes inward away from the community.

This great transformation, which goes by many names, marks the experience of the Jewish people in the modern era. Although many people and cultures have undergone a similar crisis, the instance of the Jews is unique on two counts. In Western Europe the process of secularization unfolded over the course of several centuries; for most Jews the ordeal was accelerated and compressed into one or two generations. Although for many newly emerging nations exposure to modernity has been equally jolting, it is only in the case of the Jews that this confrontation has involved a high literary and intellectual culture not in the possession of a hieratic class alone.

What happened? How did it happen? Differing and related answers to these questions are offered by the responses of the Jewish people to the crisis of tradition: modern Jewish history, politics, literature, and

This conclusion was previously published in *ORIM: A Jewish Journal at Yale*.

philosophy, and the branches of academic study that arose to interpret them. For the purposes of this conclusion I privilege one of these responses, modern Hebrew literature, and make a case for its special powers in illuminating the great transformation in Jewish life. The case is based on the provenance of Hebrew, its unique mediation between tradition and modernity, and the multivalence of its recent history. In the second part of this conclusion I go a step further; I take Hebrew not only as an explanatory account for the dilemmas of modern Jewish identity but as something much more—a source for restoration. In its very secularity modern Hebrew literature can be used as a source for Jewish theology.

There is, to begin with, the mystery of the Hebrew language. Mystery is not a term that sits comfortably in Jewish theological discourse, and I use it for its strangeness and, perhaps, its aptness. That Hebrew *literature* should be revived and take on new forms is astonishing, but it is not beyond belief because of the continuous and creative employment of the literary language down through the ages. That the *spoken* language should be brought back to life and become a natural and ambient medium for a significant portion of the Jewish people, literate and nonliterate alike—this surpasses astonishment. If many of the original visions of Zionism have failed or been compromised, the revival of the Hebrew language succeeded beyond imagining. For any religiously sensitive person there are signals of hope to be picked up here. The note that needs sounding, however, is not one of piety but of calculation. If the deep cleavages within the Jewish people are one day to be lessened, it will be the result in part of the power of the Hebrew language. It is that language—and it seems sometimes that it is *only* that language— that constitutes an arc of continuity between the tradition and the culture of the modern Jewish state that supplanted it. Lodged deep within the recesses of the Hebrew language are both the meanings that were lost and the resources for their reappropriation and transformation.

It is both the discontinuity and continuity of Hebrew that makes it a special case. What is modern about Hebrew literature are the new ends for which Hebrew began to be written at the end of the eighteenth century and the new forms in which this program was realized. Make no mistake. Before this time Hebrew had had a vital and unbroken history as a compositional medium not just in the chain of postbiblical interpretation and not just in the vast corpus of liturgical poetry and not just in the flowering of the Spanish Golden Age but in many modes and genres less conspicuously sacred or secular: historical chronicles, romances, treatises on logic and astronomy, essays in philosophical consolation, travel literature, ethical wills, and personal correspondence.

What changed at the beginning of the modern era was that Hebrew was made into the chief instrument of the movement to modernize Jewish life, the Haskalah. For the first time Hebrew was pressed into use (through parody and satire) as a medium for social criticism, and the novels, ballads, and lyric poems written in imitation of Western models claimed for themselves, beyond their didactic function, nothing less than the autonomous dignity of art itself. When the hopes of the Haskalah foundered on the realities of Russian anti-Semitism at the end of the nineteenth century, Hebrew became the language of romantic nationalism and embodied the vision of establishing a Jewish homeland. The revival of a people was inconceivable without the revival of its language. Yet once revived, Hebrew could not be limited to this proper civic mission. A generation of intellectuals had been born into the world of faith only to be banished from it by the disintegration of Jewish life in Eastern Europe at the close of the nineteenth century. The new Hebrew literature became the modernist medium through which their uprootedness and dislocation were explored. By the late 1920s the venue of Hebrew literature—its writers, periodicals, and publishing houses—had been transferred to Tel Aviv and Jerusalem. From that time forward Hebrew became, largely but not exclusively, the literary (besides the popular) culture of a particular society, the Yishuv (the Jewish settlement in Palestine), and the State of Israel.

I have adduced the provenance of modern Hebrew literature to make an obvious but important point. In confronting the dilemmas of identity and belief, to write in Hebrew represented a choice *not* to write in a Western language. A language such as German provided such Jewish writers as Freud, Kafka, and Walter Benjamin with a powerful lexicon of modernity and with immediate access to the advanced questions of culture. Their contributions to modern culture were truly awesome; yet to the degree to which they sought to address the crisis of Jews and Judaism their linguistic medium kept them on the outside. For Hebrew writers, however, no matter how cut off they felt from the world of piety from which Hebrew had emerged and no matter how artificial and unsuitable Hebrew must first have been for engaging issues of modernity, the choice of Hebrew was a choice to work from the inside. To write in Hebrew, especially before the success of the Jewish national enterprise, was itself a statement of faith and a declaration of where one stood within the hermeneutical circle of modern culture. But it was far more than a matter of allegiance. Because Hebrew literature had become both the repository of classical Judaism and the record of a reawakened people's adventure in modernity, Hebrew was thought to possess the internal resources to negotiate the distance between old and new. Substitution, retrieval, containment, synthesis, reconciliation—all the dynamics of cultural change could take place *within* Hebrew literature because in that medium alone did the new meanings and old meanings exist simultaneously.

If one grants the importance of Hebrew literature, what, then, is the account it renders about the great transformation of Jewish experience and consciousness in modern times, about what happened and how it happened? As befits the complexity of modern Jewish history, the explanation turns out to be not one but two. In literary history, the branch of criticism that studies literature diachronically, there have been until recently two principal models for explaining the origins and development of modern Hebrew literature. These explanatory accounts are important because they close certain options and open others in the endeavor of making literature "available" to Jewish thought and theology.

The first is the rebirth model associated with the ideas of Joseph Klausner and Simon Halkin. It views the appearance of the new forms of writing in modern Hebrew literature—novel, short story, essay, lyric, epic, idyll, ballad—not as an imitation of fallen Western models but as the expression of a newly expanded and invigorated national life, at the center of which stood themes of love, nature, power and art. This argument holds that the Jewish soul, released from prolonged constriction, had been freed to appropriate the full reach of its humanity. This is to be understood as a rebirth rather than a modern creation ex nihilo because the new forms of the imagination were extensions or delayed outgrowths of ancient, biblical forces that had lain quiescent through the long night of exile. There is a radical and a conservative version of this model. The aim of the new literature according to the radical version (M. Y. Berdichevsky [1865–1921]), is to revolt against the old, usurp its place, and stop at nothing less than a total "transvaluation of values." In the conservative version (Ahad Ha'am [1856–1927]), the new culture can be made an evolutionary development from the old by translating the religious values of the past into usable spiritual and ethical ideals through a process of hermeneutical recovery. Common to all of these approaches to modern Hebrew literature is a conception of sectors of experience and imagination that have been newly appropriated and restored. A spatial image may help. The "house" of the modern Jewish spirit, one might say, has been enlarged; new rooms have been built on and inhabited. In the meantime, the old rooms remain standing, esteemed but unused, and from them the objects deemed still valuable have been taken and installed in the new living space.

According to the second approach, the catastrophe model associated with the work of Baruch Kurzweil (1907–1972), the house of the Jewish spirit was destroyed, its foundation razed, and in its place was erected a totally new and flimsy structure whose claim to connection with what preceded it is a lie. The total usurpation, envisioned welcomingly by the young Berdichevsky, had, in Kurzweil's eyes, sadly come true. Modern Hebrew literature was the medium that documented and described the collapse of the world of Torah and the disinheriting of the Jewish mind. In the vacuum created by this disaster, eros had become demonic sexuality and belief self-deluding ideology. Modern Hebrew was a significant literature when it dramatized these transformations as acts of evasion and bad faith (Bialik and Agnon); it was a trivial literature when it represented the new life of the Jewish people in Israel as a healthy redemption from a benighted past (Palmah-generation writers). Kurzweil's reaction is neither reactionary nor nostalgic but tragic, with full awareness that the term *tragedy* is alien to the Jewish tradition. The wholeness of the world of Torah is irretrievably lost, and human's life in the aftermath can be nothing other than absurd. Signs from the past are, of course, not wholly absent in modern Hebrew literature: biblical motifs, allusions to classical texts, transformed religious symbols. According to the rebirth model, these are consoling survivals and markers of cohesion that support the status of the new literature as the legitimate successor to the classical civilization of the people. According to the catastrophe model, however, these survivals are the flotsam of a great shipwreck that reveals both the hollowness of the victory and the impossibility of complete divestiture.

In the face of these two models, I argue that the question of religion and literature can be put otherwise. To say that in the life of modern Jewish imagination religion has been either tragically lost or absorbed and superseded is to miss some of the unexpected directions in which this transaction can move. Both approaches hew close to the bone of modern Jewish history and take literature as a record of the pathos of that history. This linkage is accomplished, it seems to me, at the expense of the literariness of literature. By this I mean the way in which literature, especially modern literature, in addition to holding up a mirror to reality, determines an autonomous space of its own, both at the level of the literary object and the literary system as a whole. In this space of its own, certain maneuvers become possible in addition to certain experiments in the mimicking of transcendence—and this precisely because the grip of history is held at bay. There are potential materials here for use in the construction of a modern Jewish theology, but that ambitious undertaking is scarcely my purpose in the following pages. I present an itinerary of locations, four in all, where such materials may be found and what they may look like and, by doing so, support my claim for a repositioning of the question as a whole. The tack I shall not take is the one most commonly followed in such discussions: taking a motif such as the *akedah* (the binding of Isaac) or a biblical figure such as David and tracing its persistence and transformation in modern literature. These are useful exercises, to be sure, but they often reflect more on the ironizing energies of modern texts than on an engagement with the theological meanings represented by the motifs and figures. In that sense the issues I raise are adjacent to, but not part of, the widely discussed topic of modern Hebrew literature and the tradition.

The Text as Scripture/Scripture as Text

I begin with a phenomenon that is admittedly not unique to Hebrew literature but that is, nevertheless, central to this theme. It has been commonly observed that the modern literary text has come to resemble the Bible in the way it is read. Literary texts, which were once regarded simply as the object of appreciation and evaluation, are now approached by contemporary literary critics as a hidden universe of infinite complexity and inexhaustible meanings. The hallmark of modern literary texts—or simply "the text"—is its polysemy, its "many signedness." Constructed of multiple intersecting sign systems, the text does not necessarily yield up its meaning to the tracing of the surface sequence of events and gestures. In ways that resemble the midrashic techniques of the rabbis, the decoding of the text requires nonlinear procedures that make connections among different systems of signs at different levels of meaning. The very proliferation of meanings and the impossibility of fixing their number or containing the text's productions of them are reasons why some strong texts called classics seem to have something to say, often something different to say, in each generation. The fact that the meanings of the text are not just *there*, but can be realized only through interpretation, has placed new emphasis on the role of the interpreter. Far from being an ancillary or subsidiary activity, interpretation and the aggregating body of discrete interpretations have enlarged the conception of the text and blurred the sharpness of its boundaries. If the text cannot be realized without interpretation, the text must come to include within it the history of its interpretations. Not all texts possess the surplus of meaning that makes them worthy of this kind of intensive reading. Those that do are said to be part of a cannon, and although the cannon of modern literature is open to change in a way in which the biblical canon is not, the aura of canonization privileges the text in not dissimilar ways. Finally, as an object the modern literary text has undergone changes in status that recall the vicissitudes of Scripture in the hands of its students. A period in which the text was regarded as the ineffable creation of genius was followed by a period in which the text's sources of influence were searched out and its philosophy elucidated. The focus next moved inside the text to discover there a complex organic unity, only to have that structure challenged by the claim that the text's meaning is produced by shifting codes of signification whose turbulence makes the idea of a single, stable organization impossible.

How are readers to take this analogy between Scripture and text? I think one should be suspicious of those who would urge too close a historical tie between the two. This position takes the form of the argument that the new status and methods of interpretation represent either a secularization or a displacement of the ways in which the rabbis of the midrash read the Bible. There is a necessary presumption here of historical influence or transmission that is simply not defensible. Even if the rabbis could be claimed as precursors of the critics, and this is doubtful, to suggest their influence is to ignore the many, many cultural transformations that mediate between then and now. The Scripture/text analogy is evocative, moreover, precisely because its two terms are ontologically unassimilable one to other. The modern work of art, no matter how mystified or demystified its metaphysics may be, is grounded in humanly produced meanings, whereas the Bible and some of its commentaries claim for themselves a different kind of sanction.

The Scripture/text analogy, nevertheless, remains interesting, but on other grounds. It is the nature of human beings as sign-producing and meaning-generating creatures to set apart certain beautiful and powerful artifacts, to reverence them, and to make their interpretation a guarantee of the continuity of culture. In an age in which God no longer speaks audibly to humankind, endowing texts with the authority of His utterance, it should not be surprising that the need persists to be in the possession of such texts and to approach them in ways that mirror, even mimic, the ways the Bible was once approached.

The whole question, in fact, needs to be reversed. Rather than looking to the rabbis to teach one how to read modern literature, one should look to modern literature to teach one how to read the rabbis and *their* great text, the Bible. What could be more ironic and more wonderful than that the late fruits of secular humanism in the form of literary theory should help one to recuperate one's relationship to the founding texts of one's religious tradition?

The phenomenon I speak of is not a speculative proposal but a fact that is being repeatedly demonstrated, with impressive results, in the current study of the Bible and midrash and being tentatively extended to other bodies of traditional material. The application of these methods is more than a happy accident. It was because students read Eliot and Faulkner, Agnon and Zach, because they trained on the devices of the modernist text, because they learned about point of view, metaphor, allusion, gap filling, and analogical structure—because, in short, of the creation of this new sensibility of reading, it became possible to take up the text of the Bible and rediscover in it a religious drama that had been missed for a very long time.

This is much more than a simple case in which "modern methods" have been usefully applied to ancient texts. Form criticism, archeology, and comparative Semitics have in their time yielded much useful knowledge about the Bible and its world; but little has approached literary theory in recovering the primary inner excitement of the experience of reading the text of Scripture. To speak of excitement in this context is not out of place. The original source of this excitement for modern readers was not the Bible but modernist texts. It was in the deep analysis of the poem and the novel that the revelatory power of the text was first reexperienced. The shimmering overdeterminacy of the text, the serious play of meanings, the significance and inseparability of interpretation, the drama of sequential reading—all of these were factors in reconditioning the faculty of wonder in the presence of the text's aura. It was only then that this sense of discovery could be retrojected in a way that makes one into the kind of reader the Bible and midrash truly deserve. It is not my intention to demote the importance of studying modern literature by making it merely propaedeutic to the "divine sciences." Yet that function has, in fact, been served, perhaps incidentally, and it provides one with a suggestive illustration of how signals of transcendence may be imbedded in the secularity of the modern text.

Negation and Creativity

I return now to modern Hebrew literature proper to ask what its complex history can tell about the possibilities of belief and disbelief. A starting point is the fact that the emergence of modern Hebrew literature ineluctably presupposed a rejection at some level of the metaphysics of normative Jewish belief: the sovereignty of God, the covenant with Israel, the divine origin of the Torah, the authority of the commandments. Doctrine, to be sure, was not necessarily at the center of this movement, as befits its role in Jewish culture generally; the target of rejection was the whole fabric of traditional Jewish life in Eastern Europe. Yet the failure of belief was an inseparable part of things, whether conceived of as a patrimony outgrown and pushed aside (the rebirth model) or as a structure of plausibility that collapsed and was lost (the catastrophe model). It is the *moment* and *process* of negation that need to be more finely examined, for, as it is represented in the life of Hebrew literature, apostasy is a complex experience in which negation and creativity are intimately entwined.

A good example is to be found in the very originating moment of modern Hebrew literary history. In 1819 a Galician Maskil (a proponent of the Hebrew Enlightenment) named Joseph Perl published a satire of Hasidic tales called *Megalleh Temirin* (The revealer of secrets). The work is made up of imaginary letters circulating among Hasidic leaders and adherents concerning frantic efforts (including bribery, blackmail, and other reprehensible measures) to locate the whereabouts of the German manuscript of a book revealing damaging information about the inner workings of the Hasidic movement. The literary material being parodied, incidentally, was the writings of Nahman of Bratslav, whose parabolic tales are today so admired by students of literature. What for Perl was so ridiculous and discrediting about this material, in addition to its obvious distastefulness to Enlightenment principle, had to do with language; the Hebrew in which it was written was crude and vulgar and awkwardly translated from Yiddish speech with many Yiddishisms still intact.

Ironically, it turned out to be precisely the uncouth and graceless stylistic qualities of Perl's satire that, unbeknownst to him, made the work significant. The revival of Hebrew as a modern literary language at this time had been based on the purity of high biblical models and conducted according to the most elevated and ornate stylistic principles. The artificiality of this medium made it scarcely suitable for dealing with the real business of life. Therefore, Perl's parodying of the "fallen" models of Hasidism infiltrated into Hebrew vitality, resourcefulness, and raw humor that, although essential to the growth of new literature, could not be acquired "legitimately."

A more thematic example comes from the late-nineteenth-century confessional novel *Le'an* (Whither?) by M. Z. Feierberg. The work is set in the heart of pious Ukrainian Jewish society of that period and traces the intellectual coming-of-age of the young protagonist as he passes from the first inklings of childhood doubts to a tragic sense of permanent loss in young adulthood and, finally, to an impassioned affirmation of a nationalist rebirth in the East. From a compositional point of view, what is striking about the novel is the disproportion between its main sections and the proto-Zionist declaration at the end. The sections describing the journey toward apostasy are marvelously realized; by focusing on the child's fantasies and daydreams, Feierberg succeeds in presenting disbelief as a process that unfolds from within the tradition and that is linked to the development of the moral and spiritual imagination of the child. These richly evoked reveries contrast sharply with the depleted rhetoric of the concluding visionary passages. The difference is more than simply the difference between what is known and what is yet to be, and it characterizes the autobiographical genre in Hebrew as a whole. The story of the struggle to disengage from the toils of the tradition inevitably makes for better art than the life of disengagement that follows.

Rejection draws its strength from the power of the object rejected, and disbelief lives off the strength of the culture of faith. From the ex-

amples above and from many others that could be furnished, it becomes clear that although modern Hebrew literature is a secular literature of revolt, in its genesis and at crucial moments in its development
it drew its creative force from the tradition it was revolting against. Victory did not come without costs; the emancipation of Hebrew literature from its embroilment with faith and tradition has at times left it
perilously denuded of subject and vitality. The struggle between faith
and apostasy is, then, an embrace in which a secret exchange of
strengths takes place, an exchange that lasts, of course, only as long as
the struggle is joined.

Allegory and the Theological Life of Literary Forms

Literary genres possess their own theological suggestiveness. The
lyric poem presupposes the possibility of presence represented in the
fresh articulation of the human voice. Epic implies the cohesion of the
created social world and its rapport with a transcendent order. Narrative guarantees temporal duration and the successiveness of experience,
and the more self-conscious forms of the novel play continually on the
analogy between God's providence and the flawed but protean authority of the narrator or implied author over the world of the novel. Allegory, however, is a special case because, unlike lyric, epic, and novel, it is
not a modern, Western genre but a literary form found throughout
classical sources of Judaism and, for that matter, of Christianity as well.
From the prophetic and wisdom literature of the Bible, to the rabbinic
mashal (parable) to the rationalist hermeneutics of medieval philosophy, to the extravagant symbolizations of the Kabbalah, to the tales of
Nahman of Bratslav mentioned earlier, allegory has provided a way of
speaking otherwise about matters that do not lend themselves to being
spoken about directly. The modern tradition is a rich one as well: the
verse dramas of S. D. Luzzatto, the satire of Erter, the long poems of
Bialik, the existential fables of Agnon, the theater of Hanoch Levine,
and the fiction in the 1960s and 1970s of Oz, Yehoshua, and Appelfeld.
It would be easy, perhaps too easy, to take Agnon as an example,
that great classicist-modernist who made such obvious use of the para-

bolic materials of the tradition. To demonstrate how deep this tendency goes, I turn instead to the fiction of A. B. Yehoshua, whose work is fully domesticated into the milieu of secular Israeli society. In Yehoshua's short fiction of the 1960s, the hero is typically a well-educated, often nameless, native-born Israeli male (a high school Bible teacher, a philosophy lecturer, an aging university student) who is isolated from family and friends even as he moves among them. Deprived for so long of confirmation by others, and unaware of his desperation, he momentarily loosens the controls that bind him to civilization and longs to participate in and even precipitate a cataclysmic disaster, only in the end to recede back into his isolation unchanged.

Yet even though these figures seem to embody the quintessence of individual alienation, the stories manage at the same time to speak of much larger issues: the effects of perpetual war on Israeli society, the image of the Arab in the Israeli mind, the relationship to the Diaspora. In such stories as "Facing the Forests" (Mul ha-ya'arot), "Early in the Summer of 1970," and "Missile Base 612," the connection is made through subtle devices of background detail and submerged systems of reference rather than through the one-to-one correspondence one is used to associating with allegory. The centrifugal forces of allegory, which point the reader in a direction beyond story, are held in close balance with the centripetal forces of textuality, which focus the reader's interest on the workings of the story itself. The reader becomes aware of the allegorical possibilities only after the first reading, and in contrast to classical allegory, there may be no single "solution" but an ambiguous set of alternative interpretations.

In good hands allegory provides a defense against the solipsism of the modern work of art. It is a defense against nakedness as well. Nietzsche observed that it is in the nature of modern knowledge to seek to rip off the veil surrounding truth and to lay it open to direct description. In permitting the possibility of speaking otherwise, allegory "clothes" its difficult truths in narrative forms whose textures make the reader want to touch and feel them and thereby draw close to what they encloak. For the Israeli writer, allegory has proven itself to be an alternative to the techniques of socialist realism with its insistence on the representativeness of fictional characters. Through allegory the writer can keep faith with the great national themes without sacrificing fineness of focus and symbolic movement. In modern Hebrew literature the national focus inevitably takes the form of a critical assessment of the state of Israeli society and of the Jewish people as a whole. This preoccupation with the commonweal is the most significant aspect of Israeli literature as a Jewish literature. The allegorical mode represents a strong link between this contemporary concern and the dominant themes of classical Hebrew literature. It may no longer be transcendental realities that are pointed to by the allegorical counters; nevertheless, the "otherness" enforced by allegory, even as a modern device, cannot help performing a function that in the end is not so very different.

Truth-Telling and Critical Theology

The eclipse of traditional faith in the late-nineteenth century creates a vacuum that a variety of ideologies rushed to fill, functioning in turn very much like religions. The devotion and enthusiasm with which Jews committed themselves to communism and socialism—and many other movements, Zionism among them—bear witness both to the internal weakness of Judaism in that moment and to the tenacious persistence of the need to believe. The nature of these "deconversions" from traditional religion to an ideological surrogate religion is complex, and it has been the role of the best literature written in the West to examine the phenomenon with particular reference to the deformations that result from this displacement. In the case of modern Hebrew literature, it was, of course, Zionism that had to be submitted to scrutiny. In this context Zionism means not so much the Zionist *idea* of the establishment of a national homeland in Palestine as the potent blend of Zionist-Socialist *ideology* brought from Russia by the young settlers of the Second Aliyah in the years just before the First World War. It was according to this ideology that the kibbutzim were founded and the major political and educational institutions of the Yishuv were set up. Although much had changed by the time of Ben Gurion and the establishment of modern Israel, the original impulse was still evident in nearly all sectors of the new society.

At the very beginnings of Zionist ideology, Hebrew fiction was already there and involved in preparing a critique of the hubris of Zionism. The critique was an internal one, conducted in Hebrew within a broad consensus of national goals, yet the fact that it took place within the family did not make it any less radical or acrimonious. At issue was the claim of Zionism to solve the problem of the modern Jew, both as Jew and as modern man, and to offer a framework of belief and action that effectively replaced the piety of "exilic" Judaism. The founding figure in this truth-telling tradition was Yosef Haim Brenner, whose magisterial novels from the period of the Second Aliyah present the soul of the Jew, in the extremity of its theological and existential dispossession, as untransformed by the experience of the new land. Brenner was prophetic about the dangers of acting as if man had already been redeemed; the actual consequences of this presumption could only be observed at a remove in time.

In the friction of the 1960s, Amos Oz examined the later life of this ideological inheritance as it was realized in that most rationalist of utopian experiments, the kibbutz. In *Elsewhere, Perhaps* and *Where Jackals Howl and Other Stories,* Oz finds the kibbutz an endangered community, not only prey to the forces of hatred at large in the world, but more significantly, vulnerable to the turbulent passions of the reconstructed human material contained within. Oz's stories are particularly insightful at reading the costs paid by the sons for the ideological purity and romantic self-dramatization of the father. Although the kibbutz in Oz's fiction is intended to be a metomony for the Zionist enterprise as a whole, it remains a special case. Vividly presented in Yaakov Shabtai's novels of the 1970s *Past Continuous* and *Past Perfect* (Sof davar) the cityscape of Tel Aviv cuts even closer to the bone. Although his characters may have fantasies of going off to a settlement to put themselves back together, they are mired in the degraded aimlessness of their urban lives. The psychological space occupied by these figures is a vacuum created, again, by the passions, ideological and otherwise, of the generation of the founders. The absence left behind becomes in turn entropic and in turn demonic.

To speak of these writers as having theological ambitions would be inappropriate if not ridiculous. Yet if anything has been learned from literary theory in recent years, it is that the significance of a text depends on the interpretive community that reads it. So while such writers as Oz and Shabtai may have no intentions in this direction, there is nothing illegitimate about a desire to make theological use of their work. What I have in mind relates to the tradition of negative theology in medieval Jewish philosophy; this is the position that holds that because of God's transcendent otherness one is limited to making statements about what God is not rather than describing his positive attributes. One of the roles of modern literature, I submit, is to tell readers where in the world God is *not*. This is not simply a way of labeling all social criticisms as essentially religious. It applies specifically to literature that investigates the consequences of systems that have usurped the role of religion and operated in its place. Hebrew literature makes wonderfully good reading in this regard. If the picture drawn of Israeli society is unpretty, it need not be depressing. The demystifying and truth-telling force of the Jewish people depends on an honestly renegotiated relationship to the religious heritage of Judaism. In that endeavor, knowing where God is not is valuable intelligence,

I have named four ways in which theological insights can be derived from modern Hebrew literature. There are other ways as well. I have deliberately avoided invoking the magisterial figures of Bialik, Agnon, and Uri Zvi Greenberg, in whose works the crisis of the tradition is directly thematized. This territory is known, for all its richness, too well, and an overreliance on it begs the question of whither the sources of inspiration after these spirits fade. Moreover, I have sought to demonstrate that viewing modern literature theologically is not the same as theologizing it. Beware the voices that declare the departures and rebellions of modernity to have all been anticipated by our sages! For if Hebrew literature is to help shape a vision of the Jewish spirit in the future, it will do so only from within its stubborn secularity.

Epilogue

CONCERNING THE FUTURE of Israeli writing, only two things can be said with certainty: it will continue to be a provocative and engaging enterprise, and it will continue to become increasingly inclusive. The explosion of writing by and about women, Sephardim, and Holocaust survivors and their children has been one of the major developments in Israeli literature since the mid-1970s. The literature of the next decades is likely to include voices from groups who are now becoming part of the society and its culture. Among the hundreds of thousands of immigrants from the former Soviet Union there will surely be those who seek out the prism of art to reflect on the extraordinary transplantation of a people from one milieu to a radically different one. From among the community of Ethiopian Jews in Israel there will be writers who will tell of an even more stunning transformation. The circle will be widened, and the results will be illuminating.

Perhaps the most difficult challenge for Israeli writing will be less visible. The most dramatic cleavage within Israeli society is between secular Jews and Orthodox Jews. It is a profound conflict that goes far beyond issues of pluralism and "lifestyle preference" to the very center of the crisis of Judaism in modern times and the rise of Zionism. As the cultural imagination of Zionism, Hebrew literature—with the complex exception of S. Y. Agnon—has been a literature of secularity that in its early career represented the world of observant Jews only to submit it to withering satire. What was true at the end of the nineteenth century is true again today at the end of the twentieth century. The ear-locked and gabardine-wearing Jew of the shtetl represented to the Hebrew writers then the impotent spiritual corruption inherent in diaspora existence. The same iconographic image is in the minds of secular Israelis today as they view ultra-Orthodox Jews although the perception of impotence has changed to a sense of intimidation and resentment. There is no little curiosity on the part of the secular, whose lives are openly visible, about what takes placed behind the cordon of privacy among the ultra-Orthodox. This desire for a kind of literary voyeurism has been satisfied by a minitrend of books written by formerly Orthodox authors who purport to reveal the secrets, mostly about male-female relations, of Bnai Brak and Jerusalem.

An enormous sadness born of missed chances is the emotion evoked by this conflict when viewed through American Jewish eyes. Because of the politicization of religion in Israel, secular Israeli Jews have come to equate Judaism with the current formation of militant Orthodoxy and ultranationalism. That Judaism is a religious-cultural civilization that extends backward in time over millennia through many golden ages of poetry, narrative, and philosophy besides legal codes and commentaries—this awareness seems to lie beyond imagining in the present ahistorical confrontation. American Jews who observe Israel from a distance realize—and perhaps this is their meager compensation for living outside the thick texture of Israeli life—that to confuse the present array of Orthodoxy with the religious civilization of the Jewish people is a mistake with tragic consequences. The direness of the mistake lies not so much in the trodden rights of non-Orthodox religious Jews in Israel—a serious matter in its own right—as in the price paid by the secular culture. Because of disdain for the state rabbinate and for ultra-Orthodoxy, Israeli culture often views the spiritual achievements and imaginative creations of Jewish civilization over the ages as so much poisoned fruit. What is unattractive in the present moment is confused with what was glorious in its classical manifestations.

The price paid for this confusion, I argue, is not insubstantial. The imaginative reservoir of the Jewish past is made up of myths, symbols, stories, motifs, images, tropes, commentaries, and supercomentaries, and other linguistic and cultural materials. For Israeli culture to deny itself access to this body of resources because of a quarrel with its latter-day custodians means giving up a great deal. It means living off the resources of the past hundred years, and in many cases of the past fifty years, if that much. Now, there is much in this recent history of Israel to be proud of and to make meaning from, but no culture, however thickly substantial, can forgo its past, especially when it extends so far back in time, without running the risk of desultory shallowness. As evidenced by many of the works discussed in this volume, Israeli literature remains vigorous, at least in its major innovators. Yet around the margins there are signs of cultural insufficiency that may signal more serious problems if a deeper connection to the past is not made.

For American readers, especially American Jewish readers, the issue becomes one of shared relevance and shared interest. As Israeli literature becomes—to speak in gross terms—less Jewish and more Israeli, it becomes more limited to time and place. To be sure, there will always be great works of art that transcend their origins to become universal, but then again, American readers have many places they can look for universality. The attraction Israeli literature will exert because of its Israeliness will be a factor in the attentiveness of American readers who seek a deeper and more truth-telling encounter with Israel. This is, of course, not the "fault" of Israeli literature but a symptom of the growing divergence between the lives and fate of Israeli and American Jews. Yet that divergence is itself the result of a shared distancing from the common core of Jewish civilization. In the century that has now concluded, American Jews drifted away from the core out of indifference and an eagerness to become Americans; Israelis undertook a more complex ideological negation of much of classical Jewish culture while appropriating and amplifying the national idea. It is one of the dialectical surprises of modern Jewish history that it is now American Jews who, in their own heterodox ways, are reconnecting with that core.

Whether in the future American readers will discover in Israeli literature reflections of a parallel but exotic universe or something "of the essence," it is too soon to say.

NOTES

———————

INDEX

Notes

Introduction:
Israeli Literature in the Minds of American Readers

1. I thank Rona Sheramy for her help in preparing the materials for this essay. I am grateful for the helpful suggestions made by Naomi Sokoloff, Gilead Morahg, and James Diamond.

2. Unfortunately, it seems nearly impossible to obtain reliable sales figures. Publishers regard these figures as proprietary information, and, for a variety of reasons, they are not willing to disclose them. What figures mean altogether is also rather slippery because the number of books *shipped* to book stores is often many more than the number actually sold, and this discrepancy is further complicated by subsidiary rights of various sorts. In the end, because authors are paid only for the books sold, it is only from royalties that sales figures are derived. The availability of information depends upon authors' willingness to share it and their recordkeeping. I wrote to the authors mentioned later in this introduction with the hope that I could shed more light on their relative success in America. Some responded sympathetically, some not at all. But none was able to provide the information I was seeking.

3. For a useful summary of these attitudes, see Eytan Gilboa, *American Public Opinion Toward Israel and the Arab-Israeli Conflict* (Lexington, Mass.: Lexington Books, 1987).

4. I am grateful to the Institute for the Translation of Hebrew Literature and its director, Nili Cohen, for its generous help and for sharing the information about the sales of Hebrew literature in Europe.

5. I know of only two of her major stories that are widely available in English. "Na'ima Sasson Writes Poetry," a moving and beautiful story, can be found in *Meetings with the Angel: Seven Stories from Israel,* ed. Benjamin Tammuz (London: A. Deutsch, 1973), 225–49, and in *Ribcage: Israeli Women's Fiction: A Hadassah Anthology,* ed. Carol Diament and Lily Rattok (New York: Haddasah, the Women's Zionist Organiza-

tion of America, 1994), 48–70. "Bridal Veil" can be found in *New Women's Writing from Israel,* ed. Risa Domb (London: Vallentine Mitchell, 1996), 90–108.

6. An exception is Hillel Halkin's English translation of *Sippur Pashut* (A simple story) (New York: Schocken Books, 1985); I also hope that translations of some of the shorter texts escape this fate, such as those collected in *A Book That Was Lost and Other Stories by S. Y. Agnon,* ed. Alan L. Mintz and Anne Golumb Hoffman (New York: Schocken Books, 1995).

7. Alan L. Mintz, "Fiction: A Major Israeli Novel," *Commentary* 88 (July 1989): 56–60.

8. An additional subject should be mentioned in passing without making it a separate category—the tendency to compare Israeli writers to better-known Western writers. Oz is compared to Hemingway, Camus, Pavese, and Sylvia Plath and is even called a Levantine Jane Austen; the heroine of *My Michael* is called an "Israeli Madame Bovary." In Yehoshua's case names invoked include Kafka, Mann, Chekhov, Faulkner, Simenon, Gide, Hawthorne, and Pinter. Shabtai reminds reviewers of Proust, Balzac, Faulkner, and Joyce. Appelfeld evokes Edward Hopper, Mann, Kafka, and Proust; *Badenheim 1939* is called a "scherzo on a theme by Arendt." In Grossman's case it is Garcia-Marquez, Faulkner, Rushdie, Melville, Joyce, and Kafka, in addition, of course, to Bruno Schulz. The purpose of all of this glorious name calling is both to domesticate the foreignness of these writers by comparing them to familiar masters and to make claims for their nonparochial importance.

9. Although the focus of this survey is on the reception of Israeli literature in America, where it is appropriate I have occasionally brought in comments from English reviewers, mostly from the *Spectator,* the *Listener,* and, as here, the *Times Literary Supplement,* Dec. 7, 1979.

10. James S. Diamond, "The Israeli Writer as Mass Psychotherapist," *Conservative Judaism* 32 (winter 1979): 95–102.

11. Writing of *The Lover* in a similar kind of journal, the *Reconstructionist* (Apr. 1979), David Rabi concludes his review along similar lines: "[*The Lover*] warrants reading because of its sincere and penetrating look at modern Israel as well as its prophetic vision of Israel in the future."

12. The real breakthrough came in the introduction of the character Naim in Yehoshua's *The Lover.* This represents the first time in Hebrew literature, to my knowledge, that the inner life of an Arab character is explored and the character is allowed to speak in his own voice. Yet this genuine innovation goes largely unnoticed in the review literature.

13. The anonymous reviewer in *Choice* (May 1977) offered this caution about *Early in the Summer of 1970*): "One admires Yehoshua's noteworthy technique, but his negativistic, almost nihilistic, philosophy makes one hesitate to recommend this work to

a general college audience, and then only after they had been exposed to other writers, such as Agnon."

1. Nostalgia and Apocalypse:
Israeli Literature in the 1970s

1. Elliot Anderson, ed.*Contemporary Israeli Literature,* with poetry ed. Robert Friend (Philadelphia: Jewish Publication Society of America, 1977); Ezra Spicehandler and Curtis Arnson, eds. *New Writing in Israel* (New York: Schocken Books, 1976); Shulamith Hareven, *City of Many Days,* trans. Hillel Halkin (Garden City, N.Y.: Doubleday, 1977); A. B. Yehoshua, *Early in the Summer of 1970,* trans. Miriam Arad and Pauline Shrier (Garden City, N.Y.: Doubleday, 1977).

2. Amos Oz, *Where the Jackals Howl and Other Stories,* trans. Nicholas De Lange and Philip Simpson (New York: Bantam, 1982), 177–78.

3. Agnon as Modernist:
The Contours of a Career

1. This letter can be found in the autobiographical collection *Me'atsmi el 'atsmi* (From myself to myself) (Tel Aviv: Schocken Publishing, 1976), 9.

2. S. Y. Agnon, *A Book That Was Lost and Other Stories,* ed. Alan L. Mintz and Anne Golumb Hoffman, trans. Arthur Green (New York: Schocken Books, 1995), 141.

3. For historical and biographical data the editors are indebted to Arnold Band's *Nostalgia and Nightmare: A Study in the Fiction of S. Y. Agnon* (Berkeley and Los Angeles: Univ. of California Press, 1968).

4. *Me'atsmi,* 25–26.

5. Israel Cohen, ed. *Sefer Buczacz* (Tel Aviv: Am Oved, 1968), 95; Avinoam Barshai, ed. *Haromanim shel Shai Agnon* (Tel Aviv: Everyman's Univ., 1988), 16–17.

6. Gershon Shaked, *Shmuel Yosef Agnon: A Revolutionary Traditionalist* (New York: New York Univ. Press, 1989).

7. See his reminiscence in *Me'atsmi,* 111–12.

8. On Agnon's literary development in Jaffa, see my "Agnon in Jaffa: The Myth of the Artist as a Young Man" and Hillel Halkin's translation of "Nights," an early story from those years, both in *Prooftexts* 1 (1981): 43–95.

9. Gershom G. Scholem, *From Berlin to Jerusalem: Memoirs of My Youth* (New York: Schocken Books, 1980), 91.

10. Dan Miron, "German Jews in Agnon's Work," *Leo Baeck Institute Yearbook* 23 (1978): 265–80.

11. Scholem, *From Berlin to Jerusalem,* 92–93.

12. Emuna Yaron, ed., *Shai Agnon—Sh. Z. Schocken: Ḥilufei igarot 1916–1959* (Tel Aviv: Schocken Publishing, 1991).

13. Emuna Yaron and Hayyim Yaron, eds., *Sippure habest,* (Tel Aviv: Schocken Publishing, 1987).

14. Hayim Nahman Bialik and Yehoshua Hana Ravnitzky, eds., *Sefer Haggadah* (The book of legends), trans. William G. Braude (New York: Schocken Books, 1992).

15. As cited in David Canaani, *Shai Agnon be'al peh* (Tel Aviv: Hakibbutz Hameuchad, 1971).

4. The Critique of the
German-Jewish Ethos in Agnon's *Shira*

1. S. Y. Agnon, *Shira,* trans. Zeva Shapiro, with an afterword by Robert Alter (New York: Schocken Books, 1989).

5. Between Holocaust and Homeland:
Agnon's "The Sign" as Inauguration Story

1. These include *Kisui Hadam* (Covering the blood), which appears in the posthumous volume *Lifnim Min a Haḥomah* (Tel Aviv: Schocken Publishing, 1975), 51–104; "Laila Min Halelot" (The night) and, perhaps, "'Im Kenisat Hayom" (At the outset of the day) in *'Ad Henah,* 171–78 and 207–17.

2. Dan Laor, *Shai Agnon: Hebetim ḥadashim* (Tel Aviv: Sifriat Poalim, 1955), 60–97. See also Sidra DeKoven Ezrahi, "Agnon Before and After," *Prooftexts* 2 (1982): 78–94.

3. See Laor, *Shai Agnon,* 71–73; note also that in the 1944 fragment the narrator has only indistinct knowledge of the destruction of his city.

4. It should be recalled that there is a long tradition of association between Shavuot and catastrophe. Many pogroms in medieval Ashkenaz, from the Rhineland Valley to the Ukraine to Bessarabia, took place during the month of Sivan when the roads had become passable and Easter observances had inflamed anti-Jewish sentiments.

5. Quotations are taken from the graceful and sensitive translation by Arthur Green, which first appeared in *Response* 19 (1973): 5–31; it was reprinted subsequently in David G. Roskies, ed., *The Literature of Destruction* (Philadelphia: Jewish Publication Society of America, 1989), 585–604, and in Mintz and Hoffman, *A Book That Was Lost and Other Stories by S. Y. Agnon,* 378–409.

6. See also the end of chapter 14 when in the midst of telling his wife and children about the observance of Shavuot in Buczacz, the narrator observes: "I was able to tell the things calmly and not in sorrow, and one would not have known from my voice what had happened to my town, that all the Jews had been killed. The Holy One, blessed be

He, has been gracious to Israel: even when we remember the greatness and glory of by-gone days, our soul does not leave us out of sorrow and longing. Thus a man like me can talk about the past, and his soul doesn't pass out of him as he speaks."

7. Compare Hillel Weiss, "Between Mourning and Commemoration: An Examination of the Stories *Hasiman* and *Lefi hatsa'ar hasekhar* of S. Y. Agnon" (in Hebrew), in *Diyuqan shel halohem: 'Al gevurah vegibborim basifrut ha'ivrit shel ha'esor ha'aharon* (Bar Ilan, 1975), 237: "In my opinion, this story contains no irony or theodicy and certainly no sarcasm."

8. The description of Shavuot in Buczacz stresses the change in communal rhythms following Rosh Hodesh Sivan with the coming of warm weather and emergence from the semimourning of the *sefirah* period. Buczacz exists under the sign of an innocent epic complementarity between the cosmos and Jewish communal life: "The world is also glad and rejoices with us. The lids of the skies are bright as the sun, and glory and beauty cover the earth."

9. Mintz and Hoffman, eds., *A Book That Was Lost and Other Stories by S. Y. Agnon*, 387.

10. Agnon is making an intertextual reference to his earlier story, titled "Hamitpahat" (The kerchief), in *Eilu ve'eilu*, 256–67. The prayer book is a gift given by the father upon his return from an extended trip to the great trade fair in Lashkovtz. This episode in Hasiman resonates with the theme of the earlier story, which concerns the acknowledgment of the existence of evil and unredemption as a sign of coming of age.

11. The piyyut can be found in Dov Yarden, ed., *Shirei hakodesh lerabi Shelomo ibn Gabirol* (The liturgical poetry of Rabbi Solomon ibn Gabirol) (Jerusalem, 1973), 2:494–95. For an English translation see Rabbi Solomon ibn Gabirol, "A Song of Redemption," trans. Nina Davis, in *Jewish Quarterly Review* 8 (1896): 269–70.

12. There are clear resonances here from the tradition of mystical testimony in Judaism. The angelic revelation to Rabbi Yosef Karo on the night of Shavuot stands in the background. A connection to Zoharic mystical experience is conveyed through the term *nitgalfu* (carved, incised) used to describe the way in which every word the poet speaks was "carved into the form of letters, and the letters joined together into words, and the words formed what he had to say" (chap. 35). The risk attendant upon such a transcendental encounter is also stressed. When the narrator takes courage to respond to the poet, he does so *besumi et nafshi bekhapi* at the beginning of chap. 36 and again at the beginning of chap. 38. My thanks to Arthur Green for pointing out these connections.

6. The Unknown Appelfeld

1. *'Ashan* (Jerusalem, 1962), *Bagai Haporeh* (Jerusalem and Tel Aviv, 1963), *Kefor 'Al Ha'arets* (Givatayim-Ramat Gan, 1965), *Beqomat Haqarqa'* (Tel Aviv, 1968), *Adenei Hanahar* (Tel Aviv, 1971). Translations from these collections are my own. For

critical work on Appelfeld see Gila Ramras-Rauch, *Aharon Appelfeld, the Holocaust and Beyond* (Bloomington: Indiana Univ. Press, 1994). For an especially valuable study see Yigal Schwartz, *Qinat hayaḥid venetsaḥ hashevet* (Individual lament and tribal eternity: Aharon Appelfeld: The picture of his world) (Jerusalem: Keter and Magnus, 1996).

2. See Appelfeld's remarks about his changing attitudes toward Bialik's writings in *Masot beguf rish'on* (Essays in the first person) (Jerusalem, 1979), 87–92.

3. The idea of primordial catastrophe *(shevirat hakelim)* is echoed here. In public lectures Appelfeld has remarked upon the great influence on him of Jewish mysticism as discovered through the writings of Gershom Scholem.

4. The only other writer in the stories is the sometime narrator of "Cold Heights" *(In the Fertile Valley,* 135–53).

7. Constructing and Deconstructing the Mystique of Sephardism in Yehoshua's *Mr. Mani* and *Journey to the End of the Millennium*

1. A. B. Yehoshua, *Mr. Mani,* trans. Hillel Halkin (New York and San Diego: Harcourt Brace, 1992), 172.

2. I am grateful for conversations with Anne Golomb Hoffman in developing these ideas.

3. A. B. Yehoshua, *Journey to the End of the Millennium,* trans. Nicholas De Lange (New York: Doubleday, 1999), 211.

8. David Grossman's Postmodernist Ambitions

1. David Grossman, *See Under: Love,* trans. Betsy Rosenberg (New York: Farrar Straus and Giroux, 1989).

2. David Grossman, *The Book of Intimate Grammar,* trans. Betsy Rosenberg (New York: Farrar Strauss Giroux. 1994).

Index

Abelman, Paul, 23–24

Above in Montifer (Lemala
    be-Montifer) (Kahana-Carmon), 73

Acrophile, The (Ha-yored lemala)
    (Kaniuk), 11

Adenei Hanahar (Foundations of the
    river) (Appelfeld), 141, 160–71

After the Holidays (Aharei ha-hagim)
    (Kenaz), 11

"After the Wedding" (Ahar hahatunah)
    (Appelfeld), 167

Age of Wonders (Tor hapela'ot)
    (Appelfeld), 137, 152

Agnon, S. Y., 75–130; "Agunot," 84;
    allegory in, 238; anomalous status
    of, 77; Appelfeld's connections with,
    38; autobiographical myth of,
    81–86; "Betrothed," 90; and
    Brenner, 90; *The Bridal Canopy*
    (Hakhnasat kalah), 12, 102; and
    Buber, 94; Buczacz as birthplace of,
    78, 83, 86, 87, 100–101, 109;
    classical Jewish culture as animating,
    99–101; *The Collected Works of S. Y.
    Agnon,* 95; education of, 86–88;
    English translations of, 11–12,
    250n.6; father of, 83, 86, 87, 91;
    first sojourn in Palestine, 89–91,

100–101; in Germany 1913–24,
    91–94; *A Guest for the Night*
    (Ore'ah natah lalun), 12, 88–89,
    102, 108, 115, 125; "Hamitpahat,"
    253n.10; Hasidism as influence on,
    86; Hebrew as chosen language of,
    83–84; and Hebrew literature
    between the wars, 2; historical
    associations of, 82–83; and the
    Holocaust, 78–79, 108–9, 114;
    Homburg home destroyed, 94;
    imaginative chronicle in, 109; "Im
    Kenisat Hayom," 252n.1; *'Ir
    Umelo'ah,* 109, 110, 111; during
    Israeli literary explosion, 1; Jaffa as
    preferred milieu of, 90; Jewish
    books and manuscripts collected by,
    86; *Kisui Hadam,* 252n.1; *Korot
    Bateinu,* 109; in Kurzweil's model
    of Hebrew literature, 231; Lag
    B'Omer in life of, 82, 83; "Laila Min
    Halelot," 252n.1; as liaison between
    Western and Eastern European
    Jewry, 92; "A Little Hero," 82;
    marriage to Esther Marx, 94; as
    modernist, 80–101; Ninth of Av as
    birth date of, 82, 83; Nobel Prize
    speech of, 80–81, 85–86; the novel

"Bridal Veil" (Kahana-Carmon),
 249–50n.5
British Mandate, 31, 48–49
Brit Shalom, 104
"Bronda" (Appelfeld), 162–63
Brown, Norman O., 190
Broyard, Anatole, 28
Buber, Martin, 92, 94
Buczacz (Galicia): as Agnon's
 birthplace, 78, 86; in Agnon's "The
 Sign," 110, 112, 116–19, 123–26,
 128–29; Jewish life in, 87–88, 100;
 Sefer Buczacz,, 87–88

Call It Sleep (Roth), 207
Canaani, David, 95
Castel-Bloom, Orly: *Dolly City*, 15; in
 explosion of women writers, 68; as
 not translated into English, 5
"Changing the Watch" (Ḥilufei
 mishmarot) (Appelfeld), 164–65
Chernaik, Judith, 24–25
Chicago Tribune, 14, 22
Christos of the Fish (Kristus shel
 ha-dagim) (Hoffman), 72
The City and the Fullness Thereof ('Ir
 umelo 'ah) (Agnon), 109, 110,
 111
City of Many Days ('Ir yamim rabim)
 (Hareven): nostalgia in, 48–49;
 publication data, 22; yearning for
 Mandate Period in, 31
"Cold Heights, The" (Bagovah haqar)
 (Appelfeld), 144–45, 147, 154
"Cold Spring" (Aviv qar) (Appelfeld),
 142–44, 147
Collected Works of S. Y. Agnon, The
 (Agnon), 95
coming-of-age novels, 208–9

Commentary, 14, 16–17, 31
Commonweal, 17
concentrationary universe, 140–41
Conservative Judaism (journal), 25
Contemporary Israeli Literature
 (Anderson), 47–48
Czaczkes, Esther Farb, 86
Czaczkes, Shalom Mordecai ha-Levi,
 83, 86, 87, 89, 91
Czaczkes, Shmuel Yosef. *See* Agnon,
 S. Y.

Day of Holocaust and Bravery (Yom
 hasho'ah vehagevurah), 147
Days of Ziklag, The (Yemei ziqlag)
 (Yizhar), 9–10
De Lange, Nicholas, 12, 189
detective novels, 8, 56
Diamond, James S., 25–26
diaspora Jewry: Israeli literature
 critiqued from standpoint of, 33–37;
 reviewers representing to Israeli
 culture, 18–19; settlers' view of,
 220–21; shift in relations between
 Israeli Jews and, 63. *See also*
 American Jews
Dolly City (Castel-Bloom), 15
Doubleday, 8

Early in the Summer of 1970 (Bi-thilat
 kaiytz 1970) (Yehoshua): and
 diaspora Jewry, 250–51n.13; the
 family in, 32; 1967–73 period in,
 52–54; publication data, 22; on
 realities of Israeli life, 25; universal
 themes in, 32–33
"Early in the Summer of 1970"
 (Yehoshua), 53–54, 173, 239

Haskalah (Enlightenment) (*cont.*)
100; and Grossman's *See Under:
Love,* 195, 200; and modern
Hebrew literature, 97, 229; turn-of-
the-twentieth-century writers
breaking with, 99; Zionism breaking
with, 98
"Hasoḥer Bartfus" (The merchant
Bartfuss) (Appelfeld), 170–71
Ha-Yored Lemala (The acrophile)
(Kaniuk), 11
Hazaz, Haim, 11–12
Hebrew language: Agnon choosing,
83–84; American Jews' limited
knowledge of, 2; Appelfeld
acquiring, 139, 161; choosing
Hebrew as not choosing a Western
language, 229–30; discontinuity and
continuity of, 228; Galician Jews
reading, 100; in Grossman's *The
Book of Intimate Grammar,* 215; of
Grossman's *See Under: Love,* 195,
198, 202; of Hasidic tales, 237;
Haskalah on, 97, 229; as minor
language, 12; revival of, 228;
Sephardim adopting, 65–66; of
Yehoshua's *Journey to the End of the
Millennium,* 188–89; of Yehoshua's
Mr. Mani, 175. *See also* Hebrew
literature
Hebrew literature: Agnon's Nobel Prize
as recognizing, 96; allegory in,
238–40; catastrophe model of,
231–32; and collapse of the religious
tradition, 98–99; creative periods as
demarcated for, 61; Eastern Europe
and Israel contrasted in, 117–18;
Eastern European flowering of, 2;
English translations of, 2, 7–12;
increasing number of works since

1970s, 55–56; interwar high point
of, 2; long history of, 55; models of
development of modern, 230–32;
negation of traditional Judaism and
creativity in, 236–38; origins of
modern, 97; rebirth model of,
230–31, 232; as secular, 243–44; as
shifting from Europe to Palestine,
96, 229; signs from the past in
modern, 232; social criticism
tradition in, 19, 26, 59–60; as
source of modern Jewish thought,
227–42; translation of, 7–12,
58–61; as truth-telling literature, 41,
240–42; Zionism scrutinized by,
240–41. *See also* Israeli literature;
and writers and works by name
Hebrew University, 105
Heichal Ha-Kelim Ha-Shvurim (The
palace of shattered vessels) (Shahar),
49
"Ḥilufei Mishmarot" (Changing the
watch) (Appelfeld), 164–65
His Daughter (Bitoh) (Kaniuk), 11
historical novels, 56, 186, 189
Hiuch Ha-Gedi (Smile of the lamb)
(Grossman), 193
Hoffman, Adina, 36–37
Hoffman, Yoel, 72
Holland, 4
"Hollow Stone, A" (Oz), 51
Holocaust, the: Agnon and, 78–79,
108–9, 114; American fascination
with, 137; in Appelfeld, 50, 66, 108,
133, 136–37, 194; the
concentrationary universe, 139–40;
Day of Holocaust and Bravery, 147;
explosion of titles about, 4; in
Grossman's *See Under: Love,* 37, 66,
135, 193, 194, 201, 203, 205; in

Mojtabai, A. G., 29

Molkho (Yehoshua). *See Five Seasons*

moshav, 219–20

Mr. Mani (Mar Manni) (Yehoshua), 172–86; autobiographical aspect of, 174; as best-seller and critical success, 174; complexity of, 184; 1848 as start and end of, 183; English translation of, 175–76; the family in, 32; five "conversations" comprising, 72–73, 175, 176; formal experimentation in, 72–73, 134; games and devices in, 185; Hebrew of, 175; ideologies versus idées fixes in, 181; in Israeli press, 15; "Mani" as name of characters in, 184; on masculinity, 69; plot of, 176–78; reader invited to participate in, 185–86; reverse telling of story in, 176, 178; Sephardism in, 135, 172–86; sexuality versus political consciousness in, 181–84; speakers in, 184–85; ventriloquizing of discourse in, 71; womb as preoccupation in, 183–84; Yehoshua's dovish politics in, 180

"Mul Ha-ya'Arot" (Facing the forests) (Yehoshua), 239

Murder on a Kibbutz (Gur), 9

My Michael (Michael she'li)(Oz): Arab theme in, 29–30, 67; compared with Western works, 250n.8; as debut work in English, 8; English translation of, 2; feminist criticism of, 36; Israeli versus American reception of, 33–34; publication data, 22; versus stereotypes of Israeli society, 23–24

mysteries, 8–9

Nahman of Bratslav, 123, 236–37, 238

"Na'ima Sasson Writes Poetry" (Kahana-Carmon), 249n.5

Nation, 14

negative theology, 242

New Leader, 14

New Republic, 14, 17, 21

News from Jerusalem (Shahar), 49

New Wave: Appelfeld and, 133; Grossman contrasted with, 206; high modernism influencing, 70; Shalev contrasted with, 224; and the Zionist master narrative, 68, 218

New Writing in Israel (Spicehandler and Arnson), 48

New Yorker magazine, 192, 193

New York Review of Books, 2, 14

New York Times Book Review, 2, 13–14, 17, 21, 23

Nietzsche, Friedrich, 239

Nikmat Avot (Revenge of the fathers) (Shami), 67

Ninth of Av, 82, 83

Nochahim Nifkadim (Sleeping on a wire) (Grossman), 192

Notsot (Feathers) (Be'er), 10

novels: beginnings of Hebrew, 60; coming-of-age novels, 208–9; genre novels, 8–9, 56; Israeli writers' experimentation with, 72; as problem genre for Agnon, 102, 105–6; serious novels as genre of choice for translation, 8; as truth-telling, 41

Only Yesterday (Temol shilshom) (Agnon), 102

On the Ground Floor (Beqomat haqarqa') (Appelfeld), 141, 154

prose: shift from poetry to, 56–57. *See also* fiction
Publishers Weekly, 13
publishing industry, Israeli, 7–8, 57–58

Raab, Esther, 68
Rabi, David, 250n.11
Rabin, Yitzhak, 61
Rachel (poet), 68
Rapoport, S. Y., 100
Ravnitzky, Y. H., 94
reception: dynamics of, 7–20; getting noticed, 13–20; getting translated, 7–12. *See also* reviews
"Regina" (Appelfeld), 168–69
religious Zionism, 110, 112
"Revenge of the Fathers" (Nikmat avot) (Shami), 67
reviews: in community newspapers, 21; in disseminating a book, 13–20; interpretive frameworks in, 28
Rokeah, Elazar, 89
romances, 56
Roman Rusi (Shalev). *See Blue Mountain*
Rosenberg, Betsy, 12, 195, 206
Rosenzweig, Franz, 94
Roth, Henry, 207
Russian (Soviet) Jews, 62, 243

sales figures, difficulty in obtaining reliable, 249n.2
Sandbank, Shimon, 47
Saturday Morning Murder, The (Gur), 9
Schocken, Salman, 93–94, 95
Schocken publishing house, 57, 93, 95
Scholem, Gershom G., 91, 254n.3

Schulz, Bruno: Grossman influenced by, 71; Grossman's *See Under: Love* quoting, 197–99, 201, 202, 203, 204
Scripture, 233–36
Second Aliyah, 240–41
"Second Generation" writers, 194
secularization, 60, 227
See Under: Love (Ayien erech: Ahavah) (Grossman), 193–205; ambitions of, 194–95; *The Book of Intimate Grammar* compared with, 207–8, 212; criticized on literary grounds, 33; encyclopedia concept in, 201–2; English translation of, 2, 195; first section of, 195–97; formal experimentation in, 72; four sections of, 72, 195; fourth section of, 200–201; Hebrew of, 195, 198, 202; the Holocaust as theme of, 37, 66, 135, 193, 194, 201, 203, 205; on imagination redeeming suffering of the past, 195, 205–6; in Israeli press, 15; Jewish literary tradition ignored in, 205; and juvenile adventure literature, 135, 196, 202, 204; magic realism of, 70–71, 198; Mintz's review of, 18; moral vision of, 204; on the Nazi Beast, 197; political criticism of, 36–37; as postmodernist, 70, 202; previous literature recycled in, 71, 196, 202; publication data, 22; Bruno Schulz in, 71, 197–99, 201, 202, 203, 204; second section of, 197–99; Shalev's *Blue Mountain* compared with, 219; storytelling in, 71; style changes in, 195; third section of, 199–200
Sefer Buczacz (The book of Buczacz), 87–88

Sefer Ha'aggadah (The book of legends) (Bialik and Ravnitzky), 94
Sefer Ha-Dikduk Ha-Pnimi (Grossman). *See Book of Intimate Grammar, The*
Sefer Hama'asim (The book of deeds) (Agnon), 115, 125
"Sense of Smell, The" (Agnon), 84–85
Sephardim: arriving in Israel, 65; Ashkenazis privileged over, 63; Hebrew adopted by, 65–66; literature by, 66; *Sefaradi tahor,* 182; Yehoshua as Sephardic, 134–35, 172, 189; in Yehoshua's *Journey to the End of the Millennium,* 186–91; in Yehoshua's *Mr. Mani,* 172–86
Seventy-Three (Yom Kippur) War, 45, 61, 173
Shabtai, Yaakov: on hope as possible only through art, 72; in Israeli literary explosion, 1; *Past Perfect,* 241–42. *See also Past Continuous*
Shahar, David, 49
Shaked, Gershon, 11, 16, 89
Shalev, Meir: *Esau,* 39; storytelling in work of, 71. *See also Blue Mountain*
Shamas, Anton, 67
Shami, Yitzhak, 67
Shamir, Moshe, 69
Shamosh, Amnon, 66
Shapiro, Zeva, 12, 103
Shavuot, 112–13, 122, 127, 252n.4, 253nn.8, 12
"Shemesh Shel Ḥoref" (The winter sun) (Appelfeld), 170
"Shevuat Emunim" (Betrothed) (Agnon), 90
Shimoni, Yoav, 73
Shira (Agnon), 102–7; as Agnon's most contemporary novel, 78; alternative endings of, 103; bibliomania in, 104; English translation of, 103; German Jews as depicted in, 104–5; Herbst as central character of, 103; as incomplete, 103, 106–7; as problem novel, 102–3, 105; setting of, 103; Shira, 103, 104, 105–6
Shlonsky, Avraham, 198
Shlosha Yamim Ve-Yeled (Yehoshua). *See Three Days and a Child*
Sholem Aleichem, 202
short stories, translation of, 8
Shrimpton, Nicholas, 32
Sifriyat Poalim, 7
"Sign, The" (Hasiman) (Agnon), 108–30; Buczacz in, 110, 112, 116–19, 123–26, 128–29; English translation of, 252n.5; Ibn Gabirol in, 110, 111, 112, 115, 116, 119–21, 122, 124–25, 126–30; as inauguration story, 110; in *'Ir Umelo'ah,* 110–11; loss and rebuilding in, 95; narrator's breakdown in, 127; one-page version of, 1944, 111–12, 252n.3; *qetsat qasheh* in, 121–22; Revelation linked to the Holocaust in, 114; the revelatory experience in, 126–30; Shavuot as setting of, 112–13, 122, 127, 253nn.8, 12; strength as motif in, 115; Talpiyot in, 112, 115, 116–18; three forms of imaginative experience before the revelation in, 122–26; two parts of, 112
Simckes, Seymour, 12
Simple Story, A (Sippur pashut) (Agnon), 102, 250n.6
Simpson, Philip, 12
Sippur Pashut (A simple story) (Agnon), 102, 250n.6

Where Jackals Howl and Other Stories
(Artsot hatan) (Oz): and the Arab
question, 29; Broyard on, 28; English translation of, 8; on the
founding fathers, 218–19; the
kibbutz in, 51, 241; publication
data, 22; versus stereotypes of Israeli
society, 24
White, Edmund, 38
Wiesel, Elie, 108
"Winter Sun, The" (Shemesh shel
horef) (Appelfeld), 170
Wisse, Ruth, 37
women: in Appelfeld's work, 167–71;
feminism, 36, 63; increase in women
writers from 1970s, 46, 68; in
Shalev's *Blue Mountain*, 220,
222–23; Zionist view of, 68

Yaron, Emuna, 94, 110
Yehoshua, A. B., 172–91; allegory in,
238, 239; on Appelfeld, 136; Arabs
in work of, 29; and Ashkenazic
intelligentsia, 172; compared with
Western writers, 250n.8; contract
with American publishing house, 8;
and diaspora Jews, 34–35; "Early in
the Summer of 1970," 53–54, 173,
239; "Facing the Forests," 239; the
family in work of, 32; *Five Seasons,*
69, 173, 189; and the Holocaust,
194; international stature of, 58;
Israeli life as depicted in, 19; in
Israeli literary explosion, 1; Kahana-
Carmon compared with, 9, 68; later
works of, 39; on masculinity, 69;
"Missile Base 612," 52–53, 239; as
moralist, 54; 1967–73 period in
work of, 52–54; obligation to his

material, 54; *Open Heart,* 18, 32;
postmodernist practices in, 135; as
Sephardic, 134, 172, 189; Sephardic
identity in work of, 134–35; short
stories of, 134; thesis-laden big ideas
in work of, 190; universal themes in
work of, 32. *See also Early in the
Summer of 1970; Journey to the End
of the Millennium; Lover, The; Mr.
Mani; Three Days and a Child*
Yehoshua, Yaakov, 174
Yellow Wind, The (Ha-zeman
ha-tzahov)(Grossman), 36–37, 192,
193
Yemei Ziqlag (The days of Ziklag)
(Yizhar), 9–10
Yiddish language, 100, 188, 237
Yidisher Veker, Der (weekly), 89
Yizhar, S., 9–10, 29, 67, 69, 206
Yom Hasho'ah Vehagevurah (Day of
Holocaust and Bravery), 147
Yom Kippur (Seventy-Three) War, 45,
61, 173

Zemora-Beitan, 7
Zikhron Devarim (Shabtai). *See Past
Continuous*
Zionism: Agnon's association with, 89,
94, 110; Appelfeld as Zionist writer,
133; breaking with Haskalah, 98; in
Galicia, 100; Hebrew language
revived by, 228; labor Zionism, 63;
literature as leading politics, 2; on
masculinity, 69; and minorities,
64–65, 243; modern Hebrew
literature scrutinizing, 240–41;
religious Zionism, 110, 112;
Russian and Ethiopian Jews
renewing, 62; and Sephardim, 65,

Zionism (*cont.*)
243–44; on women, 68; in
Yehoshua's *Mr. Mani,* 178–81;
Zionization of American Jewish life,
3–4. *See also* Zionist master plot
Zionist master plot: Kahana-Carmon
sidestepping, 9, 68–69; as model of

Israeli literature, 64; New Wave
demythologizing, 68, 218; Oz
engaging, 68; rewriting of,
131–226, 243–45; the settlers as
pioneers in, 212; women writers in
assault on, 46, 69; Yehoshua
engaging, 68, 134

Judaic Traditions in Literature, Music, and Art
Ken Frieden & Harold Bloom, *eds.*